Father, Son and Spirit

Titles in this series:

NEW STUDIES IN BIBLICAL THEOLOGY 24

Series editor: D. A. Carson

Father, Son and Spirit

THE TRINITY AND JOHN'S GOSPEL

Andreas J. Köstenberger

and

Scott R. Swain

APOLLOS

INTERVARSITY PRESS
DOWNERS GROVE, ILLINOIS 60515

APOLLOS (an imprint of Inter-Varsity Press)
Norton Street, Nottingham NG7 3HR
Website: www.ivpbooks.com
Email: ivp@ivpbooks.com

InterVarsity Press, USA
P.O. Box 1400, Downers Grove, IL 60515-1426
World Wide Web: www.ivpress.com
Email: email@ivpress.com

Inter-Varsity Press, England, is closely linked with the Universities and Colleges Christian Fellowship, a student movement connecting Christian Unions throughout Great Britain, and a member movement of the International Fellowship of Evangelical Students. Website: www.uccf.org.uk

InterVarsity Press®, USA, is the book-publishing division of InterVarsity Christian Fellowship/USA® <www.intervarsity.org> and a member movement of the International Fellowship of Evangelical Students.

UK ISBN 978-1-84474-253-0
USA ISBN 978-0-8308-2625-4

Set in Monotype Times New Roman
Typeset in Great Britain by Servis Filmsetting Ltd, Manchester

Printed in the United States of America ∞

British Library Cataloguing in Publication Data

A catalogue record for this book is available from the British Library.

Library of Congress Cataloging-in-Publication Data

Köstenberger, Andreas J., 1957-
  Father, Son and Spirit: the Trinity and John's Gospel / Andreas J.
  Köstenberger and Scott R. Swain
    p. cm.—(New studies in biblical theology; 24)
  Includes bibliographical references and indexes.
  ISBN 978-0-8308-2625-4 (US: pbk.: alk. paper)—ISBN
  978-1-84474-253-0 (UK: pbk.: alk paper)
1. Bible. N.T. John—Religious aspects—Christianity.   2.
Trinity—Biblical teaching.   I. Swain, Scott R.   II. Title.
BS2615.52.K665   2008
226.5'06—dc22
                 2008008906

P 24 25 23 22 21 20 19 18 17 16 15 14 13 12 11 10 9 8 7 6 5 4 3 2

Y 29 28 27 26 25 24 23 22 21 20 19 18 17 16 15 14 13 12 11 10 09

This book is offered humbly
To the triune God
Revealed in the Scriptures
Believed on in the church
Father, Son and Spirit
Whom we serve with gratitude and gladness

May this volume be
'to the praise of his glory'
(Eph. 1:14)

Contents

Series preface

New Studies in Biblical Theology is a series of monographs that address key issues in the discipline of biblical theology. Contributions to the series focus on one or more of three areas: (1) the nature and status of biblical theology, including its relations with other disciplines (e.g. historical theology, exegesis, systematic theology, historical criticism, narrative theology); (2) the articulation and exposition of the structure of thought of a particular biblical writer or corpus; and (3) the delineation of a biblical theme across all or part of the biblical corpora.

Above all, these monographs are creative attempts to help thinking Christians understand their Bibles better. The series aims simultaneously to instruct and to edify, to interact with the current literature, and to point the way ahead. In God's universe, mind and heart should not be divorced: in this series we will try not to separate what God has joined together. While the notes interact with the best of scholarly literature, the text is uncluttered with untransliterated Greek and Hebrew, and tries to avoid too much technical jargon. The volumes are written within the framework of confessional evangelicalism, but there is always an attempt at thoughtful engagement with the sweep of the relevant literature.

One trap we would not want a series devoted to biblical theology to fall into is a kind of implied depreciation of systematic theology. Biblical theology and systematic theology are differentiable but overlapping and complementary disciplines. The former tends to ask theological questions about individual biblical books and corpora and about the trajectories that run right through the biblical corpora; the latter tends to ask theological questions that are primarily atemporal (e.g. 'What is God like?' and not 'What does the Gospel of John tell us about God?'). For those of us who hold that Scripture must be the norming norm, both disciplines, to be responsible, no matter how much they learn from each other and from other contributing fields such as historical theology and philosophical theology, must ground themselves in the exegesis of Scripture. And of course, that exegesis is itself shaped, inevitably, by antecedent theological understanding.

This present volume is the joint product of a *Neutestamentler* and a systematic theologian. In their collaboration they have simultaneously attempted a detailed exegetical and theological understanding of what the Fourth Gospel says about God, using the categories of that Gospel itself, *and* mature understanding of the links between that text and the systematic formulations of what came to be called the doctrine of the Trinity. In what sense is it proper to think of the doctrine of God in John's Gospel as trinitarian? Some are so suspicious of links between biblical exegesis and systematic theology that they will deplore any ostensible connections between the two, afraid that the latter will domesticate the former and stain it with anachronism, or that the former will dilute the latter and render it insipid. Drs Köstenberger and Swain, thankfully, are not numbered among them. For those who want to know what they *ought* to believe – surely one of the functions (though not the only one) of constructive systematic theology – out of God's self-disclosure in Scripture, this book will be a stimulating delight. In addition to its contribution to Christian understanding of God (can there be any higher subject?) it stimulates serious thought about how we move from careful study of biblical text to theological formulation. Nothing would please us more than if this book were to become a model for a lot more theological work of the same order.

D. A. Carson
Trinity Evangelical Divinity School

Authors' preface

We are grateful to our dear wives for their unwavering love, support and partnership.

I (Andreas) would also like to express my heartfelt gratitude to my mentor in things Johannine and others, Don Carson, for his theological acumen and commitment to excellence, and to the school where I teach, Southeastern Baptist Theological Seminary (SEBTS), for the administration's continued affirmation of my writing ministry. In the spirit of 'ironing sharpening iron', may I also acknowledge the stimulating influence of my doctoral students at SEBTS and of the readers of my blog, www.biblicalfoundations.org, and its Spanish version, www.fundamentosbiblicos.com.

Several others deserve thanks as well. Fred Sanders and Josh Leim read and helpfully commented upon earlier portions of the present manuscript. Michael Farrell, Associate Librarian at Reformed Theological Seminary, Orlando, provided assistance in obtaining vital resources, and Matt Lytle compiled the indexes. Pete Schemm was the original catalyst for this work.

Finally, we wish to express our gratitude to Don Carson for the opportunity to contribute to the present series, a series from which we have both benefited so much, and the dedicated staff at Inter-Varsity Press, especially Philip Duce and the copy editor, Eldo Barkhuizen, for the phenomenal speed and competence with which they processed the manuscript. Our prayer is that the present volume will be a fitting contribution to an already excellent series. Even more, we pray that this volume will be a blessing to the church, that community gathered into the fellowship of the Father and the Son by the indwelling of the Holy Spirit (1 John 1:1–3; 4:13). *Soli Deo gloria!*

Andreas J. Köstenberger
and Scott R. Swain

Abbreviations

1 Apol.	*Apologia i* (Justin Martyr)
1 En.	*1 Enoch*
1QS	*Rule of the Community*
1Qsa	*Rule of the Congregation*
2 Clem.	*2 Clement*
2 Esdr.	*2 Esdras*
4Q246	*Apocryphon of Daniel*
4QFlor	*Florilegium*
4Qmess	*Messianic Apocalypse*
11QMelch	*Rule of Melchizedek*
AB	Anchor Bible
ABD	*Anchor Bible Dictionary*, ed. D. N. Freedman, 6 vols., New York: Doubleday, 1992
AGJU	Arbeiten zur Geschichte des antiken Judentums und des Urchristentums
Ant.	*Jewish Antiquities* (Josephus)
ANTC	Abingdon New Testament Commentaries
Aram.	Aramaic
AV	Authorized (King James) Version
b. 'Erub.	*Babylonian Talmud 'Erubin*
b. Ketub.	*Babylonian Talmud Ketubbot*
BBCS	Blackwell Bible Commentary Series
BBET	Beiträge zur biblischen Exegese und Theologie
BBR	*Bulletin for Biblical Research*
BECNT	Baker Exegetical Commentary on the New Testament
BETL	Bibliotheca ephemeridum theologicarum lovaniensium
BFCT	Beiträge zur Förderung christlicher Theologie
Bib	*Biblica*
BSac	*Bibliotheca sacra*
BNTC	Black's New Testament Commentaries

BRev	*Biblical Review*
b. Ta'an.	*Babylonian Talmud Ta'anit*
b. Yeb.	*Babylonian Talmud Yebamot*
BZNW	Beihefte zur Zeitschrift für die neutestamentliche Wissenschaft
C. Ar.	*Orationes contra Arianos* (Athanasius)
CBQ	*Catholic Biblical Quarterly*
Civ.	*De civitate Dei* (Augustine)
CTJ	*Calvin Theological Journal*
Dial.	*Dialogus cum Tryphone* (Justin Martyr)
Did.	*Didache*
DSS	Dead Sea Scrolls
EBS	Encountering Biblical Studies
EDNT	*Exegetical Dictionary of the New Testament*, ed. H. Balz and G. Schneider, 3 vols., ET Grand Rapids: Eerdmans, 1990–3
EMSS	Evangelical Missiological Society Series
ESV	English Standard Version
ET	English translation
ExpTim	*Expository Times*
FAT	Forschungen zum Alten Testament
Fid. orth.	*De fide orthodoxa* (John of Damascus)
Haer.	*Adversus haereses* (Irenaeus)
HBT	*Horizons in Biblical Theology*
Hist.	*Histories* (Tacitus)
Jo.	*In divi Joannis* (Cyril of Alexandria)
Inst.	J. Calvin, *Institutes of the Christian Religion*, trans. F. L. Battles, London: SCM; Philadelphia: Westminster, 1961
Int	*Interpretation*
IVPNTC	InterVarsity Press New Testament Commentary
JBL	*Journal of Biblical Literature*
JETS	*Journal of the Evangelical Theological Society*
John	J. Calvin, *The Gospel According to St. John*, 2 vols., trans. T. H. L. Parker, Edinburgh: Oliver & Boyd, 1959 and 1961
JSNT	*Journal for the Study of the New Testament*
JSNTSup	Journal for the Study of the New Testament, Supplement Series
JSOTSup	Journal for the Study of the Old Testament, Supplement Series

JTS	*Journal of Theological Studies*
Jub.	*Jubilees*
LXX	Septuagint version
Mir ausc.	*De mirabilibus auscultationibus* (Aristotle)
Mos.	*De vita Mosis* (Philo)
NAC	New American Commentary
m. Ber.	*Mishna Berakot*
Mos.	*De vita Mosis* (Philo)
NASB	New American Standard Bible
NICNT	New International Commentary on the New Testament
NIDOTTE	*New International Dictionary of Old Testament Theology and Exegesis*, ed. W. A. VanGemeren, 5 vols., Grand Rapids: Zondervan; Carlisle: Paternoster, 1997
NIV	New International Version
NSBT	New Studies in Biblical Theology
NT	New Testament
NTS	*New Testament Studies*
NTSI	New Testament and the Scriptures of Israel
NZSTh	*Neue Zeitschrift für systematische Theologie und Religionsphilosophie*
Opif.	*De opificio mundi* (Philo)
Orat.	*Orationes* (Demosthenes)
Or. 29	*Oratio theologica tertia: de Filio* (Gregory of Nazianzus)
Or. 30	*Oratio theologica quarta: de Filio II* (Gregory of Nazianzus)
OT	Old Testament
PNTC	Pillar New Testament Commentary
Prob.	*Quod omnis probus liber sit* (Philo)
ProEccl	*Pro ecclesia*
Pss Sol.	*Psalms of Solomon*
QG	*Quaestiones et solutiones in Genesin* (Philo)
Quis div.	*Quis dives salvetur* (Clement of Alexandria)
SBLDS	Society of Biblical Literature Dissertation Series
SBLMS	Society of Biblical Literature Monograph Series
SHR	Studies in the History of Religions (supplement to *Numen*)
SJT	*Scottish Journal of Theology*

SNTSMS	Society for New Testament Studies Monograph Series
StudBib	*Studia biblica*
TDNT	*Theological Dictionary of the New Testament*, ed. G. Kittel and G. Friedrich; trans. G. W. Bromiley, 10 vols., Grand Rapids: Eerdmans, 1964–76
TJ	*Trinity Journal*
T. Jud.	*Testament of Judah*
T. Levi	*Testament of Levi*
TNIV	Today's New International Version
TNTC	Tyndale New Testament Commentaries
Trin.	*De Trinitate* (Augustine)
TynBul	*Tyndale Bulletin*
VC	*Vigiliae christianae*
VE	*Vox evangelica*
WBC	Word Biblical Commentary
WMANT	Wissenschaftliche Monographien zum Alten und Neuen Testament
WUNT	Wissenschaftliche Untersuchungen zum Neuen Testament
ZNW	*Zeitschrift für die neutestamentliche Wissenschaft und die Kunde der älteren Kirche*
ZRG	*Zeitschrift für Religions- und Geistesgeschichte*

Introduction

John's Gospel and the church's doctrine of the Trinity

From the patristic period until today, John's Gospel has served as a major source for the church's knowledge, doctrine and worship of the triune God. The Fathers found in the Fourth Gospel both a primary text concerning the trinitarian mystery of salvation[1] and ammunition for the refutation of heresies such as modalism and Arianism.[2] In expounding their full-orbed trinitarianism, major fourth-century pastors and theologians were 'drawn like a magnet' to John's Gospel.[3] The reason for this lies close at hand:

> Among all New Testament documents the Fourth Gospel provides not only the most raw material for the church doctrine of the Trinity, but also the most highly developed patterns of reflection on this material – particularly, patterns that show evidence of pressure to *account* somehow for the distinct personhood and divinity of Father, Son, and Spirit without compromising the unity of God.[4]

In John's Gospel, the distinct personal identities of Father, Son and Spirit and their unity in being, will and work are equally affirmed. While there are important personal differences in the roles of the triune God along salvation-historical lines (the Father sends, the Son is sent and sends, the Spirit is sent) the *missio Dei* is characterized by a deep underlying unity among the participants in this mission. As

---

[1] See Wiles 1960: 148–161.
[2] See Plantinga (1991: 303, n. 2), citing Hilary of Poitiers, the Nicean *homoousios* clause and Tertullian's refutation of Sabellianism. Pollard (1957: 334–349) documents the use of John 10:30 in early trinitarian controversies.
[3] Plantinga 1991: 305.
[4] Ibid.

the fourth evangelist puts it, Father and Son are 'in' one another, and they are 'one' (10:30, 38; 14:10–11).

Given John's perennial impact on the church's trinitarian confession, it is surprising that, with the exception of Royce Gruenler's *The Trinity in the Gospel of John*,[5] no contemporary, book-length study of John's trinitarian theology is available. Fine studies related to aspects of John's doctrine of God have been published by M. M. Thompson,[6] Bauckham[7] and others,[8] but none that summarizes and synthesizes what John has to say about God as Father, Son and Holy Spirit. This void is a subset of the larger neglect of theology proper in NT studies,[9] which is itself a symptom of the systematic separation of dogmatics and exegesis in the modern era.[10]

The tide of NT studies is turning, however. A recent spate of articles and books devoted to God and/or the Trinity in the NT has emerged.[11] Contemporary with this revival in trinitarian NT studies is a shift in the playing field of the theological disciplines and theological method. On the one hand, many theologians increasingly acknowledge the role that biblical interpretation must play in their own discipline. Biblical exegesis is not only the territory of professional Bible scholars and biblical theologians.[12] On the other hand, many biblical scholars recognize the role that theological reflection must play in the exegetical enterprise. The Bible is, after all, a profoundly *theological* document.[13] Readings that fail to move beyond literary and genetic/historical issues

---

[5] Gruenler's (1986) work treats trinitarian themes by way of a brief, running commentary on John's Gospel. Though not without its problems (see below), the book is full of excellent insights. However, the scope of Gruenler's book limits its engagement with much of the ancient and contemporary literature on Johannine and/or trinitarian theology. Moreover, Gruenler's work is dedicated to demonstrating the problematic thesis that John's is a 'social' view of the Trinity. For these reasons, we believe there is still much work to be done.

[6] M. M. Thompson 2000, 2001.

[7] Bauckham 1998, 2005.

[8] See e.g. Stibbe 2006.

[9] See Dahl 1991.

[10] This separation was enshrined in Johann Philipp Gabler's famous address delivered in 1787 at the University of Altdorf, 'An Oration on the Proper Distinction Between Biblical and Dogmatic Theology and the Specific Objectives of Each'.

[11] See Yeago 1994; Bauckham 1998a; N. T. Wright 1991, 1992; Fee 1994, 2007; Watson 2000; M. M. Thompson 2000, 2001; Jenson 2002; Das and Matera 2002; Witherington and Ice 2002; Rowe 2000, 2002, 2003, 2006; and Bockmuehl 2006.

[12] On the 'theological interpretation of the Bible' movement, see Fowl 1998; and Vanhoozer 2005b.

[13] I. H. Marshall 2004: 19.

to substantive doctrinal ones thus fail to grasp the Bible's main subject matter.[14]

Corroborating this (re)new(ed)[15] methodological approach is an increased historical awareness that the church's great dogmas, including the doctrine of the Trinity, originated not as a consequence of a priori theological reflection but instead as interpretative principles, principles that were derived from a believing engagement with Scripture.[16] Indeed, Augustine traces his understanding of the Trinity to 'all the Catholic *commentators*' whom he 'read on the divine books of both testaments' (*Trin.* 1.7; italics added).

To be sure, there is a danger associated with speaking of the Bible's, or even of John's, 'trinitarianism'. We must not import fourth-century discussions into our exegesis of biblical texts.[17] Anachronism should be avoided. Nevertheless, we believe it is legitimate to label John's teaching about God 'trinitarian' for at least two reasons.

First, John's Gospel is 'trinitarian' in an obvious, non-controversial sense: John presents Father, Son and Spirit as three characters whose identities are bound together in a profound and mutually determining way. Admitting this point does not concede a full-blown doctrine of the Trinity. Even Arius spoke of a 'trinity' of 'three *hypostases*' in this sense (Arius simply denied that two of the three characters were fully divine!).[18] The present point simply justifies our concentrated focus on Father, Son and Spirit as they are portrayed in their mutual relationships and actions in the Fourth Gospel. It also assures us that such a focus will not lead us away from John's own interests and intentions.

Second, in keeping with an increasing body of literature (see n. 11), we believe there is a strong and natural link between the canonical books of the Old and New Testaments and later trinitarian formulations and terminology (e.g. the Nicene Creed, *trinitas*, *hypostasis*, *homoousios* etc.). Simply put, John's portrayal of Father, Son and Spirit (along with the rest of the Bible) put 'pressure'[19] on fourth-century discussions about the nature of God in such a way that later formulations and terminology should be viewed less as evolutionary developments beyond the NT data and more as attempts 'to describe

---

[14] Childs 1993: 80–85; N. T. Wright 1992: 467–476.

[15] Before the modern era, the history of theology simply *is* the history of biblical interpretation.

[16] Behr 2001: 1–70; O'Keefe and Reno 2005; cf. Jenson 2002: 338–339.

[17] See Dunn's comments (1996: 9).

[18] See Arius' 'Letter to Alexander of Alexandria', in Rusch 1980: 31.

[19] See the quotation of Plantinga above; and Rowe 2002.

and analyse the way in which Jesus Christ and the Spirit' were 'intrinsic to' Scripture's way of speaking about God.[20] In other words, the creeds represent a 'descriptive grammar' of the Bible's own *intrinsically* trinitarian discourse.[21] Jenson explains:

> The real question about the relation of church doctrine to biblical witness is not about the development of ideas, but about whether the church's Trinity doctrine and Christology make – and then develop and analyze – the same judgments about Jesus that Scripture does.[22]

Admittedly, the present point is more controversial than that of the preceding paragraph.[23] But we believe the present volume will bear it out, at least in the case of the Fourth Gospel.[24]

The approach of the present study

In the light of the preceding discussion, we believe that a fresh examination of the Fourth Gospel's trinitarian teaching is in order. To accomplish this fresh examination of John's trinitarian vision, we have employed a variety of interpretative tools and methodologies:

1. We have sought to build on the fine work done by scholars like Bauckham, Hurtado and others in reconstructing John's historical and cultural milieu, especially pertaining to Second Temple Jewish monotheism.
2. We have attempted to pay close attention to the Gospel's literary art, including its storyline, characterization and ideology.
3. We have read John's Gospel in its canonical, salvation-historical context.
4. We have enlisted the aid of the church in our study, including its official doctrinal pronouncements (e.g. the Nicene–Constantinopolitan Creed, the Chalcedonian Creed etc.) and its

[20] Hays (2002: 141) is describing Paul's trinitarian logic; but the same point goes for John as well. For an excellent historical account of the present point, see Behr 2001, 2004.
[21] Of course, this is not the *only* thing that creeds do. Creeds make assertions about reality, form and inform the church's praise etc.
[22] Jenson 2003: 194. Jenson here follows Yeago 1994. Cf. Dunn 1996: 250.
[23] For the historical factors that gave rise to this controversial state, see Babcock 1991; and Muller 2003: 120–140.
[24] For further discussion of the relationship between Scripture and trinitarian dogma, see Yeago 1994; and Rowe 2002.

most trusted teachers (e.g. Augustine, Cyril of Alexandria, John of Damascus, John Calvin etc.).
5. Finally, we have read the Fourth Gospel with awe and wonder and with prayerful dependence upon 'the Spirit of truth' (14:17; 15:26; 16:13).

In each case, our various reading strategies are rooted in convictions concerning the Johannine 'thing' (*res*) we have attempted to understand. Our approach is thus one of 'confessional criticism'.[25] We read John's Gospel in its *historical and cultural context* because we believe that the book was not written in a vacuum but instead was penned in order to engage the world at a specific time in a specific place. We read the Fourth Gospel using the tools of *narrative criticism* because, when John set out to publish his trinitarian Gospel, he told a story. Because John claims that his trinitarian story constitutes the fulfilment of the OT storyline,[26] we read the Fourth Gospel within the salvation-historical context of the *canon*. We read John's Gospel in and with the *church* because Jesus promised to lead that body of *lectors* into 'all truth' (16:13) and because we believe that the church's great trinitarian creeds do not represent corruptions of the biblical message but instead constitute mature, exegetically trustworthy pathways into Holy Scripture.[27] Finally, we read with *humility, prayer and faith* because we recognize that many who encountered Jesus still rejected him and, in doing so, rejected the Father who sent him. Reading, as Graeme Goldsworthy recently observed, is 'spiritual warfare'.[28] We therefore acknowledge our utter dependence upon the same Spirit who inspired John's Gospel to illuminate our minds that we might know the only true God and Jesus Christ whom he sent (17:3). But dependence is not despair. For Jesus promised, 'I have made you known to them, and will continue to make you known in order that the love you have for me may be in them and that I myself may be in them' (17:26; cf. 16:13–15). In the light of his promise, we trust that our labour of reading is not in vain (1 Cor. 15:58; cf. 2 Tim. 2:7).

The present volume proceeds in three parts. In part 1, we attempt to situate John's trinitarian teaching within the context of Second

[25] Wolters 2000: 91.
[26] See Evans 2000.
[27] O'Keefe and Reno argue that the patristic exegetical tradition bears similarities to a modern scientific research programme (2005: 114–139). The wager of the present study is that a more traditional approach to reading John will prove more exegetically fruitful than critical traditions inherited from Spinoza and Socinus.
[28] Goldsworthy 2006: 314.

Temple Jewish monotheism. Part 2 is devoted to the characterization of God (*theos*),[29] Father, Son and Spirit in John's Gospel, followed by a brief synthesis of these individual treatments. In each case, the Johannine narrative will be followed in order to trace the development and contextual nuances of the Fourth Gospel's characterization of God as Father, Son and Spirit. The careful, exegetical tracing of John's trinitarian story in part 2 identifies the tracks upon which our theological reflection in part 3 may run. Part 3, then, deals more fully with major trinitarian themes in the Fourth Gospel, including its trinitarian account of Jesus Christ, the Holy Spirit and mission. A final chapter discusses the significance of John's Gospel for the church's doctrine of the Trinity. A brief conclusion summarizes some of the practical implications of the present study.

---

[29] Stibbe (2006) does not provide an adequate treatment of *theos* in his study of the Father in the Fourth Gospel. We seek to remedy this omission in the present study.

Part 1: Historical Context

Chapter One

John's Gospel and Jewish monotheism

John's Gospel was not written in a vacuum. One's construal of the most likely context in which the Gospel was written will significantly affect the way in which one understands the Gospel's teaching on God, Jesus and the Spirit. In this chapter, the ensuing study of John's presentation of God, the Father, the Son and the Spirit, will be set within the larger framework of the notion of monotheism in the OT and Second Temple literature. In this context, it will also be helpful to consider the most likely background for John's portrayal of Jesus' pre-existence. This will enable a more accurate assessment of John's teaching on this subject in relation to notions of God in the larger Jewish and Greco-Roman world in which he lived.

John's context

The traditional view holds that the apostle John, at the urging of some of his disciples, wrote the Gospel toward the end of the first century AD in Ephesus in Asia Minor.[1] On this view, John's Gospel, alongside the Synoptics, occupies a place well within the mainstream of first-century Christianity. The sources underlying the Gospel not merely comprise what may be called 'Johannine tradition' (i.e. material independent of the so-called 'Synoptic tradition') but the Gospel is ultimately grounded in eyewitness testimony on the part of one of the key participants in the actual story and history leading to Jesus' crucifixion (cf. e.g. 19:35; 21:24).[2]

[1] Irenaeus, *Haer*. 3.1.2. For a more detailed account, see Köstenberger 2005a: 205–242. Though see the recent challenge of this reading of Irenaeus' testimony by Bauckham 2006: 452–468 and the response by Köstenberger and Stout (forthcoming). It should be noted that the internal evidence, in our view decisively, supports the apostolic authorship and the eyewitness character of John's Gospel, and that patristic testimony has a subordinate, though nonetheless significant, role in confirming authorship. See further the discussion and critique of Bauckham below.
[2] Note the recent case made for the Gospels as eyewitness testimony by Bauckham 2006.

In the wake of the Enlightenment, scholars began to question the traditional attribution of apostolic authorship to the Gospel of John. Edward Evanson believed the author was familiar with Platonic philosophy.[3] Karl Gottlieb Bretschneider construed the background as Philonic Alexandrian philosophy.[4] David Friedrich Strauss viewed the Gospel as mythological, an understanding refined and further developed by Rudolf Bultmann, a proponent of the history-of-religions school. Bultmann, for his part, believed John was aligned with Mandaean Gnosticism and saw numerous parallels in Hellenistic mystery religions.[5] Similarly, C. H. Dodd detected parallels in the Hermetic literature.[6]

Others, however, such as Adolf Schlatter and B. F. Westcott, maintained that John's Jewish background predominates.[7] Schlatter adduced detailed rabbinic parallels, while Westcott located the context of John's Gospel in the matrix of three major events: (1) the Pauline Gentile mission; (2) the destruction of the Jerusalem temple; and (3) the emergence of Gnosticism.[8] In the second half of the twentieth century, a rather novel construal of the setting of John's Gospel emerged, the 'Johannine community hypothesis' in its various permutations. J. L. Martyn proposed that the reference to synagogue expulsion in John 9:22 actually refers to a then-recent event in the life of the Johannine sect: its expulsion from its parent synagogue.[9]

According to Martyn, the primary setting of John's Gospel is not its overt location in Jesus' earthly ministry (c. AD 30), but rather the life of the 'Johannine community' (c. AD 90). In order to unearth this latter history, Martyn devised a 'two-level hermeneutic' that substitutes symbolic or allegorical references to the 'Johannine community' for language overtly pertaining to the historical Jesus. An important historical datum for Martyn's fully fledged version of the 'Johannine community hypothesis' was the 'curse of the Christians' (*birkat-ha-mînîm*) that was allegedly added to Jewish synagogue liturgy around AD 90 and applied to messianic, Christian Jews.[10]

---

[3] See Köstenberger 2001b: 17–47.
[4] See Baird 1992: 312–314.
[5] Bultmann 1925: 100–146.
[6] Dodd 1953.
[7] Schlatter 1902, 1948; Westcott 1975 (1881).
[8] Westcott 1975 (1881): xxxvii–xxxviii, cited in Köstenberger 2005a: 207 = 2006: 71.
[9] Martyn 2003 (1968, 1979); 1977: 149–175.
[10] For a cogent critique of Martyn's thesis in general and his reading of 9:22 in particular, see Carson 1991: 360–361, 369–372.

Others, such as Raymond Brown, held to a form of 'Johannine community hypothesis' without mentioning the *birkat-ha-mînîm*. Brown, for his part, postulated a five-stage trajectory of development of the 'Johannine community' inferred from the Gospel's and the epistles' internal evidence.[11] However, many forms of the 'Johannine community hypothesis' are essentially sectarian,[12] which was recognized by some to be rendered unlikely by the manifest mission thrust of the Gospel.[13] For this reason, efforts were made to refine the hypothesis to accommodate the mission emphasis.[14] The alleged role of the *birkat-ha-mînîm*, as well as the 'Johannine community hypothesis' in its various forms, has undergone extensive critique in recent years.[15]

The demise of the 'Johannine community hypothesis', especially in its sectarian form, is apparent in that a substantial recent volume on the contexts of John's Gospel does not even mention this hypothesis.[16] Instead, a plurality of studies is presented on a variety of Johannine topics, and an integrative approach is urged that combines smaller detailed investigations into a coherent whole. Tellingly, however, the work itself does not actually attempt such a larger synthesis. In another important development, the recent substantive rehabilitation of the historical reliability of John's Gospel has rendered the essence of the traditional view more plausible once again (or at least the view that John contains eyewitness testimony), and studies of the OT background of John's Gospel underscored the predominance of its Jewish background.[17]

In this context, Richard Bauckham's work *Jesus and the Eyewitnesses* (2006) has broken new ground by showing that the Gospels constitute

---

[11] Brown 1978, 1979. See the helpful summary in Carson 1991: 35–36.

[12] E.g. the widely influential article by Meeks 1972: 44–72.

[13] See esp. the discussion in Köstenberger 1998b: 203–206 *et passim*.

[14] See e.g. Onuki 1984; Okure 1988.

[15] See esp. Hengel 1993; Bauckham 1998b; Hill 2004; Köstenberger 2006.

[16] Frey and Schnelle 2004.

[17] See Blomberg 2001; Köstenberger 2001a: 1–216; 2007. Bauckham 2006 believes that John's Gospel was written by John the Elder, not John the apostle. But in keeping with Bauckham's own argument, John's Gospel is not merely eyewitness testimony, but *apostolic* eyewitness testimony (see Bauckham 2006: 93–113 on the role of the Twelve as 'authoritative collegium'). Also, it is highly unlikely (and in fact in conflict with Mark 14:17 and Luke 22:14, who indicate that Jesus was at the final Passover with the Twelve/apostles; see further below) that a person outside the apostolic circle participated with Jesus in the Last Supper (13:23; cf. 21:20), as Bauckham contends, much less occupied a place next to Jesus (ironically, the cover of Bauckham's book features Jesus at the Last Supper with his *twelve* disciples). What is more, Bauckham's reading of the patristic material is doubtful as well, on which see Köstenberger and Stout (forthcoming).

eyewitness testimony. According to Bauckham, the ideal source in ancient Greco-Roman literature is not the dispassionate observer, but the eyewitness.[18] The written Gospels, Bauckham contends, contain oral *history* related to the personal transmission of eyewitness testimony, not merely oral *tradition* that is the result of the collective and anonymous transmission of material.[19] Bauckham (2006: 93) states his own thesis as follows:

> It is the contention of this book that, in the period up to the writing of the Gospels, gospel traditions were connected with named and known eyewitnesses, people who had heard the teaching of Jesus from his lips and committed it to memory, people who had witnessed the events of his ministry, death, and resurrection and had formulated the stories about these events that they told. These eyewitnesses did not merely set going a process of oral transmission that soon went its own way without reference to them. They remained throughout their lifetimes the sources . . .

In this context, the Twelve served as 'an authoritative collegium'.[20] Especially important in this regard is the phrase 'from the beginning', which is found at several strategic points in the Gospels and the NT record (e.g. Luke 1:2; 1 John 1:1; cf. John 1:1). Several other literary devices are used to stress the Gospels' character as eyewitness testimony, such as 'the *inclusio* of eyewitness testimony' (see esp. Mark 1:16–18 and 16:7 for Peter; John 1:40 and 21:24 for the Beloved Disciple). According to Bauckham, the transmission process of the Jesus tradition resulting in our written canonical Gospels is best understood as a formal controlled tradition in which the eyewitnesses played an important, and continuing, part.[21]

What is more, the Gospel material was transmitted not merely in a given community's quest for self-identity but for profoundly theological reasons, in the conviction that the events of Jesus' history were of epochal historical significance when understood in the larger framework of the (salvific) activity of Israel's God. Jesus was viewed not merely as the founder of a movement, but as the source of salvation, and Christianity was not just a new movement: it celebrated the

[18] Bauckham 2006: 8–11.
[19] See esp. ibid. 36.
[20] Ibid. 94.
[21] Ibid. 264 *et passim.*

fulfilment of God's promises in Jesus the Messiah who had now come, died and risen.

With regard to John's Gospel, Bauckham contends that the Beloved Disciple should be regarded as the author, but he identifies John the Elder (not John the apostle, the son of Zebedee) as the author, primarily, it appears, because of his reading of the patristic evidence (Papias, Polycrates and Irenaeus) and because of his understanding of the reference to the 'sons of Zebedee' in John 21:2. Regarding the latter point, Bauckham finds the Beloved Disciple's anonymity throughout the Gospel an insurmountable obstacle to the apostolic authorship of John's Gospel, since the 'sons of Zebedee' are named (though not by first name); he believes the Beloved Disciple is one of the two unnamed disciples in that list.

This may be so, but there seems to be no good reason why John the apostle (if he was the author) could not have put himself inconspicuously at the scene without lifting his anonymity as the author. Put a different way, since the Beloved Disciple must be one of the seven disciples mentioned in 21:2, but since he cannot be Peter, Thomas or Nathanael, there is at least a one in four possibility that he is John the son of Zebedee, and if his brother James is ruled out (as he should be), the probability rises to one in three. The argument for John the apostle as the author becomes all the more compelling when one considers the following list of concerns with Bauckham's argument:

1. Mark 14:17–18 clearly places the Twelve in the upper room with Jesus at the Last Supper (cf. Luke 22:14: the 'apostles'); this militates against Bauckham's thesis that the author was not one of the Twelve and seems to pit one apostolic eyewitness (Peter as the source for Mark) against another eyewitness (that of the Beloved Disciple).

2. What is the historical plausibility of someone other than one of the Twelve being at Jesus' *side* at the Last Supper, even more so as we know that Judas (one of the Twelve) was on the other side?

3. Bauckham makes nothing of the strong historical link between Peter and John the apostle in all of the available NT evidence (all four Gospels, Acts and Galatians); this is especially significant in the light of the fact that Peter and the Beloved Disciple are indisputably and consistently linked in John's Gospel.[22]

4. The presence of the phrase 'I suppose' (*oimai*) in John 21:25 as a device of authorial modesty (in keeping with the label 'Beloved

---

[22] See Quast 1989.

31

Disciple') supports the integrity of the entire Gospel as from the same author, who is identified as an eyewitness at strategic points in the Gospel (e.g. 13:23; 19:35; cf. 21:20).[23]

5. Methodologically, the question arises as to how legitimate it is to put a large amount of weight on one's reading of the patristic evidence over against the internal evidence of the Gospels themselves.

6. How likely is it, in the light of Bauckham's own theory, that the primary eyewitness behind John's Gospel is a non-apostle, yet one whose testimony is superior even to that of Peter? In this regard, the question arises whether the early church would ever have received such a gospel, especially if written a generation after the Synoptic Gospels and in the light of the crucial importance placed on apostolicity in the canonization process.

7. Why did the author leave out the name John, other than for the Baptist? Surely, it is surprising that someone as important as John the apostle would not be mentioned in the Gospel at all (apart from 21:2). Would it not be considerably more likely that he is in fact the Beloved Disciple and author of the Gospel?

8. Which other John was ever credited with the authorship of the Gospel of John in the early church?[24]

The cumulative force of this list suggests that Bauckham's argument, while generally sound when he affirms the importance of eyewitness testimony for the Gospels, is unduly biased when examining the evidence for the authorship of John's Gospel. In fact, one gets the impression that non-apostolic authorship is all but assumed at the outset of Bauckham's argument. This is all the more surprising as it seems to follow most naturally from Bauckham's overall thesis. After all, Bauckham's point is not merely that eyewitness testimony is important for the Gospels, but that we are dealing here with *apostolic* eyewitness testimony, that is, eyewitness testimony that is credible because it comes from those who were closest to Jesus during his earthly ministry. In this regard, it is hard to see how the testimony of one largely unknown 'John the Elder' (not mentioned in any of the Synoptics or other non-Johannine NT writings)

---

[23] Köstenberger 2004b; cf. Jackson 1999.

[24] Polycrates' possible conflation of the John mentioned in 13:23 with the John referred to in Acts 4:6 (adduced by Bauckham 2006: 439) is no real exception. Contra Bauckham (2006: 444), there is no evidence that Polycrates thought the author of John's Gospel was anyone other than John the apostle (such as John the Elder; see Köstenberger and Stout forthcoming).

would satisfy Bauckham's own criterion. On the other hand, the apostolic authorship of John's Gospel, coupled with Peter's importance as a secondary witness, would fit perfectly with Bauckham's overall theory.

For these and other reasons we welcome and concur with Bauckham's overall thesis on the Gospels' eyewitness character, yet do not find his case against the apostolic authorship of John's Gospel convincing. Much more likely, in our opinion, is the view that John's Gospel, like the other three canonical Gospels, is founded on apostolic eyewitness testimony, and that John, in fact, is the Gospel written by the apostle who was closest to Jesus during his earthly ministry, a claim that fits historically only with the apostle John, who, according to the unified witness of Matthew, Mark and Luke was one of three members of Jesus' inner circle together with Peter, and John's brother James.

With regard to the occasion for writing John's Gospel, recent studies have focused particularly on the Johannine temple theme and explored the possible connection between the destruction of the Jerusalem temple in AD 70 and the composition of John's Gospel.[25] It has been argued that now that the temple has been destroyed, the resurrected Jesus is without peer or rival as the new tabernacle, the new temple, and the new centre of worship for a new nation encompassing all those who are united by faith in Jesus as Messiah. Over against non-messianic Jewish hardening against the Christian message and the formation of rabbinic Judaism, and over against the emergence of proto-gnosis (see 1 John), John seized the opportunity for evangelizing Jews and Diaspora proselytes.

In the light of this plausible reconstruction of the Johannine context, how is one to understand John's teaching on God and the deity of Jesus within the framework of Second Temple Judaism, Greco-Roman thought and early Christianity? Only the broad contours of such an approach can be sketched here. As will be seen, first-century Jews held to a strict form of monotheism rather than blurring the lines between God and other divine mediator figures. At the same time, John did not violate exclusivist Jewish monotheism by attributing divinity and pre-existence to Jesus, because he understood Jesus as belonging to the identity of God rather than as a second, separate, distinct God, resulting in his portrayal of Jesus as Son of the Father.

---

[25] See Köstenberger 2005a (slightly revised, 2006) and the literature cited there.

John's portrayal of Jesus and Jewish monotheism

The Jews' belief in one God was firmly grounded in the Shema: 'Hear, O Israel: The LORD our God, the LORD is one' (Deut. 6:4). The Decalogue, likewise, in the first two commandments forbade Israelites from having (monotheism) or worshipping (monolatry) any gods other than Yahweh (Exod. 20:2–6; Deut. 5:6–10). Everywhere in the Hebrew Scriptures, it is this one God who manifests his character and acts in human history both redemptively and in terms of revelation.[26] This includes seminal events such as the exodus (Exod. 20:2; Deut. 4:32–39; Isa. 43:15–17), the giving of the Law, and the Assyrian and Babylonian exiles. This God is the Creator and sole and sovereign Ruler of all things.[27]

Not only is God recognized as the one and only God; he alone is worshipped. As Bauckham notes, 'Judaism was unique among the religions of the Roman world in demanding the exclusive worship of its God. . . . Jewish monotheism was defined by its adherence to the first and second commandments.'[28] This sharp distinction between God as being alone God and worthy of worship stood in distinct contrast to Hellenistic conceptions which held that worship was a matter of degree because divinity, likewise, was a matter of degree, so that worship was to be rendered to the extent appropriate to its object. Judaism, on the other hand, viewed God as unique, and thus uniquely worthy of worship.[29]

The belief in, and worship of, one and only one God set Israel apart from the polytheistic beliefs and practices of its pagan neighbours, including the Greco-Roman pantheon, which was made up of dozens of gods. While the Jews had lapsed into the worship of other deities in the period prior to the exiles,[30] post-exilic Judaism, including that of the first century AD, was committed to monotheism and monolatry.[31] In fact, this became an important distinguishing characteristic

[26] See esp. Machinist 1991, who notes that affirmations of the uniqueness of Israel's God are found in every genre and at every stage of OT literature; similarly, Clements 1984; and the chart in C. J. H. Wright 2006: 104.

[27] See esp. Isa. 43:11; 44:6; 45:5–6, 14, 18, 21–22; 46:9; Bauckham 1998a: 10–11.

[28] Bauckham 1992, 3: 816. See also Gnuse 1997; MacDonald 2003, 2005; Bauckham 2004 (including a critique of Gnuse); C. J. H. Wright 2006: 73–74.

[29] Bauckham 1998a: 15. Cf. Hurtado 2003: 31, who notes, 'For devout Jews, the core requirement of Judaism was the exclusive worship of Israel's God.' Hurtado also points out that none of the 'divine agents' of God were 'treated as rightful recipients of cultic worship in any known Jewish circles of the time' (2003: 31).

[30] See Lang 1981, 1983; Olyan 1988; M. S. Smith 1990, cited in Hurtado 2003: 29–30, n. 5.

[31] See esp. Hurtado 1998a.

of Jewish religion in a polytheistic environment and was recognized as a hallmark of Jewish faith by Greco-Roman historians such as Tacitus, who wrote, 'The Jews conceive of one God only' (*Hist.* 5.5).

As C. J. H. Wright (2006: 105) observes, faith in the one and only God anchored 'the theocentric, monotheistic worldview of first-century Jews' and constituted 'the assumptive bedrock of Jesus and all his first followers'. 'This God', Wright continues, 'was acknowledged now by Israel, his covenant people. But the God of Israel was also the universal God to whom all nations, kings, and even emperors must finally submit.'[32] As the NT attests, strikingly, Jesus claimed, and his followers believed, that he shared the identity of Yahweh, the one and only God of Israel and of the nations, indicated by the application of *maranatha* (Aram. 'O Lord, come') to Jesus (1 Cor. 16:22; Rev. 22:20) and the appellation of Jesus as *kyrios* (Lord) in the Christian confession *kyrios Iēsous* ('Jesus is Lord'; see esp. Acts 2:36; Rom. 10:9; 1 Cor. 12:3; Phil. 2:11 cf. Isa. 45:22–23).[33]

In the light of the Jewish context of John's Gospel noted above and the Jewish belief in monotheism, it is apparent that any claims to deity by an individual such as Jesus would have been fiercely opposed by pious first-century Jews. Numerous passages in John's Gospel suggest that this is in fact what occurred when Jesus' Jewish contemporaries repeatedly attempted to stone Jesus on account of blasphemy (e.g. 5:18; 8:59; 10:31–33; cf. 11:8). Also, at Jesus' trial before Pilate, the Jews, after initially insinuating Jesus was a political threat to Roman imperial power, eventually insist that Jesus 'must die, because he claimed to be the Son of God' (19:7). Hence Jesus died first and foremost because he claimed to be God (cf. Matt. 26:65; Bock 2000).

Some believe that Second Temple Judaism held to a strict monotheism that rendered it impossible to attribute divinity to anyone other than God. In this case, only a radical break with Judaism would have allowed his followers to attribute divinity to Jesus. Hence Maurice Casey contends that 'the deity of Jesus is . . . *inherently* unJewish. The witness of Jewish texts is unvarying: belief that a second being is

---

[32] C. J. H. Wright 2006: 105.

[33] See ch. 4 in C. J. H. Wright 2006, esp. pp. 106–109; and Rowe 2000, 2003, 2006. Contra Dunn, who claims that 'only in the Fourth Gospel can we speak of a doctrine of the incarnation' (1996: 259; but see e.g. the critique by Cranfield 1987 with regard to Romans; and Fee 2007: 500–512). A full critique of Dunn's work is beyond the scope of the present volume. It should be noted, however, that the recent works by Bauckham, Lee and Hurtado et al., discussed in this chapter, have decisively undercut Dunn's thesis.

God involves departure from the Jewish community.'[34] Others favour the view that Second Temple Judaism was more flexible, pointing to various intermediary figures such as angels, exalted humans or personified divine attributes, claiming that these provide Jewish precedents for identifying Jesus as divine.[35]

Indeed, the OT and Second Temple literature feature several passages where beings other than God are called 'god'. Philo refers to Moses as 'god' (*Mos.* 1.155–158; *Prob.* 42–44; cf. Exod. 7:1).[36] Human judges are called 'gods' in the LXX (Exod. 22:27), as are angels (Pss 8:6; 82:1, 6; 97:6; 138:1) and the mysterious figure of Melchizedek (11QMelch 2.24–25).[37] Yet intermediary figures such as these were understood as creatures, and the line between God and created beings was clearly drawn (cf. Ezek. 28:2; Hos. 11:9). In passages such as these, rather than blurring divine–human distinctions, beings who are not God are shown to exercise divine prerogatives.[38] Hence these instances cannot serve as genuine precedents.

Rather than pointing to Jewish intermediary figures, therefore, it is most plausible that the early Christians identified 'Jesus directly with the one God of Israel' and included 'Jesus in the unique identity of this one God'.[39] If correct, this view has revolutionary implications for understanding the Christology of the NT. In Bauckham's words:

[T]he highest possible Christology, the inclusion of Jesus in the unique divine identity, was central to the faith of the early church even before any of the New Testament writings were written. . . . Although there was development in understanding this inclusion of Jesus in the identity of God, the decisive step of so including him was made at the beginning . . .[40]

[34] Casey 1991: 176, cited in M. M. Thompson 2001: 28. See the critique of Casey's work in Hurtado 2003: 43–44; and Dunn 1994.

[35] Cf. Hurtado 1998a, 2003. Though see the important clarification in Hurtado 2003: 29, n. 3, where Hurtado notes that he believes Jewish 'divine agency' traditions 'were *not* by themselves sufficient to explain the emergence or distinctive character of devotion to Jesus'.

[36] Philo also calls the Logos 'a second god' (*QG* 2.62; cf. Justin Martyr, *1 Apol.* 63.15; *Dial.* 56.4).

[37] See Jesus' citation of Ps. 82:6 per John 10:34, on which see the discussion later in this volume.

[38] So rightly, M. M. Thompson 2001: 45.

[39] Bauckham 1998a: 4.

[40] Ibid. 27. Bauckham's findings stand in sharp contrast to those of Dunn 1996 (except for a new foreword, unchanged from 1980).

What is more, this high Christology was entirely possible within strict Jewish monotheism. This explains why neither John nor the other NT writers evidence any consciousness of tension between the attribution of deity to Jesus and their Jewish monotheistic beliefs. Jesus' inclusion in the unique deity was novel, but did not compromise Jewish monotheism. John's Gospel also shows Jesus appropriating the divine name *'anî hû'* (LXX: *egō eimi*).[41] At times, the expression is used simply meaning 'I am' without indicating a claim to deity on Jesus' part. At other times, especially in the seven absolute 'I am' sayings, Jesus' deity is clearly implied.[42]

In keeping with Isaiah's vision of a new exodus for God's people, the Gospels provide a new narrative of God's acts.[43] Just as Israel knew God as the one who delivered the nation out of Egypt and told the story of that God, the NT writers identify God as the God of Jesus Christ and tell the story of Jesus as the account of the deliverance of God's people from sin.[44] This new story is consistent with the OT account of God and his acts on behalf of his people, yet it is new in the way God now has revealed himself and provided redemption in a final and universal way (1:18; cf. Heb. 1:1–3). In Jesus, the Creator and Ruler of the world has become its universal Saviour (4:42; cf. Luke 2:1).

Jesus' inclusion in the identity of God means that God must be conceived in relational terms, uniting God as Father, Son and Holy Spirit. God thus transcends one-dimensional conceptions of human identity. This entails an element of novelty: 'Nothing in the Second Temple Jewish understanding of divine identity contradicts the possibility of interpersonal relationship within the divine identity, but on the other hand there is little, if anything, that anticipates it.'[45] Jesus is now 'God with us' (Matt. 1:25) and 'will be with' his people (Matt. 28:20).[46] 'The Father, the Son, and the Holy Spirit' names the newly disclosed identity of God revealed in the Gospels' account of Jesus (e.g. Matt. 28:19).[47]

---

[41] Harner 1970; Ball 1996; Williams 2000; Bauckham 2005: 153–163.

[42] 4:26; 6:20; 8:24, 28; 13:19; 18:5, 6, 8. Both Isa. 40–66 and John's Gospel feature a total of nine (seven plus two) references to God or Jesus as 'I am'.

[43] Bauckham 1998a: 71; 2006: 277. See also Vanhoozer 2005a, in further development of Balthasar 1988, 1990, 1992, 1994.

[44] See esp. John 1:14–18 with its repeated allusions to Exod. 33–34, esp. 33:18 and 34:6.

[45] Bauckham 1998a: 75.

[46] See the important monograph-length treatment by Kupp 1996.

[47] Bauckham 1998a: 76.

With this we have come full circle, and yet have come to realize a massive advance in God's self-revelation in and through his Son. As noted at the outset, OT Israel's belief in one God is grounded in the Shema of Deuteronomy 6:4. In 1 Corinthians 8:4–6, Paul applies this most foundational of all Jewish monotheistic texts decisively and unmistakably to Jesus, inserting Jesus into the 'one God, one Lord' formula and connecting him with the creative work of God the Father:

> We know that an idol is nothing at all in the world and that there is no God but one. For even if there are so-called gods, whether in heaven or on earth . . . , yet for us there is but one God, the Father, from whom all things came and for whom we live; and there is but one Lord, Jesus Christ, through whom all things came and through whom we live.

Richard Bauckham aptly draws out the implications of Paul's statement for biblical monotheism:

> The only possible way to understand Paul as maintaining monotheism is to understand him to be including Jesus in the unique identity of the one God affirmed in the Shema'. . . . Paul is not adding to the one God of the Shema' a 'Lord' the Shema' does not mention. He is identifying Jesus as the 'Lord' whom the Shema' affirms to be one. In this unprecedented reformulation of the Shema', the unique identity of the one God consists of the one God, the Father, and the one Lord, his Messiah (who is implicitly regarded as the Son of the Father).[48]

This shows that Paul and the early church, as well as John, included Jesus within the identity of the one God confessed in the Shema and believed that Jesus shared in the identity of Yahweh, in keeping with Jesus' own claim that he and the Father are one. Contrary to the Jewish charge that Jesus' claim constituted a breach of their monotheistic beliefs (cf. e.g. John 10:31–33), Jesus' followers understood that Jesus' claim did not imply that he was a second God alongside, and in addition to, God the Father (ditheism), but that his deity

---

[48] Bauckham 2004: 224, cited in C. J. H. Wright 2006: 111–112. See also N. T. Wright 1991: 120–136; Hurtado 2003: 123–126 (with implications for Jesus' pre-existence, on which see also Moo 2005: 178–179 and the discussion below) *et passim*; Capes 1992; and Fee 2007: 88–94.

was to be accommodated within the framework of Jewish monotheism in such a way that the one and only God affirmed in the Shema could accommodate the notion of Father, Son and Spirit – three in one – as God.[49]

The background of John's portrayal of Jesus' pre-existence

One important question that has received considerable attention in recent years is what led the early church to conclude that Jesus pre-existed with God in eternity past. In a recent study, A. H. I. Lee demonstrated convincingly, and against the preponderance of much contemporary scholarship, that neither Jewish angelology nor the pre-existent Messiah ever exerted sufficient influence on early Christology to serve as ready-made categories for viewing Jesus as a divine and pre-existent being alongside God. Rather, the early Christian understanding of Jesus as the pre-existent Son of God is the result of early Christian exegesis of Psalms 110:1 and 2:7 in the light of Jesus' self-understanding as the Son of God.[50]

According to Lee, Jewish wisdom traditions never issued in personified divine attributes that took on divine hypostases separate from God. Rather, these enabled Second Temple Jews to speak of God's activity in the world without sacrificing the notion of his transcendence. Viewing himself as sustaining a unique personal relationship to God as his Father, Jesus was the Messiah because he was the Son of God, and his consciousness of divine sonship played a significant role in the developme : of early Christology. Hence Jesus' self-understanding is foundational for the early Christian conception of Jesus as the pre-existent Son of God. The parable of the wicked tenants, for example, makes clear that Jesus was God's Son sent into this world from above.[51]

In particular, Jesus' consciousness of divine sonship laid the foundation for the early church's messianic exegesis of Psalms 110:1 and 2:7

---

[49] This is why there is no contradiction between the church's worshi⸗ of God as the Trinity and its claim that its God is Israel's God, a question addressed by B. D. Marshall, who notes that '[t]he lack of referential fixity in Christian discourse about the God of Israel teaches us . . . that the Father is the God of Israel, the Son is the God of Israel, and the Holy Spirit is the God of Israel, yet they are not three gods of Israel, but one God of Israel' (2001: 258).

[50] A. H. I. Lee 2005; see also Juncker 2001. See already Bauckham 1998a: 29–31; and Gathercole 2006 on the Synoptic material (though see the critique by Dunn 2007).

[51] See the important discussion of Mark 12:1–9 in Bockmuehl 2006: 215–220.

with reference to Jesus (rooted, again, in Jesus' own usage). Through its messianic exegesis of these two Psalms references and other similar passages, the early church came to confirm what it was already beginning to believe on the basis of Jesus' self-consciousness and his resurrection. In Psalm 110:1, the early church found biblical grounding for the notion of Jesus' resurrection as his exaltation to God's right hand (see esp. Acts 2:34–35). Importantly, the early Christians did not view Jesus' resurrection as conferring on him an essentially new status but as confirming the status he already possessed.

The early Christian understanding of Jesus as Lord finds an important point of departure in Jesus' treatment of Psalm 110:1 with reference to himself as David's Lord who stands and exists before David. This implies Jesus' claim of pre-existence, which is also confirmed by his statement before the Sanhedrin in Mark 14:62. Psalm 2:7, likewise, was understood by the early church as a prophecy concerning Jesus' divine sonship that was decisively fulfilled at his resurrection and exaltation (Acts 13:33; cf. Acts 4:25–26). Jesus did not become God's Son at the resurrection; he already was God's Son prior to the crucifixion, and his resurrection and exaltation merely confirmed his status as Son of God.

Conversely, wisdom Christology is not clearly present in Paul's writings.[52] Rather, the early Christian understanding of Jesus as the pre-existent Son of God, aided by its messianic exegesis of certain psalms, led it to express this conviction by using Jewish wisdom traditions. Hence the church expressed the implications of its conviction that Jesus was the Son of God, namely that Jesus was active in creation and coeternal with God the Father, in terms provided by Jewish wisdom traditions. Thus the latter were not the *source* for the church's understanding of Jesus' pre-existence but rather one way of expressing the *implications* of this conviction at which the church had arrived on different grounds.

If Lee is correct, John did not derive his Christology from Jewish wisdom traditions,[53] but rather chose to contextualize his understanding of Jesus' pre-existence and divine sonship by couching some of the implications in Jewish wisdom categories, a different procedure altogether.[54] This hypothesis comports well with the internal data of John's Gospel, mentioned above, regarding the grounds of Jewish opposition to Jesus during his earthly ministry, namely Jesus' implicit

[52] Fee 2007: 594–619.
[53] Contra e.g. Witherington 1995 (following Dunn).
[54] See also Ebert 1998.

and explicit claims to deity. Intermittent attempts to stone Jesus on account of blasphemy throughout John's Gospel and the Jews' remark before Pilate that Jesus deserved to die because he claimed to be the Son of God confirm that Jesus claimed to be God.

Christ-devotion and exclusivist Jewish monotheism

In his work *Lord Jesus Christ*, Larry Hurtado argues three basic inter-related theses: (1) 'devotion to Jesus emerges phenomenally early in circles of his followers, and cannot be restricted to a secondary stage of religious development or explained as the product of extraneous forces'; (2) 'devotion to Jesus was exhibited in an unparalleled inten-sity and diversity of expression, for which we have no true analogy in the religious environment of the time'; and (3) 'this intense devo-tion to Jesus, which includes reverencing him as divine, was offered and articulated characteristically within a firm stance of exclusivist monotheism, particularly in the circles of early Christians that . . . helped to establish what became mainstream . . . Christianity'.[55]

According to Hurtado, 'the exclusivist monotheism of ancient Judaism is the crucial religious context in which to view early Christ-devotion', and this monotheism helped shape Christ-devotion 'espe-cially in those Christian circles concerned to maintain a fidelity to the biblical tradition of the one God'.[56] Central to this exclusive monotheism is a sharp distinction between legitimate and illegitimate recipients of worship: 'Jesus is not reverenced as another deity of any independent origin or significance; instead, his divine significance is characteristically expressed in terms of his relationship to the one God.'[57] Hence Jesus-devotion was binitarian (worshipping both God and Jesus), but not ditheistic.[58]

John's claim that Jesus is 'Christ' and 'Son of God' amounts to more than asserting that Jesus is Israel's rightful king. Rather, these designations express the belief that Jesus was also divine and of heav-enly origin.[59] Other than in the Synoptics, where the charge of blas-phemy surfaces only at the trial of Jesus, in John's Gospel Jesus is charged with blasphemy throughout his ministry (cf. 5:18; 8:59;

---

[55] Hurtado 2003: 2–3.
[56] Ibid. 48.
[57] Ibid. 51.
[58] Ibid. 52–53.
[59] Ibid. 362.

10:31–33). John's adaptation of the Isaianic 'I am' formula and of the 'glory' and 'lifted up' motifs also intimately associate Jesus with God in a way unparalleled by any other Jewish tradition of the period.[60] Remarkably, Jesus is given 'glory' by God (e.g. 17:5, 24) despite the fact that God does not share his glory with another (Isa. 42:8; 48:11).[61]

On the basis of the identification of Jesus with Isaiah's suffering Servant, which is doubtless grounded in Jesus' own self-understanding (e.g. Luke 4:18), John read Isaiah 40 – 55 as referring, not to one, but to two divine figures, God on the one hand and the suffering Servant on the other.[62] In Isaiah, John found warrant for seeing Jesus as a figure properly identified with the 'I am' of Isaiah and the exodus (cf. Exod. 3:14) and sharing the glory of God as the one who bore the transgressions of many and who was 'lifted up' and exalted by God.[63] Indeed, the Gospel's portrayal of Jesus as the Word sent by God, which, once it has accomplished its purpose, returns to the one who sent it, derives directly from Isaiah 55:11.[64]

Other startling attributions of divinity in John's Gospel are entailed by its emphasis on Jesus being given God's name (e.g. 17:11–12), the requirement of believing in Jesus' name (e.g. 1:12) and by the frequent references to prayer being rendered in Jesus' name (e.g. 14:13–14). At the same time, Jesus is portrayed by John as both obedient to the Father and yet equal to him (compare 14:28 with 10:30); and as both human and divine (compare 4:9 or 11:35 with 8:58 or 17:5).[65] Jesus is a historical, earthly, human figure who is primarily perceived by his contemporaries as a rabbi, a Jewish religious teacher, though, at the same time, he is also the Son of God.[66]

Jesus' humanity (his 'flesh', 1:14) is required particularly for the efficacy of his redemptive cross-death (e.g. 6:51–58).[67] Significantly,

[60] Ibid. 379.

[61] Note the possible connection between the Johannine 'glory' and 'temple' motifs, to be further developed in Köstenberger forthcoming.

[62] Hurtado 2003: 380, citing Juel 1988: 119–133 and Bauckham 1998a: 47–69.

[63] On the 'I am' motif, see briefly above. Regarding the phrase 'lifted up', compare 3:14, 8:28, 12:32 with Isa. 52:13, which speaks of the suffering servant being 'raised and lifted up and highly exalted' in the context of a reference to the disfigured servant 'sprinkl[ing] many nations' (v. 15). On the use of Isaiah in John's Gospel, see esp. Evans 1987: 221–236.

[64] Köstenberger 2004c: 27.

[65] On the former, see Cowan 2006; on the latter, see M. M. Thompson 1988 (contra Käsemann 1968).

[66] See Köstenberger 1998a: 97–128.

[67] On the nature of Jesus' work, see Köstenberger 1998b: 74–81.

the fourth evangelist bears witness to Jesus' full humanity at the cross (19:34–35). Jesus is also shown to be endowed with the Spirit (1:32–33; 3:34) and as performing a series of startling signs confirming his messianic identity (e.g. 2:11). The Spirit's role as 'other helping presence' and as sent by both God and Jesus ties him intricately to Jesus the Son. The triunity of Father, Son and Spirit forms the paradigm and basis for the love and unity among Jesus' followers and for their mission to the world as they re-present his message and follow their Lord (20:21; cf. 17:18).[68]

Implications for John's Gospel

The understanding of the Jewish monotheistic framework for the characterization of Jesus in John's Gospel is relevant for a proper reading of John's prologue and for understanding the portrayal of Jesus throughout the Gospel as the Son of the Father, as one with the Father, and as the 'I am'.[69] The depiction of the Word in John 1:1 and of its instrumentality in creation in 1:3 makes clear that the Word, rather than being a creature, belongs to God's own unique, uncreated identity and thus has life in itself (1:4; cf. 5:26). John's Christological retelling of Genesis has several Second Temple precedents, though it is of course unique in its reference to Jesus as the Word.[70]

According to John, the Word, while distinct from God, is at the same time intrinsic to his own identity: it existed with God 'in the beginning' (1:1).[71] In the Gospel proper, however, the designation of Jesus as the Word is, naturally, superseded by Jesus' own way of speaking of himself as the Son of the Father. In its portrayal of Jesus as distinct from God and yet intrinsic to his identity, John's Gospel does not compromise Jewish monotheism, since, while being 'with God', the Word 'was God' in its own right, and hence one with God (1:1–2; cf. 10:30; see also 5:26), rather than a second God, that is, a

[68] See Köstenberger 1998b; and chapter 9 below.

[69] See esp. Bauckham 2005: 148–166.

[70] Bauckham 2005: 150.

[71] Note in this regard Bauckham's (2006) thesis that the four canonical Gospels, including John, constitute eyewitness testimony and his proposal that John, like Mark and Luke, features an *inclusio* of eyewitness testimony, in 1:40 and 21:24. This may be so, but, more importantly, it seems that 1:1, in conjunction with 1:18, indicates that Jesus himself, who was 'in the beginning' with God, serves as the ultimate eyewitness (cf. 18:37), whose testimony is foundational for the Beloved Disciple's testimony (compare Jesus' position *eis ton kolpon* per 1:19 with the Beloved Disciple's position *en tō kolpō* of Jesus per 13:23 [reiterated in slightly different terms at 21:20]).

divine entity apart from the one and only God revealed in Scripture as the Creator and Ruler of all things.

Implicit in Jesus' inclusion in the identity of God is his right to receiving worship (5:23; cf. 9:38; 20:28). His inclusion in the divine identity is also indicated by the possible allusion to the Shema of Deuteronomy 6:4 in John 10:30 (cf. 1 Cor. 8:6).[72] As Bauckham writes:

> Without contradicting or rejecting any of the existing features of Jewish monotheism, the Fourth Gospel, therefore, redefines Jewish monotheism as Christological monotheism. Christological monotheism is a form of monotheism in which the relationship of Jesus the Son to his Father is integral to the definition of who the one true God is.[73]

With this, we are ready to embark on our study of John's characterization of God: the Father, the Son and the Spirit.

---

[72] The change from masculine to neuter 'one' is a necessary adaptation of language (Bauckham 2005: 163).

[73] Bauckham 2005: 165.

Part 2: Biblical Foundations

Chapter Two

God in John's Gospel

Introduction

As Culpepper (1983: 113) astutely notes, God never appears in the Fourth Gospel, and the only words he speaks are 'and I have glorified it, and will glorify it again' (12:28).[1] Hence 'God is characterized not by what He says or does but by what Jesus, His fully authorized emissary, says about Him.'[2] Moloney (1998: 47), likewise, registers the incisive point that according to the fourth evangelist (1:18), Jesus is telling God's story. What this means, then, is that it is not so much the evangelist who is telling Jesus' story but Jesus who is telling the story of God, and the fourth evangelist retreats dutifully into the background to allow Jesus to tell his story.[3]

From these initial observations it follows, then, that according to John's Gospel, God is characterized by Jesus, and once one has understood the Gospel's characterization of Jesus, one has understood its characterization of God.[4] Nevertheless, Jesus and God (the

---

[1] But see Stibbe (2006: 177), who notes that 'it is precisely through this lack of disclosure that John manages to preserve a sense of the Father's [God's] transcendence'. Later in his discussion, Stibbe (2006: 184–186, citing M. M. Thompson 1993: 198) relates 12:27–28 to 12:32 and ties Jesus' glorification of the name of the Father in with Gentiles as well as Jews coming to Jesus subsequent to his glorification. Scripture references are from the NIV unless noted otherwise. The renderings 'one-of-a-kind Son' for *monogenēs* and 'helping presence' for *paraklētos* are the present authors' (see chapter 5, n. 1, in the present volume).

[2] Culpepper 1983: 113. Similarly, Meyer (1996: 255): 'The only "presentation of God" in the Fourth Gospel is the self-presentation of Christ in its narratives and discourses.' For some literary-critical comments on the characterization of God in John's Gospel, see M. M. Thompson 1993: 177–187.

[3] See esp. Stibbe 2006, who makes the point that John's Gospel is not so much a 'life' (*bios*) of Jesus as it is a 'life' of God (*bios theou*) or, better still, a 'life' of God the Father (*bios patrou*). See also Olsson (1999: 143), who writes, 'The Gospel of John is in form a narrative about Jesus, but its contents are in fact a narrative about what God has done and continues to do through Jesus.'

[4] Meyer (1996: 256) also makes the converse point, 'everything in the Gospel's presentation of Christ is also a "presentation of God"'. Meyer is rightly critical of both Bultmann's reductionistic reading of Jesus as revealing nothing but that he is the

47

Father) are separate and so must be considered individually.[5] The present chapter surveys all references to *theos* in John's Gospel, whether the referent is God the Father or Jesus. Subsequent chapters will deal with the Fourth Gospel's characterization of the Father, the Son and the Spirit seriatim before a synthesis will be attempted and the theological implications of John's portrayal of the triune God be explored.

The prologue

John's prologue serves to provide the reader with the proper lens through which to interpret the subsequent narrative.[6] Two critical issues are addressed: (1) the relationship between God and the Word (Jesus); and (2) the possibility of a close relationship between God and human beings.[7] The prologue includes eight references to *theos* (1:1 [*bis*], 2, 6, 12, 13, 18 [*bis*]). Of these, six refer to God the Father (1:1, 2, 6, 12, 13, 18), and two to the Word or Jesus Christ (1:1, 18).[8] The term *theos* is familiar to John's readers as a reference to the God revealed in the OT. The word occurs in Genesis 1:1 to refer to the Creator. While the Greco-Roman pantheon was made up of dozens of deities, the Jews believed in only one God (Deut. 6:4).[9]

In 1:1a, the 'beginning' of the story, God is set in relation to the Word.[10] He subsisted as an eternal being (note the four instances of

---

Revealer and of Käsemann's famous characterization of the Johannine Jesus as God striding across the earth. Neither does theology collapse into Christology (Bultmann 1955, 2: 66) nor does Christology collapse into theology (Käsemann 1968: 9 *et passim*; 255–256). The Father–Son relationship retains a distinction in persons, and John's 'very Christocentricity is theocentric' (256, with reference to the influential essay by Barrett 1982: 1–18).

[5] As M. M. Thompson (1993: 188) puts it (citing Culpepper), 'the Gospel does not confuse or conflate Father and Son'. Yet Thompson agrees that 'it is the words and deeds of Jesus that serve as a characterization of God' (though note the indefinite article).

[6] Cf. Tolmie 1998: 61: '[T]he primary purpose of the prologue is to serve as a comprehensive introduction that will enable the implied reader to gain a firm hold on the basic ideological perspective presented in the Gospel'.

[7] Tolmie 1998: 62–63.

[8] John's favourite expression for God in his Gospel is 'Father' of Jesus (cf. 1:14, 18). On 'God' and 'Father' in the Gospel of John, see the monographs by M. M. Thompson (2000, 2001). On the characterization of God in the Fourth Gospel, see also Tolmie 1998: 57–75; on God the Father, see Meyer 1996: 255–273; and Fisher 2003.

[9] See chapter 1 above.

[10] As Stibbe (2006: 175) rightly notes, it is the Word, rather than God (who 'is introduced here as an indeterminate figure'), who is placed in the foreground in John 1:1. This pattern continues throughout the remainder of the prologue (see e.g. 1:6: 'sent by God'; 1:12: 'children of God').

ēn, 'was', in 1:1–2) prior to creation. In 1:1b, it is the Word that is referred to as *theos*. Hence in 1:1 two different persons are referred to as God, God [the Father] and the Word.[11]

Now it is one thing for the Word to be *with* God (so were Isaiah's personified Word and Wisdom); it is quite another for the Word itself to *be* God.[12] Having distinguished the Word (Jesus, not mentioned by name until 1:17) from God, John shows what they both have in common: they are God. Clearly, calling Jesus 'God' stretched the boundaries of first-century Jewish monotheism.[13] From the patristic era (Arius) to the present (Jehovah's Witnesses), it has been argued that this verse merely identifies Jesus as *a* god rather than as God, because there is no definite article in front of the word *theos*. Yet this is dubious for several reasons.[14]

First, John, as a monotheistic Jew, would hardly have referred to another person as 'a god'. Second, if John had placed a definite article before *theos*, this would have so equated God and the Word that the distinction established between the two persons in the previous clause ('the Word was *with* God') would have been all but obliterated. Third, in Greek syntax it is common for a definite nominative predicate noun preceding a finite verb to be without the article, so that it is illegitimate to infer indefiniteness from the lack of the article in the present passage.[15]

In fact, if John had merely wanted to affirm that Jesus was divine, there was a perfectly proper Greek word for it (*theios*).[16] Nevertheless, the force of the anarthrous *theos* is probably not so much that of definiteness but that of quality: Jesus 'shared the *essence* of the

---

[11] Stibbe (2006: 175) aptly observes that the dynamic of the prologue significantly revolves around the progressive characterization of the Word–God relationship in terms of a Father–Son relationship. On the complex grammatical and theological issues involved in the interpretation of John 1:1, see Harris 1992: 57–71, 301–313; Erickson 1995: 198–201; and Köstenberger 2004c: 25–29.

[12] For a brief survey of the divinity and uniqueness of Jesus, particularly claims of Jesus' pre-existence, see Köstenberger 1998b: 46–47 (see relevant bibliography in nn. 7–8).

[13] Though see Bauckham 1998a; and Hurtado 1998b, 2003.

[14] See Hartley 1999 for an interaction with the arguments by Jehovah's Witnesses against Jesus' deity from 1:1c. Hartley first surveys the history of the debate, starting with Colwell (1933: 12–21), followed by contributions by Harner (1973: 75–87), Dixon (1975) and Hartley himself (1996). Hartley concludes that 'the Word was *theos* (1:1c) in every *sense* the Father was *ton theon* (1:1b), rather than *a god* in a particular sense the Father was not' (1999: 1, summarizing 1996). See also MacLeod 2003: 59–60.

[15] Colwell 1933: 12–31; McGaughy 1972; and Wallace 1996: 256–270.

[16] Brown 1966: 5; Bultmann 1971: 33–34; and Carson 1991: 117.

Father, though they differed in person'.[17] All that can be said about God can also be said about the Word.[18]

The Word's eternal subsistence with God 'in the beginning' (eternity past) is reiterated in 1:2.[19] In 1:3, the flow moves from pre-existence to creation. The Word is presented as God's agent in creation. By implication, God is the Creator, using the Word in his creation of 'all things'. The emphatic way in which this is stated (and the converse denied) focuses on the Word as God's *exclusive* agent in creation.

In 1:6, God is said to be the sender of John (the Baptist). God as the sender is implicit in the divine passive of *apestalmenos* (sent) and explicit in the phrase 'from God'. Hence God is shown to take the initiative not only in creation but also in redemptive history.

In the likely pivot of the prologue,[20] 1:12, believers are referred to as children (*teknia*) of God.[21] In the following verse, they are said to be 'born from God' (*ek* points to God as the source of this spiritual birth). This clearly implies that God in a special sense is the spiritual Father of believers.[22] From Creator in 1:3 John's presentation of God has moved to portraying him as Saviour in 1:12 via John the Baptist being sent (1:6–8) and the Light coming into the world (1:9–11).

The final reference to God completes the panorama from the eternity of God in 1:1 to the invisibility of God in 1:18 (cf. 5:37; 6:46). The logic of John's argument here is that the invisibility of God necessitates revelation. This revelation was accomplished by the *monogenēs theos* (cf. 1:14), that is, Jesus Christ (1:17). The evangelist here emphasizes the closeness of relationship between Jesus and the Father as the grounds of the 'full account' (*exēgēsato*) borne by Jesus of the Father (1:18).[23] This comes on the heels of allusions

[17] Wallace 1996: 269; cf. Erickson 1995: 200.

[18] Morris 1995: 68; and Wallace 1996: 735.

[19] 'In the beginning' appears to serve the dual purpose of anchoring John's creation theology (cf. 20:22) and salvation-historical presentation (cf. 1:6–8, 17) and of rooting the Gospel's eyewitness testimony to Jesus in Jesus' own pre-existent witness from 'the beginning'. This insight builds on, yet transcends, the proposal by Bauckham 2006.

[20] Köstenberger 2004c: 19–23, 38–39 (following Culpepper 1980–1: 1–31).

[21] As Stibbe (2006: 176) observes, believers are called 'children' rather than 'sons' or 'daughters', perhaps because at this early point in the Gospel the evangelist is still trying to establish the uniqueness of the relationship between the Logos and God as Son and Father; for the same reason they are also called 'children of God' rather than 'children of the Father'.

[22] So rightly, Stibbe 2006: 175: 'The words "children" and "born" set up a picture of God as a parent.'

[23] Cf. Moloney 1998: 47, who notes that the verb has the basic meaning 'to tell at length', 'to relate in full', 'to recount a narrative'; and Stibbe 2006. See again the

to God manifesting his presence to his people in the Tent of Meeting (1:14) and to God's giving of the Law through Moses (1:17) at previous junctures of salvation history. But the fullness of grace and truth were revealed only in and through Jesus Christ (1:14, 16–17).

In sum, God is presented in the prologue as eternal and as subsisting in close relationship with the Word prior to creation (1:1–2; cf. 1:18). He is the Creator (1:3), as well as the sender of John the Baptist (1:6) and the source of spiritual rebirth for believers (1:12–13). God is invisible; hence he used Jesus Christ as his vehicle of revelation (1:18; cf. Heb. 1:1–2). As Stibbe (2006: 175) notes, through the course of the prologue, 'the God/Logos distinction is redefined as a Father/Son distinction. This means that the word "God" can refer to at least two figures, a father and a son.'[24]

Table 2.1 The Word-made-flesh and the Son–Father relationship in John's Gospel

1:1	Word (*logos*) = God (*theos*)	God (*theos*)	eternity past
1:14	Word (*logos*) → flesh		then-recent history
1:14–18	Son (*huios*; 'sent')	Father (*patēr*; 'sender')	

The Book of Signs

The vast majority of references to *theos* in this Gospel are found in what has been called 'The Book of Signs' (1:19 – 12:50). The references are not evenly spread. Chapter 2 does not contain a single instance of *theos*; chapters 7 and 12 contain only one instance; and chapter 4 includes a mere two passages. This may indicate that theology proper is subordinated to Christology in John. References to God are often clustered together, particularly (but not limited to) the following passages: 3:2–5, 16–18, 33–36; 5:18; 6:27–29; 8:40–42, 47; 9:29–33; and 10:33–36.

---

possible secondary component of Jesus' coexistence with God 'in the beginning' as the foundation for Jesus' witness and the resultant witness of the author of this Gospel.

[24] Stibbe's (2006) entire essay repays careful reading. One weakness, however, is that Stibbe does not distinguish rigorously enough between the terms *theos* and *patēr* in John's Gospel.

1:19–51

All of the references to *theos* in the remainder of chapter 1 are in the genitive, placing God in relation to Jesus 'the Lamb of God' (1:29, 36) and the 'Chosen One' or 'Son of God' (1:34, 49) and to the 'angels of God' (1:51). John the Baptist uses both Christological titles: 'Lamb of God' in his initial reference to Jesus as the one 'who takes away the sin of the world' (1:29; he uses the title by itself on the subsequent day, 1:36), 'Chosen One of God' as his concluding, climactic confession at the end of the unit 1:29–34.[25]

Hence the Son's redemptive mission is firmly grounded at the very outset of John's Gospel and of Jesus' ministry in God as his source. John's baptizing ministry, in turn, is shown to centre in the purpose of manifesting Jesus, 'God's Lamb', to Israel. Toward the end of the chapter Jesus is confessed as 'Son of God' by Nathanael, who also calls Jesus 'the King of Israel' (1:49). The reference to 'the angels of God' in 1:51 extends God's reach even beyond the Son to other messengers of God.

2 – 4

After a considerable hiatus, the next instances of *theos* appear in John's interchange with Nicodemus. The latter refers to Jesus in conventional terms as a 'teacher who has come from God', acknowledging that unless God were with him, he could not perform the 'signs' he did (3:2). Jesus, in reply, asserts the necessity of a spiritual rebirth in order for anyone to enter God's kingdom (3:3, 5; cf. 1:12–13). These references to God present Jesus in a subordinate role: as a teacher come from God and as herald of God's kingdom.

The remaining references to God in this chapter are probably both parts of explanatory sections provided by the evangelist, in 3:16–21 and in 3:31–36.[26] In the first unit, Jesus' words to Nicodemus regarding the lifting up of the serpent in the wilderness are further elaborated upon by the evangelist with reference to God's love as what motivated him to 'give' his *monogenēs* Son (3:16) to save the world (3:17). In the following verse (3:18), Jesus is called the '*monogenēs* Son

---

[25] On the text-critical issue associated with the reading 'Chosen One of God' in 1:34, see Köstenberger 2004c: 88. See also Charlesworth 2006, 3: 113, who notes the reference to the 'Elect of God' (*bḥyr l' h'*) in the *Elect of God Text* (4Q534 = 4QMess) at Qumran.

[26] See Köstenberger 2004c: 113–114, 133, 138.

of God' (cf. 1:14, 18).[27] The unit closes with a reference to works 'done through [in] God' (3:21).

The second unit added by the evangelist in 3:31–36 contrasts 'the one who comes from above/heaven' (Jesus; cf. 3:13) with 'the one who is from the earth' (the Baptist, representing humanity at large). The latter bears witness to what he has seen and heard (though his witness is largely rejected); the former speaks the words of God. Rejecting John's testimony is tantamount to rejecting the truthfulness of God. 'The one whom God has sent' without further qualifier in this Gospel refers to Jesus (cf. 9:7). Jesus' words are the words of God (cf. 12:47–48; 14:10).

God very likely also is implied to be the giver of the Spirit in 3:34 (cf. 4:10?).[28] God's wrath rests, and continues to rest, on those who refuse to believe in his Son (3:36).

The ensuing interchange between Jesus and the Samaritan woman, similar to that between Jesus and Nicodemus, contains only a few references to God, two to be exact (though the second is exceedingly important). In 4:10, Jesus refers rather obliquely to 'the gift of God' (an objective genitive as in 'gift from God'), 'living water', which is later identified as the Spirit (7:37–39). In 4:24, Jesus asserts that God is spirit, and those who worship him must worship him in spirit and truth. Not only is God eternal (1:1–2) and invisible (1:18); he is also spiritual (4:24).

This spiritual nature of God necessitates that worship directed toward him be likewise spiritual and in keeping with truth. The phrase 'God is spirit' does not refer to the Holy Spirit (contra TNIV), much less to the human spirit, but identifies God as a spiritual, rather than material, being.[29] Owing to God's spiritual nature, the Israelites were not to make idols 'in the form of anything' as did the surrounding nations (Exod. 20:4). Jesus' point here is that, since God is spirit, proper worship of him is also a matter of spirit rather than physical location.

5 – 10

Thus far the characterization of God as Jesus' Father has not yet led to controversy. This changes in 5:17–47.[30] In 5:18, the essence of the

---

[27] The presence of *monogenēs* only in the prologue and the present section constitutes strong evidence that 3:16–21 is by the evangelist. See Carson 1991: 203.

[28] So Tolmie 1998: 65, who notes the effect of the ambiguity in this verse on the reader.

[29] The reference is qualitative, 'stressing the nature or essence of God' (so Wallace 1996: 270); see the similar phrase in 3:6. On the broader theological issues, see W. D. Davies 1994: 288–335, esp. 298–302.

[30] Tolmie 1998: 65.

Jewish leaders' case against Jesus is summed up in the charge that Jesus, by calling God (*theos*) his own Father, made himself equal to God. This violated their notion of monotheism. But already in the prologue, the evangelist places the Word unapologetically and unequivocally beside God as being himself God (perhaps in the sense of 'divine'). Hence the Jews' monotheism proves to be too rigid to accommodate a plurality of persons within the one Godhead.

In the ensuing verses, Jesus deals with the objection of his Jewish opponents by developing in some detail his relationship to the Father as the Son (5:19–30), calling himself 'the Son of God' in the process (5:25). Previously in this Gospel only Nathanael has applied this epithet to Jesus.

Later in the pericope Jesus charges that his opponents do not truly have love for God (5:42) (hence their rejection of him) and that they do not seek the glory of the 'only God' (5:44). Interestingly, in the same pericope in which Jesus is accused of denying the notion of monotheism by claiming to be the Son of God he affirms monotheism by calling God 'the only God'.

The next interchange between Jesus and his Jewish interrogators takes place in the aftermath of Jesus' feeding of the multitudes in chapter 6. In 6:27, he asserts that God (the Father) has put his seal on the Son of Man. In the following verses, the Jews ask, and Jesus tells them, what are 'the works God requires' (NIV; the force of the genitive in the phrase 'works of God'). Rather than accruing merit by performing religious acts, people were urged to perform the one and only 'work of God' required for salvation: to believe in the one he sent (6:28–29).

In the following controversy, Jesus calls himself 'the bread of God', who has come down from heaven and who gives life to the world (6:33). In this, he claims to be the eschatological fulfilment of God's provision of manna to wilderness Israel through Moses (cf. 6:31). Shortly thereafter Jesus also claims to be the eschatological fulfilment of Isaiah's prophecy that all will be taught by God (6:45; cf. Isa. 54:13; see 7:17 below). In language reminiscent of the prologue (cf. 1:18), Jesus here claims that, while no one has seen the Father, he, who is from God, has: hence his call for people to come to him as God's life-giving sustenance.

In Peter's climactic confession at the end of the chapter, this most outspoken member of the Twelve calls Jesus 'the Holy One of God' (6:69; cf. the variant 'Chosen One of God' in 1:34).[31] According to

---

[31] This is part of Peter's characterization throughout John's Gospel: see 13:6–10; 20:2–10; 21:7, 15–19 (cf. Matt. 14:28–33; Luke 5:8; 22:33). Note in this regard

Bauckham, this fits with the characterization of Peter in all the Gospels: his 'impetuosity, self-confidence, outspokenness, and extravagant devotion to Jesus'.[32] Through the device of 'internal focalization',[33] Peter becomes the lens through which the Fourth Gospel's portrayal of Jesus as 'the Holy One of God' is refracted for its readers.

The only reference to *theos* in chapter 7 designates God as the source of Jesus' teaching. In 7:17, anyone who is prepared to do God's will is promised that he will know whether Jesus' teaching is of human or divine origin.

God features very prominently in the paternity dispute unfolding between 8:40 and 54. The pericope continues the pattern of escalating controversy between Jesus and the Jewish leaders, which had previously climaxed in 5:18–47 and also at the end of chapter 6. In 8:40, Jesus points to God as the source from which he heard the truth. In response to Jesus' insinuation that they might have a father other than God, the Jews are insistent that their only Father is God (8:41). Jesus contends that if God were their Father, they would love Jesus (cf. 5:42), because he had come from God (cf. 3:2). The pericope climaxes in the following stinging indictment by Jesus, echoing once again the language of the prologue: 'Anyone who is from God listens to God's words. This is why *you* don't listen – because you're not from God!' (8:47: our trans.; cf. 1:12–13). Finally, 8:54 harks back to the Jews' earlier claim (8:41) that God is their Father. To the contrary, Jesus maintains that they really do not know God, though he does.

In chapter 9, the existence and character of God as revealed in the Hebrew Scriptures is everywhere assumed. The question is, 'Who is Jesus in relation to this God?' The account displays the evangelist's narrative skill in dealing with this issue by way of representative characters. In 9:3, Jesus affirms that 'the work(s) of God' are the ultimate purpose for the man's blindness rather than human sin. In 9:16, the Pharisees contend that Jesus is not from God, because he does not observe the Sabbath. The phrase 'give glory to God' (9:24) is a customary exhortation to truthfulness.[34] In 9:29, the Pharisees affirm

---

Bauckham's (2006: 165–172, 180) well-taken challenge and proposed corrective to the common notion that Peter typically serves as a spokesman for the Twelve throughout the Gospels.

[32] Bauckham 2006: 177.

[33] The term is Bauckham's, who defines 'internal focalization' as a literary device that 'enables readers to view the scene from the vantage point . . . of a character within the story' (2006: 162–163).

[34] See Josh. 7:19.

that God spoke to Moses but doubt that he spoke to Jesus: for them, he is not only human but a 'sinner'. The formerly blind man, on the other hand, argues that God does not listen to sinners but only to those who fear him and do his will (9:31). Hence, if Jesus were not from God, he could do nothing (9:33). In his concluding indictment, Jesus notes that, ironically, the Pharisees' claim to see renders them spiritually blind, while those who acknowledge their spiritual blindness will be given sight.

In 10:33, Jesus' opponents renew their charge from 5:18 (an *inclusio* bracketing chs. 5–10) that Jesus, whom they consider to be a mere man, makes himself out to be God (cf. 10:30: 'I and the Father are one'). In his defence, Jesus cites Psalm 82:6, 'I said, "You are gods"', and contends that if it is appropriate for Scripture to call the recipients of God's word 'gods' in some sense, how can it be considered blasphemy for him to call himself the 'Son of God' (as he does in 5:25, another *inclusio*; see also 11:4 below)?[35]

11 – 12

As in the case of the blind man in chapter 9, Jesus responds to the news of Lazarus' illness by saying that its purpose was the glory of both God and the Son of God (11:4). In 11:22, Martha affirms her belief that God will give Jesus whatever he asks of him (cf. 9:31) (hence placing herself opposite the Pharisees' judgment in ch. 9), and in 11:27 calls Jesus 'the Christ, the Son of God', anticipating the evangelist's eventual purpose statement for the entire Gospel (20:30–31).[36] Immediately prior to raising Lazarus, Jesus once again refers to the glory of God as the purpose of his work (11:40).

Later in the same chapter the evangelist makes reference to the gathering of God's children even beyond Israel as the purpose of Jesus' impending death (11:52).

The final reference to *theos* in the 'Book of Signs' indicts secret believers in Jesus among the Jewish leaders as seeking human praise

---

[35] See Köstenberger 2007: 464–467. For the charge of blasphemy against Jesus, see Hurtado 1999, esp. 36–37.

[36] Martha's witness to Jesus in 11:27 in terms virtually identical to the purpose statement makes her Christological confession at least the virtual equivalent to Peter's confession of Jesus as 'the Holy One of God' in 6:68–69 and beyond this renders hers the anticipatory confession of Jesus as the Christ and Son of God in John's Gospel. Like her sister, Mary, who anticipated Jesus' burial by anointing him (12:3; cf. 12:7), Martha captures (albeit not fully) the essence of Jesus' identity, a fact that is rarely given adequate attention by commentators.

rather than God's glory (12:43; cf. 5:44). This is in obvious contrast to Jesus (cf. 9:3; 11:4, 40).

The Book of Glory

References to God in the second half of John's Gospel are much less frequent than in the 'Book of Signs'.[37]

At the very inception of the 'Book of Glory' the evangelist makes pointed and programmatic reference to Jesus' awareness that he had come from God and was returning to God (13:3). Immediately subsequent to Judas' leaving the upper room, Jesus himself makes reference to glory accruing both to God and to himself (the 'Son of Man') in and through the crucifixion. This continues the string of references in the 'Book of Signs' to the glory of God as the ultimate purpose of Jesus' ministry (e.g. 9:3; 11:4, 40; see above).

Jesus' encouragement to his disciples at the onset of the dark hour of his arrest and passion is that they believe in both God and himself (14:1). Except for the incidental reference that those who kill the disciples will believe they have rendered a service to God in 16:2, virtually the entire farewell discourse is devoid of any explicit reference to *theos* (14:2 – 16:26). Only in 16:27 and 30 is there reference to the disciples having believed that Jesus has come from God (an *inclusio* with 13:3).

In Jesus' final prayer, reference is once again made to God as the 'only' true God (cf. 5:44). And once again, Jesus is mentioned in conjunction with God (cf. e.g. 13:31–32; 14:1).

The pattern of fairly sparse references to *theos* is continued in that there is no explicit reference between 17:4 and 20:16 (except for the Jews' charge before Pilate in 19:7 that Jesus deserved to die because he made himself the Son of God; cf. the likely *inclusio* of 5:18 and 10:33).

The final instances are the risen Jesus' reference to his return to 'my God and your God' in 20:17; Thomas' confession of Jesus as his Lord and his God in 20:28 (cf. 1:1, 18);[38] the reference to Jesus as the Son of God in the purpose statement of 20:31; and the reference to Peter's God-glorifying martyrdom in 21:19.

---

[37] There are a total of sixteen references in John 13 – 21, compared with sixty-seven in John 1 – 12, a ratio of about 1 to 4.

[38] Harris 1992: 128 identifies 1:1, 18 and 20:28 as literary *inclusios*, commenting, 'The Prologue ends (1:18) as it begins (1:1), and the Gospel ends (20:28) as it begins (1:1), with an assertion of the deity of Jesus.'

Summary

Almost half of the references to *theos* in John's Gospel (or thirty-nine out of eighty-three) are found on Jesus' lips.[39] Another quarter comes from the evangelist (twenty-one instances);[40] and another eighth from the Jewish leaders or Pharisees (nine).[41] The remaining fourteen references come from the Baptist (1:29, 34, 36); Nicodemus (3:2 [2]); and various disciples of Jesus.[42] Many of these references centre on the disputed nature of Jesus' relationship with God. The Jewish leaders consistently deny that Jesus is from God,[43] while Jesus himself affirms this,[44] as do his disciples.[45] Jesus, in turn, denies the Jews' claim that they know God,[46] while asserting that he himself does (7:29; 10:15).

Jesus himself is the referent of *theos* in 1:1, 18 and 20:28. He is called the 'Son of God' in 1:49; 3:18; 5:25; 10:36; 11:4, 27; and 20:31 (and possibly 1:34; his claim is disputed in 19:7). Other Christological titles involving reference to *theos* are 'Lamb of God' (1:29, 36); 'Chosen or Holy One of God' (1:34 variant; 6:69); and 'bread of God' (6:33). Jesus' claim to deity is disputed in 5:18; 10:33; and 19:7.

God is an independent referent and is characterized in the following passages as

- eternally existing (1:1, 2)
- the source of new birth (1:13)
- invisible (1:18)
- the origin of Jesus' coming (3:2; 6:46 8:42, 47; 9:33; 13:3; 16:27, 30; cf. 9:16)
- loving the world (3:16)
- true (3:33; 17:3)
- the sender of the Son (3:17, 34; this is implied in many other passages as well)

---

[39] 1:51; 3:3, 5; 4:10, 24; 5:25, 42, 44; 6:27, 29, 33, 45 [OT], 46; 7:17; 8:40, 42 (2), 47 (3), 54; 9:3; 10:34 [OT], 35 (2), 36; 11:4 (2), 40; 12:43; 13:31, 32 (2); 14:1; 16:2, 27; 17:3; 20:17 (2).

[40] 1:1 (2), 2, 6, 12, 13, 18 (2); 3:16, 17, 18, 21, 23, 34 (2), 36; 11:52; 13:3 (2); 20:31; 21:19.

[41] 5:18 (2); 6:28; 8:41; 9:16, 24, 29; 10:33; 19:7.

[42] This includes Nathanael (1:49); Peter (6:69); the formerly blind man (9:31, 33); Martha (11:22 [2], 27); the disciples as a group (16:30); and Thomas (20:28).

[43] 5:18; 9:16; 10:33; 19:7.

[44] 5:25; 6:27, 33, 46; 7:17; 8:42, 47; 10:34–36; 11:4, 27; 13:31–32; 14:1; 16:27; 17:3; 20:17.

[45] 1:20, 34, 36, 49; 6:69; 9:31, 33; 11:22, 27; 20:28.

[46] 7:28; 8:19, 54–55; cf. 15:21; 16:3; 17:25.

- spirit (4:24)
- the only God (5:44; 17:3)
- approving of Jesus (6:27)
- the Father (6:27; in many other passages this is implied in the context)
- the source of Jesus' teaching and of truth (7:17; 8:40)
- the Jews' alleged (but not real) father (8:41, 42, 47, 54)
- the one who spoke to Moses (9:29)
- the one who hears righteous prayer (9:31; 11:22)
- the one to whom Jesus is returning (13:3)
- the God of Jesus and of his disciples (20:17)

Beyond this *theos* occurs in the following genitival constructions: children of God (1:12; 11:52); angels of God (1:51); kingdom of God (3:3, 5); work(s) of God or in God (3:21; 6:28, 29; 9:3); words of God (3:34; 8:47) or Word of God (10:35); wrath of God (3:36); and gift of God (4:10).[47] God is also presented as the object of glory (9:24; 11:4, 40; 12:43; 13:31–32; 21:19; or as the one who glorifies, 13:32); love (5:42); faith (14:1); and worship (16:2). The Baptist is sent by God (1:6) and his people are taught by God (6:45).

On the whole, God is a character who remains in the background. As Culpepper (1983: 113) observes, 'God is the reality beyond, the transcendent presence.' References to God's actions are limited to his loving the world (3:16) and sending (3:17) and approving of his Son (6:27); to his hearing righteous prayer (9:31; 11:22); and to his glorifying the Son (13:32).[48] In (semantic, though not ontological) contrast, the Father is characterized in considerably more active terms in John's Gospel.[49] While the fourth evangelist therefore stringently maintains God's transcendence, he also portrays God as a loving Father who gives and draws individuals to Jesus.[50] There are also several references to God's nature or essential attributes: God is eternal (1:1–2); invisible (1:18); true (3:33; 17:3); spirit (4:24); the only God (5:44; 17:3); and the Father (6:27; cf. 1:13; 20:17).[51] These

[47] A similar list is found in Culpepper (1983: 113–114), though 'words of God' is found in 3:34 (not 3:36) and 'love of God' (5:42) is an objective genitive (with the sense 'love for God'; so e.g. Morris 1989: 128, n. 4). Also, it seems best to list Christological titles such as 'Lamb of God' separately.

[48] Culpepper (1983: 114) also lists God speaking to Moses (9:29).

[49] See the list in Culpepper 1983: 114; and chapter 3 below.

[50] So rightly Culpepper 1983: 114.

[51] Culpepper also includes 'God is light' (3:21), but this does not reflect a direct statement but an inference (1983: 114).

statements further accentuate God's distance or otherness (Culpepper 1983: 114).

Overall, God is the great Given, Known, Accepted and constant Assumed in the controversy concerning Jesus, whose support is sought and invoked by both sides in the escalating debate.[52] Jesus affirms that he has a unique relationship with God as the Son of God as firmly as this is denied by his opponents. Various Christological titles are applied to Jesus by his followers, but most striking is the application of the term *theos* itself to Jesus in the opening and closing verse of the prologue and in the final pericope of the Gospel proper (20:28). This literary *inclusio*, whereby Jesus is affirmed to be God at the beginning and at the end of the Gospel (and nowhere else in those terms) is startling in that it takes a designation, *theos*, universally applied to the God of the Hebrew Scriptures in the entire body of the Gospel and changes the referent to Jesus.

This is done without any sustained attempt at adjudicating the issue of how the God of the Hebrew Scriptures and Jesus can both be called *theos*. The major exception, of course, is found at the inception of the Gospel, where the Word (himself *theos*) and *theos* are said to have existed eternally in close proximity to one another. Yet at the same time, even the risen Jesus still refers to the God of the Hebrew Scriptures as 'my God' in 20:17, and earlier in the Gospel affirms that the Father is greater than him (14:28; cf. 10:30). This hints at a resolution of an apparent ditheism: while there is more than one referent of *theos* in this Gospel, these two persons sustain a nuanced and complementary relationship, which, as will be explored more fully in the following chapters of this volume, is most frequently described in the Johannine narrative as that of 'Father' and 'Son'.

---

[52] As Dahl (1991: 58–60) has noted, the NT writers regularly presuppose or make only indirect reference to contemporary beliefs about God. See Meyer 1996: 257 (also citing Bassler 1992: 1049).

Chapter Three

The Father in John's Gospel

Introduction

In the previous chapter, we saw that the Johannine prologue starts with the Word–God relationship in the opening verse of the Gospel and inexorably moves to the explication of this relationship via the incarnation (the Word-made-flesh, 1:14) as a relationship between Son and Father.[1] What started out as less explicitly defined, and certainly less overtly intimate, has through the incarnation expressed itself in the closest way humanly imaginable, in the form of an only Son dearly loved by his Father, what is more, a Son sent into the world by this Father to make him known (3:16) and to convey his love to a world he had made (1:3, 11), yet a world steeped in moral darkness and sin (1:11; 3:19–21).

While ubiquitous in John's Gospel, the notion of God as Father is not a common one in the Hebrew Scriptures.[2] On the whole, 'Father' tends to be applied to Israel as a nation rather than to individual Jews.[3] The situation is very different in John's Gospel. There are 136 instances of *patēr*, of which 120 have God as a referent.[4] The

---

[1] As M. Stibbe (2006: 171) observes, until not too long ago, it would have been possible to speak of 'the forgotten Father' in Johannine research. As T. Larsson (2001: 14) notes, 'Despite the fact that some have realized that a main theme of the FG [Fourth Gospel] is theology and not only Christology, we must conclude that there is no satisfactory treatment of God in the FG in twentieth-century NT scholarship.' Recently, M. M. Thompson (1993, 2000, 2001), Meyer (1996), Tolmie (1998) and Stibbe (2006), among others, have sought to fill this lacuna and have provided perceptive explorations of the Father in John's Gospel.

[2] Morris 1989: 129.

[3] See the discussion in Fisher 2003: 55–96.

[4] Morris (1989: 130) finds 122 references to God as Father in John's Gospel (he also notes that the only other NT writer that comes even close to the pervasiveness of this motif is Matthew, with forty-five references to God as the heavenly father). Culpepper (1983: 113), following Tenney (1975: 38), puts the number at 118, as does Meyer (1996: 269, n. 27). Schrenk (1967: 996) counts 115 instances, and M. M. Thompson (1993: 196, n. 17) 131. Occasionally, *patēr* refers to Jacob (4:12) or Abraham (8:39, 53, 56), the father of the servant healed by Jesus (4:53), or (in the

references to God as *patēr* are pervasive, but not evenly spread. The expression does not occur at all in chapters 7, 9, 19 and 21.[5] It is found only once in chapters 2, 3, 11 and 18, and only twice in chapters 1 and 13. Major clusters of references are concentrated primarily in the so-called festival cycle (chs. 5, 6, 8 and 10) and in the farewell discourse (14 – 16). Virtually all references are found in discourse rather than narrative material.[6] This strongly suggests that John's 'Father' language is rooted in the terminology of Jesus himself.[7] The emphasis on the Father as the one who sent Jesus and who witnesses to him portrays him as the Authorizer and Authenticator of Jesus.[8]

It should also be noted at the very outset that the Fourth Gospel's 'Father' language and the characterization of God as 'Father' and 'Son' must be understood within the context of the Jewish notion of the father's role in the family and the life of the larger community. As

---

plural) to the Jewish ancestors (e.g. 4:20; 6:31, 49, 58; 7:22). In 8:44, the repeated referent of *patēr* is the devil.

[5] The absence of the term 'Father' in ch. 7 is noted, among others, by Ashton (1991: 318, cited in Meyer 1996: 262), who does, however, draw the hardly defensible conclusion that 'nowhere in this chapter is there the slightest hint that Jesus regarded himself as the Son of God'.

[6] This is noted by Meyer 1996: 264; and M. M. Thompson 1993: 196, who provides a careful and sensitive study of the characterization of God (including that of 'Father') in John's Gospel using R. Alter's scale of characterization, moving from his actions to his appearance, his direct speech, his inward speech and finally statements by the narrator (187–204); and Stibbe (2006: 175): 'we learn most about the Father not from narrated material but rather from discourse or spoken material'.

[7] The historicity of Jesus' calling God 'Father' seems secure (but see the important remarks by Plantinga 1991: 307); space does not permit a defence of Jesus' use of this term. See the bibliographic references in Meyer 1996: 267, n. 17, and his presentation of Synoptic instances of Jesus' use of 'Father' on 267, n. 20 (citing Mark 8:38; 11:25; 13:32; 14:36; Luke 2:49; 6:36; 10:21–22; 11:2, 13; 12:30, 32; 22:29; 23:34(?), 46; 24:49; Matt. 5:16, 45; 6:1, 4, 6 [*bis*], 8, 9, 15, 18 [*bis*], 26, 32; 7:11, 21; 10:20, 29, 32, 33; 11:25–27; 12:50; 13:43; 15:13; 16:17; 18:10, 14, 19, 35; 20:23; 23:9; 25:34; 26:29, 39, 42, 53; 28:19). Meyer notes that, on the assumption of Markan priority, the earliest canonical Gospel contains the fewest references to God as Father, while the last (John) features the most (though the fairly extensive list above of Synoptic references to God as Father hardly justifies Meyer's judgment that such references are 'surprisingly scarce in the pre-Johannine gospel tradition', 258). Nor does Meyer's verdict appear to be on target (at least in the categorical way in which he states it) that the 'Father' language in the Fourth Gospel 'has its roots in post-Easter theological development and is part of the community's confessional language' (ibid.). To say that an 'appeal to Jesus' own religious usage at this point only stands in the way of examining carefully how this language functions in the evangelist's text' (ibid.) seems to overstate one's point considerably.

[8] Cf. Meyer (1996: 265), who calls the Father 'the Vindicator and Authorizer of Jesus'.

Daniel Block (2003: 40) notes, like most ancient Near Eastern cultures, Israelite families were *patrilineal* (official descent was traced through the father's line), *patrilocal* (married women became a part of their husband's household) and *patriarchal* (the father was in charge of the household).[9]

While most identify the ancient Israelite family structure by the term 'patriarchy' (rule of the father), Block (2003: 41) contends that the expression 'patricentrism' (centred around the father) may be better suited for this type of arrangement, since 'patricentrism' better reflects the 'normative biblical disposition toward the role of the head of a household in Israel'. Like the spokes of a wheel, family life radiated outward from the father as its centre. The community was built around the father and bore his stamp in every respect.[10] This background is highly instructive as we embark on a study of 'Father' language in John's Gospel.

The prologue

The prologue contains two strategic references to God as Father by the evangelist. In 1:14, at the 'middle' of the story, Jesus is referred to as the *monogenēs* from (*para*) the Father.[11] Drawing on the human and cultural phenomenon of a father's cherished only son, this denotes a very special relationship of love and trust. This only Son (Jesus Christ, 1:17) is said in 1:18 to be, literally, in the Father's 'lap' (cf. Prov. 8:30; Luke 16:22). His intimate knowledge of the Father enabled the Son to disclose fully his character and plan for humanity.[12] The one who was with God 'in the beginning' (1:1) thus renders the primary witness (18:37), which, in turn, results in witness being borne by those who have been with Jesus 'from the beginning' (15:27), especially the Beloved Disciple (21:24–25; cf. 13:23; 19:35; 21:20).

---

[9] See more fully ch. 5 in Köstenberger 2004a. See also M. Davies 1992: 131 and Reinhartz 1999: 84, both cited in Stibbe 2006: 179.

[10] Block (2003: 47) lists nine major responsibilities of fathers in ancient Israel.

[11] Cf. Stibbe (2006: 176), who notes that the narrator starts at the 'beginning' of the story, i.e. the Word's eternal pre-existence prior to creation (1:1), and then moves to the 'middle' of the story, the Word's incarnation in then-recent history. As Stibbe observes, remarkably, the 'end' of the story is left open (ibid.), though Meyer's remark that 'What is distinctively Johannine about this presentation of God as Father is that . . . eschatology has been replaced by protology' (1996: 265, cited in Stibbe 2006: 176) and speaking of 'replacement' takes matters too far.

[12] See Köstenberger 2004c: 49–50.

The Book of Signs

2 – 4

Now that the narrator has given way to the protagonist,[13] the next reference comes from Jesus himself.[14] At the occasion of the temple clearing, Jesus calls the temple his 'Father's house' (2:16).[15] The fact that the same expression is found on Jesus' lips in Luke 2:49 is a strong indication of authenticity. Jesus' concern for the state of his Father's designated dwelling place among his people on earth is displayed at his visitation of the temple. The temple clearing constitutes a prophetic sign of Jesus' messianic authority to cleanse Israel from corrupt worship and to restore the true worship of God to his people.[16] As Jesus' ensuing pronouncements make clear, this would involve his crucifixion, followed in three days' time by his resurrection.

In another section supplied by the evangelist,[17] mention is made of the Father's love for the Son (3:35). The Father has entrusted all things to the Son. The present passage, together with 1:14 and 18, may suggest that 'Father and Son' is the evangelist's preferred way of conveying the nature of Jesus' relationship with God.

The three final instances of *patēr* with reference to God in this section are found in 4:21–23. In his conversation with the Samaritan woman, Jesus refers to God as his Father. The issue is proper worship of God in spirit and truth.[18] *Patēr* is here used in parallelism with *theos* (cf. 4:24), but *patēr* is more personal and conveys the notion of an intimate personal family relationship between God and Jesus. On the basis of this intimate relationship (see discussion of 1:18 above), Jesus is able to reveal (in this case, to the Samaritan woman) who God truly is (in the present instance, that he is spirit, which has implications for the proper way of worship). Note that the Father is here said to (actively) 'seek' worshipers of a certain kind. Hence Jesus is shown

[13] Stibbe 2006: 178.

[14] As Stibbe (2006: 179) proposes, citing warnings against abstracting 'from the Gospel some detached doctrine of God' (Meyer 1996: 256; cf. O'Day 1999: 11, 16), 'we will therefore look at the references to God as Father as they appear in the landscape of the unfolding story'.

[15] It is doubtful that 14:2 represents an allusion to 2:16. Note that the word for 'house' in 14:2 is *oikia* (cf. 4:53; 8:35; 11:31; 12:3), not *oikos* as in 2:16–17 (cf. 11:20). See Köstenberger 2004c: 425–427.

[16] See Köstenberger 1995b.

[17] So e.g. Stibbe 1993: 61. Surprisingly, in his narrative study of the Father in John's Gospel (2006: 179–184), Stibbe does not discuss 3:35.

[18] See the discussion of 4:24 in the previous chapter.

to be on a mission 'recruiting' such worshippers of God, not solely among the Jews, but also among the Samaritans.

It is hardly a coincidence that the two references to the Father by Jesus in the first four chapters of John's Gospel (2:16 and 4:21–23) both involve the question of worship. At the Jerusalem temple, Jesus exposes the corruption of current Jewish worship and acts to restore proper worship. At the foot of Mount Gerizim, Jesus instructs the Samaritan woman as to true, spiritual worship rendered to God irrespective of physical location. As the evangelist makes clear in 2:20, Jesus himself, in a major paradigm shift, becomes the new temple who is to be the proper object and sphere of worship for God's people.[19]

5 – 10

Fifteen of the thirty-eight references to God as Father in chapters 5–10 are clustered in 5:17–47, the aftermath of the so-called 'Sabbath controversy' between Jesus and the Jewish leaders. Jesus' pronouncement in 5:17 that his Father is at work until the present and so Jesus is at work as well provokes fierce opposition by the Jewish leaders. This is owing to Jesus' unequivocal alignment of himself with God (5:18; see above).

In the following verses, Jesus elaborates on the Father–Son relationship. As in the case of human fathers, where sons (including Jesus) customarily followed in their fathers' footsteps by learning their trade, Jesus claims to take his cue from his Father (cf. 1:18). Jesus' statement in 5:20 echoes that of the evangelist in 3:35 (except that *agapan* is replaced by *philein*). Not only does the Father love the Son, but as an expression of this love he has shown him everything he does (cf. 15:15). An example of this is the Father's life-giving activity, which is said to be reproduced in the Son's ministry (5:21). The Father is also said to have delegated all judgment to the Son (5:22). In order that he may receive the same respect awarded the Father, in an unmistakable instance of *šālîaḥ* (messenger) terminology, Jesus affirms that whoever fails to honour the Son also fails to honour the Father who sent him (5:23; cf. *m. Ber.* 5.5). In an astounding assertion, Jesus proceeds to affirm that just as the Father has life in himself, so the Son, too, has life in himself. This clearly implies the Son's deity.[20]

---

[19] On the temple motif in John's Gospel, see esp. Kerr 2002; Coloe 2001; P. W. L. Walker 1996; and Köstenberger 2005a. See already W. D. Davies 1994: 289–302.

[20] Or, as the Puritans would call it, his *aseity* (self-sufficiency).

In 5:36, Jesus cites his works, given to him by the Father, as evidence that the Father sent him (see 5:19–20 above). Yet it is not merely the works, but the Father himself who directly bears witness to Jesus (5:37; the clearest instance of this in John's Gospel is the heavenly voice in 12:28). In 5:41, Jesus says plainly that he has come in his Father's name. Nevertheless, people reject him (another instance of *šālîaḥ* terminology, see 5:23 above). Yet not Jesus, but Moses, will accuse them before the Father. For he wrote about Jesus ahead of time (5:45–46).

Eleven references to God as Father are found in 6:27–65 in the aftermath of Jesus' feeding of the multitudes. The entire interchange is pervaded by Jesus' repeated references to his close relationship with the Father. In 6:27, *patēr* occurs in apposition to *theos*. In 6:32, Jesus asserts that it was (ultimately) not Moses but the Father who provided wilderness Israel with the manna. Most pronounced in the present context are references to the Father as 'giving' people to Jesus or as 'drawing' people to him. All those whom the Father has given to Jesus will come to him (6:37).[21] It is the Father's will that all those who believe in the Son have eternal life (6:40). No one can come to Jesus unless the Father draws him (6:44–45, reiterated in 6:65). In his ministry, the Son is totally dependent on the Father. In the remaining references to *patēr* in the present discourse, Jesus claims that he alone has seen the Father (cf. 1:18) and that 'the living Father' sent him (6:57).

The pericope 8:12–58 contains nineteen references to God as Father. In the aftermath of Jesus' appearance at the feast of Tabernacles in Jerusalem, Jesus once again affirms his close association with his sender, the Father (8:16, 18). The Father who sent Jesus testifies concerning him (8:18; cf. 5:37). When Jesus is challenged by some who ask, in effect, 'Where is your father?' (cf. 6:42), he responds that his opponents do not know the Father or else they would acknowledge him (8:19). The important point is that the Father is known through Jesus and him alone; Jesus is the sole point of access to God (cf. 10:7–9; 14:6).

The ensuing paternity dispute[22] is anticipated in 8:27, another instance of Johannine misunderstanding (cf. 6:42; 8:19). In 8:28 and 38, Jesus maintains that the Father is the origin of his teaching. In the latter passage, Jesus hints at his opponents' real (as opposed to alleged)

---

[21] On divine election in John's Gospel, see e.g. Yarbrough 1995. More broadly, see Carson 1981.

[22] See Stibbe (1993: 97), cited by Tolmie 1998: 66.

father, that is, the devil (continued in 8:41). The Jews assert that, ethnically speaking, their father is Abraham (8:39) and, spiritually speaking, their one and only father is God (8:41). Jesus acknowledges that Abraham is the Jews' father ethnically, but challenges them to do the *works* of Abraham in keeping with their claim. Their hatred of Jesus proves that their true spiritual father is none other than the devil (8:44). When in the heat of debate Jesus is charged with demon possession, he reasserts that he knows his Father and that his opponents dishonour him (Jesus; 8:49). Jesus reiterates that he does not seek to glorify himself but that it is the Father (whom the Jews claim as their God) who is glorifying him (8:54). The pericope ends on a note of increased hostility and conflict.[23]

After a hiatus in chapter 9, there are 13 references to God as Father in the aftermath of Jesus' discourse in 10:15–38. In 10:15, Jesus says that he knows his own and they know him, just as the Father and he know each other.[24] The trusting and caring relationship between a shepherd and his sheep is here used as an illustration of Jesus' relationship with his Father. The Father loves Jesus because he is willing to sacrifice his life for those in need of salvation (10:17–18). In 10:25, Jesus once again points to the witness of his works done in the name of the Father (an *inclusio* with 5:36). In keeping with previous assertions (cf. esp. 6:37, 44), Jesus affirms that no one can snatch those the Father has given him out of his hand; for the Father is greater than all (10:29).

Jesus proceeds to affirm his unity of purpose and mission with the Father by saying, 'I and the Father are one' (*hen*, neuter singular; 10:30; cf. 5:17–18). The Jews promptly pick up stones to stone Jesus. Jesus' present claim forms the climax of the chapter much as 8:58 does for chapter 8. The statement echoes the basic confession of Judaism, 'Hear, O Israel: The LORD our God, the LORD is one' (Deut. 6:4; the term 'one' is neuter, not masculine). For Jesus to be one with the Father yet distinct from him amounts to a claim to deity (cf. 1:1–2). To be sure, the emphasis here is on the unity of their works,[25] yet an ontological (not just functional) unity between Jesus and the Father seems presupposed.[26] While not affirming complete identity,

---

[23] On Jesus and the Jews in John's Gospel, see esp. S. Motyer 1997 and Kierspel 2007. Regarding the alleged anti-Semitism of John's Gospel, see Bieringer, Pollefeyt and Vandecasteele-Vanneuville 2001a, 2001b.
[24] On the OT background of John 10, see Köstenberger 2002: 67–96; and 2007: 461–467: *ad loc.*
[25] Ridderbos 1997: 371.
[26] See esp. Carson 1991: 394–395.

clearly there is more in view than a mere oneness of will between Jesus and the Father.

Consequently, Jesus' assertion of oneness with the Father challenged narrow Jewish notions of monotheism, even though there are already hints in the Hebrew Scriptures of a plurality within the Godhead, some of which Jesus was careful to expose (e.g. Matt. 22:41–46 par.). Jesus' unity with the Father later constitutes the basis on which Jesus prays that his followers be unified (17:11, 22; note again the neuter *hen*). In the following interchange, Jesus refers to his 'many good works from the Father' (NASB; better than NIV's 'many great miracles') and asks for which of these his opponents want to stone him (10:32). Their answer is that Jesus' offence is not good works but blasphemy. Jesus does not retract his claim but rather asserts that the Father set him, the Son of God, apart and sent him into the world (10:36). Again, Jesus offers 'the works of [his] Father' (NASB) as evidence that the Father is in him and he in the Father (10:37–38). And again, the Jews attempt to stone Jesus, but he eludes their grasp.

To sum up, chapters 5–10 characterize God as the Father of Jesus, who initiated and authorized Jesus' mission and who bears witness to him.[27] The festival cycle in John's Gospel ends as it began: with Jesus' unequivocal alignment of himself with God's purposes and the Jews' fierce opposition to him.

11 – 12

The term *patēr* is absent from chapter 11 except in Jesus' customary address to God in prayer in 11:41 at Lazarus' tomb.[28] The portrait of Jesus as one whose prayers are heard is in keeping with his being a righteous man who does God's will (cf. 9:31; 11:22). Jesus' prayer is uttered, not for himself, but on account of the crowds standing at Lazarus' gravesite and for the purpose of eliciting faith in the one God sent among them. The fact that Jesus prays prior to calling Lazarus (who has been dead for four days) out of the tomb underscores the Gospel's pervasive emphasis on Jesus' total dependence on God in carrying out his mission. As the ensuing events make clear, the Father hears and answers Jesus' prayer.

Later, when instructing his followers on discipleship, he promises that the Father will honour anyone who serves Jesus (12:26). In a

---

[27] Tolmie 1998: 67.
[28] Cf. 12:27–28; 17:1, 5, 11, 21, 24, 25.

struggle reminiscent of the Synoptic portrait of Gethsemane, Jesus asks, rhetorically, whether he will ask the Father to rescue him from the hour of death, only to discard the idea immediately: 'No – Father, glorify your name' (12:28; our paraphrase).[29] His prayer is promptly answered by a voice from heaven, the only direct utterance by God in this Gospel (12:27–28). Hence the intimacy between Jesus and the Father continues unabated even with the crucifixion rapidly approaching (cf. 12:24). The chapter and the entire Book of Signs concludes with Jesus' emphatic affirmation that his teaching is in keeping with that of the Father who sent him and that the purpose and end of his Father's command is eternal life.

The Book of Glory

The farewell discourse notably shifts the perspective from the vantage point of Jesus' earthly ministry to the Jews to that of anticipating his exaltation with the Father.[30] At the very outset of the Book of Glory, the evangelist makes clear that Jesus is about to return to the Father and that he faces the ensuing events in the full awareness that the Father has given everything into his hands and that he has come from God and is returning to God (13:1–3; note the clear verbal echo of 3:35, also by the evangelist).

The farewell discourse

There are a total of forty-four references to God as Father in the farewell discourse proper (chs. 14–16) plus six in Jesus' final prayer in chapter 17. This speaks of the intimate nature of Jesus' disclosure in these final moments of his earthly ministry.[31] Tolmie (1998: 72) provides two lists of references to God as Father in the farewell discourse, one that demonstrates the intricate linkage between the Father and Jesus and the other featuring passages that emphasize the benefit of this relationship for human beings.[32] With regard to *Jesus*, the Father

---

[29] For this rendering, and a discussion of alternative interpretations, see Köstenberger 2004c: 380–381.

[30] See Köstenberger 1998b: 149–153 *et passim*.

[31] Tolmie (1998: 71) points out that the events narrated in 13 – 17 are situated within an intimate atmosphere. He notes the marked change in the way in which the relationship between God and human beings is portrayed (a move from possibility to reality) and observes that there are no new traits of God revealed in these chapters (1998: 72).

[32] Though note that Tolmie does not distinguish between references to *theos* and *patēr*.

- hands all things over to him (13:3; 17:2)
- has sent him (13:3, 20; 15:21; 16:5, 28, 30; 17:3, 8, 18, 25)
- glorifies him (13:31, 32; 17:1, 5, 22)
- reveals himself through him (14:6–11; 17:6, 11, 14, 26)
- is in him (14:10–11, 20)
- instructs him what to say and do (14:10, 24, 31; 15:10, 15)
- grants his requests (14:16)
- is greater than him (14:28)
- loves him (15:9; 17:23, 26)
- gives people to him (17:6, 9)
- is one with him (17:10, 11, 21–22)

With regard to *believers*,

- there is adequate space for them in his 'house' (14:2)
- he will send the *parakletos* to them (14:16, 26; 15:26)
- he will love them (14:21, 23; 16:27)
- he will come and stay with them (14:23)
- he will prune the branches in order that they may bear more fruit (15:2)
- he will grant their requests (15:16; 16:23)
- he will protect them from the evil one (17:15)
- he will enable them to be one (17:21–22)[33]

In 14:2, Jesus tells his followers he is going to prepare a place for them in his 'Father's house'. This is the same expression as in 2:16 (though, as noted above, the Greek term for 'house' is different), which is why some have suggested that here, too, the temple is in view. However, owing to the lack of contextual indicators in the present passage, heaven is a more likely referent.[34]

The densest concentration of references to God as Father is found in 14:6–13, where twelve references occur in a span of eight verses. Thomas first asks Jesus to show the disciples the way (14:5). Jesus tells him that he *is* the way and that no one can come to the Father except through him (14:6). Philip follows up by asking Jesus to show them the Father (14:7). Jesus replies that having seen *him* is having seen the Father (14:9), an amazing statement in the light of the fact that no one can, or ever has, seen God (1:18). Jesus has made the invisible God visible.

---

[33] See the discussion in Stibbe 2006: 187–188, who also cites Meyer's (2006: 264) list of active verbs used in conjunction with the word *pater* when applied to God.

[34] Köstenberger 2001a: 137.

In 14:10–11, Jesus elaborates further on the closeness of his relationship to the Father, maintaining that he is 'in' the Father and the Father is 'in' him. Clearly, this indicates a very close personal family relationship. What is in view here is not an identity of persons, but a unity of purpose. The 'in' language should not be taken as suggesting a 'mystical' relationship between Jesus and the Father.[35] Rather, their relationship is one of intimacy, love and trust. Hence Jesus' words come from the Father who does his works in Jesus (14:11).

Jesus' return to the Father will enable his followers to do greater works than Jesus did during his earthly ministry.[36] This promise of 'greater works' (NASB; NIV: 'greater things') is predicated upon Jesus' exaltation with the Father (14:12c). Once exalted, Jesus will answer prayer so that the Father will be glorified in the Son and the disciples' mission be accomplished (14:13). At Jesus' request, the Father will also send the Spirit (14:16). Once Jesus has risen, his followers will know that he is in the Father (14:20). Those who obey Jesus will be loved by his Father (14:21).

In fact, both Jesus and the Father will come and make their home in the believer (14:23). Since the Spirit is said to be in the believer as well (14:17), this means that in a sense the entire triune Godhead will be present in that individual, though perhaps more precisely it is the indwelling Spirit who is sent by the Father in Jesus' name (cf. 14:16, 26). Jesus' message is not his own but the Father's (14:24). The promise of the Father's sending of the Spirit in Jesus' name is reiterated in 14:26. As Jesus came in the Father's name, the Spirit will come in Jesus' name.

The disciples ought to rejoice that Jesus is returning to the Father, for the Father is greater than him (14:28). This is only an apparent contradiction with 10:30. There the reference is to the Father's and the Son's unity of purpose. Here reference is made to the Son's subordination to the Father, which is consistently affirmed in the Gospel: the Father is the sender of Jesus; Jesus obeys and depends on the Father; he originates with and returns to the Father; and it is the Father who does his work and speaks his words through him.[37]

---

[35] As has been argued by some of the proponents of the history-of-religions school, evoking parallels with first- and second-century mystery religions.

[36] See Köstenberger 1998b: 71–75.

[37] This subordination is non-reversible: the Son does not send the Father; the Father does not depend on the Son etc. Contra Grenz with Kjesbo (1995: 514, with reference to Pannenberg), according to whom the persons of the Trinity are mutually dependent, so that the 'Father is dependent on the Son', not merely for his Fatherhood but even 'for his deity' (see Köstenberger 1998c: 517–518).

Jesus concludes this portion of the farewell discourse by affirming that he is committed to obeying the Father in order to show the world that he loves the Father (14:31).

The entire ensuing allegory of the vine is told by Jesus in personal terms depicting his Father as the vinedresser and himself as the vine (15:1).[38] The Father is glorified when Jesus' followers bear much fruit (15:8; note the verbal allusion to Jesus' bearing of fruit in 12:24). Critically, the disciples are the next link in the chain that connects the Father and Jesus. Just as the Father has loved Jesus, so he loves the disciples (15:9). And just as Jesus has obeyed the Father, so his followers ought to obey him (15:10; see 20:21 below *et passim*).

No longer does Jesus call his disciples his 'servants' (13:16; cf. 12:26). Rather, they are his friends, because he has made known to them all the things he has heard from the Father (15:15; cf. 5:19–20). Hence Jesus' followers are included in his close familial relationship with the Father. And once again, the disciples are enjoined to petition the Father in Jesus' name (15:16; cf. 14:13–14).

In another application of the *šālîah* principle, Jesus states that whoever hates him also hates the Father (15:23–24). For the third time, he refers to the coming of the Spirit, this time by stating that he himself will send the Spirit 'from' (*para*) the Father (15:26). This Spirit 'of truth' is said to proceed (*ekporeuomai*) from (*para*) the Father (15:26). Jesus' followers are warned that the world will persecute them, because the world has known neither the Father nor Jesus (16:3).

The Spirit's convicting work will include convicting the world of righteousness because Jesus is about to return to the Father (16:10). This may mean that the world will be convicted of its *un*righteousness (parallel to being convicted of its sin of unbelief in Jesus and Satan 'the prince of this world' [16:11] being judged) or that the world will be convicted on the basis of *Jesus'* righteousness, which will be apparent when he is raised from the dead subsequent to his crucifixion.

The trinitarian interplay between Father, Son and Spirit is evident in the Spirit's ministry of taking from what is Jesus' and revealing it to the disciples, even as all things that are the Father's are Jesus' as well (16:14–15). At present, however, the disciples do not yet understand what Jesus means when he says he is returning to the Father (16:17). Yet once again Jesus raises the spectre of answered prayer to

---

[38] Note the frequent reference to the Father as 'my' Father in this chapter (15:1, 10, 15, 23–24).

the Father in his name (16:23; cf. 14:13–14; 15:16). At that time Jesus' words to his followers were still unclear to them; later, subsequent to Jesus' departure and return to the Father, they would understand (16:25–28).

As the farewell discourse draws to a close, Jesus anticipates his disciples' wholesale defection. Yet he reaffirms his assurance that the Father will still be with him (16:32).

The final prayer

Six times in his final prayer in John's Gospel, Jesus addresses God as 'Father'. He asks that the Father glorify the Son, so that the Son may glorify him (17:1) with the glory that he had with the Father prior to the world's creation (17:5). He asks the 'holy Father' to keep his followers who remain in the world unified in his name, as he and the Father are unified (17:11). The purpose for this is that the world may believe that the Father sent Jesus (17:21). Harking back to 17:5, Jesus petitions the Father that his own see the glory he had with the Father prior to the world's creation (17:24). Jesus concludes by referring to God as 'righteous Father' (17:25).

The passion narrative

In the only reference to the Father in the passion narrative proper, Jesus expresses his resolve to drink the 'cup' the Father has given him to drink (18:11). This indicates that Jesus viewed the cross as part of God's will for him. Subsequent to the resurrection, he speaks of returning to 'my Father and your Father, to my God and your God' (20:17). Hence a distinction is maintained between the Fatherhood of God in relation to Jesus and in relation to believers.[39] The final reference to God as Father is found in 20:21 where Jesus sends the disciples as the Father sent him.[40]

Summary

Father–Son is the dominant, controlling metaphor used for Jesus' relationship with God in the Fourth Gospel. The two persons of God

---

[39] Tolmie (1998: 74) speaks of 20:17 as the 'conclusion, and indeed the climax' of the characterization of God in the Fourth Gospel, since it is only here that God is characterized, not only as Father of Jesus, but also as Father of believers. This is clearly an important point, but we will argue below that 20:21 is a more likely climax.

[40] On the theological and missiological implications of this verse, see esp. Köstenberger 1998b.

the Father and the Son are thoroughly and inextricably intertwined.[41] Jesus derives his mission from the Father and is fully dependent on him in carrying it out. The imagery of 'father' and 'son' plainly draws on Jewish cultural expectations related to father–son relationships, especially those pertaining to only sons.[42] The vast majority of instances of *patēr* in John's Gospel are found in discourse material. Emphatically, it is Jesus himself who refers to God as 'the' Father and in close to twenty instances even as 'his' Father.[43] 'The Father' is Jesus' natural, almost unselfconscious, way of referring to God. Particularly prominent are references to the Father's *sending* of Jesus.[44] One also notes the absence of the terms *theos* and *patēr* in the (in our view non-Johannine) pericope of the adulterous woman (7:53 – 8:11).[45]

[41] See esp. the 'just as' statements relating the Father and the Son in this Gospel (e.g. 5:21, 23, 26; 6:57; 8:28; 10:15; 12:50; 17:18; 20:21) and references to Jesus being 'in' the Father and the Father being 'in' him (e.g. 10:38; 14:11, 20).

[42] See Köstenberger 1998b: 115–121 in interaction with the relevant literature.

[43] 2:16; 5:17, 43; 6:32, 40; 8:19 (2), 49; 10:18, 25, 29, 37; 14:2, 7, 20, 21, 23; 15:1, 8, 10, 15, 23, 24; 20:17. Several times the evangelist uses the term 'Father' (1:14, 18; 3:35; 13:1, 3). In 8:41, Jesus' Jewish opponents claim they have one Father: God.

[44] 5:23, 36, 37; 6:44, 57; 8:16, 18; 12:49; 14:24; 20:21.

[45] See Köstenberger 2004c: 245–249. The terms *huios* and *pneuma* are absent from this pericope as well.

Chapter Four

The Son in John's Gospel

Introduction

The term 'Son' occupies a central role within the Christology of the Fourth Gospel; most frequently found is the name Jesus itself (240 times). The term *logos* (the Word) is limited to the prologue, where it serves as a shorthand of God's self-expression through Jesus in keeping with the depiction of the Word of God in the OT (see 1:18; cf. esp. Isa. 55:11). Throughout the Gospel, Jesus is repeatedly addressed as *kyrios* ('sir' or 'Lord') and *rabbi* (teacher).[1] But it is the term *huios* (Son) that pervades the Gospel, both absolutely and in combination with various Christological titles applied to Jesus.

The expression *huios* is found fifty-five times in John's Gospel, of which forty-one refer to Jesus.[2] Twice Jesus is called the 'son of Joseph' (1:45; 6:42; cf. Luke 3:23; 4:22). Twice also Jesus is called by the evangelist the 'one-of-a-kind Son' (*monogenēs*; 3:16, 18; cf. 1:14, 18). The term 'Son of God' is applied to Jesus eight times in this Gospel: by Nathanael (1:49); the evangelist (3:18); Jesus himself (5:25; 10:36; 11:4); Martha (11:27); negatively by 'the Jews' (19:7); and again by the evangelist (20:31). Another set of instances involving *huios* are Jesus' thirteen references to himself as the 'Son of Man'.[3] Finally, there are eighteen references to Jesus as 'the Son', virtually always vis-à-vis God 'the Father'.[4]

---

[1] 4:11, 15, 49; 5:7; 11:34, 39 (*kyrios*); 1:38, 49; 3:2; 4:31; 6:25; 9:2; 11:8; 13:13–14 (*rabbi*; cf. 20:16).

[2] If one includes the four references to Jesus as the 'one-of-a-kind Son' (*monogenēs*), this makes a total of forty-five references to Jesus as 'son' in John's Gospel (see the chart below).

[3] 1:51; 3:13, 14; 5:27; 6:27, 53, 62; 8:28; 9:35; 12:23, 34 (2); 13:31.

[4] The first five references to Jesus as the Son are by the evangelist (3:16, 17, 35, 36 [2]). All other instances of 'the Son' are self-references by Jesus: 5:19 (2), 20, 21, 22, 23 (2), 26; 6:40; 8:36; 14:13; and 17:1 (2). The reference in 3:17 to *God* (rather than 'the Father') sending the Son is noteworthy.

Table 4.1 Jesus as the Son in John's Gospel: overview

son of Joseph (2)	1:45; 6:42
'one-of-a-kind Son' (4)	1:14, 18; 3:16, 18
Son of God (8)	1:49; 3:18; 5:25; 10:36; 11:4, 27; 19:7; 20:31
Son of Man (13)	1:51; 3:13, 14; 5:27; 6:27, 53, 62; 8:28; 9:35; 12:23, 34 (2); 13:31
the Son (18)	3:16, 17, 35, 36 (2); 5:19 (2), 20, 21, 22, 23 (2), 26; 6:40; 8:36; 14:13; 17:1 (2)

When compared with 'Father' language in John's Gospel, one notes that references to God as Father are considerably more frequent than references to Jesus as the Son. It appears that Jesus speaks quite a bit more about the Father than he does about himself.

Rather than intermingling the various references to Jesus as the Son as reflected in the distinct usage of the Christological titles 'one-of-a-kind Son' (*monogenēs*), 'Son of God' and 'Son of Man', and references to 'the Son' in relation to the Father, and investigating all instances of *huios* in chronological order, it seems preferable to look at the string of references tied to each expression separately. As needed, a comparison with the Synoptic Gospels will prove illuminating. At the end of the chapter, in order to facilitate a concluding synthesis, we will provide a narrative survey of all the relevant references to Jesus as the Son in John's Gospel.

One-of-a-kind Son

The first set of references to be mentioned (the two instances of 'son of Joseph' do not call for extended comment) are those designating Jesus as God's 'one-of-a-kind Son' (*monogenēs*; 3:16, 18; cf. 1:14, 18). While the precise term is unique to the Fourth Gospel, there may be a parallel in the Synoptics in the language 'beloved Son' (*huios agapētos*), which is applied to Jesus at his baptism (Mark 1:11 par. Luke 3:22) and transfiguration (Mark 9:7 par. Luke 9:35) and is implied also in the parable of the wicked tenants (Mark 12:6 par. Luke 20:13).

The prologue refers to Jesus as the *monogenēs* or 'one-of-a-kind Son' from the Father (1:14) and stresses his unique relationship with him (1:18).[5] The predominant OT usage is 'only child' (Judg. 11:34;

---

[5] On Jesus as God's 'one-of-a-kind Son', see Köstenberger 2004c: 42–44, 49 and the literature cited there.

Amos 8:10; Jer. 6:26; Zech. 12:10; Prov. 4:3). Being an only child, and thus irreplaceable, makes a child of special value to its parents (cf. Luke 7:12; 8:42; 9:38; Pendrick 1995: 593–594). Hence the LXX often uses *agapētos* instead of *monogenēs* (Gen. 22:2, 12, 16; Amos 8:10; Jer. 6:26; Zech. 12:10; cf. Prov. 4:3; in Judg. 11:34, both are used).

The seminal event in OT history in this regard is Abraham's offering of Isaac, who in Genesis 22:2, 12, 16 is called Abraham's 'one-of-a-kind son' (Heb. *yāḥîd*; note the probable allusion to this text in John 3:16), even though the patriarch had earlier fathered Ishmael (cf. Heb. 11:17; Josephus, *Ant.* 1.22).[6] *Monogenēs* therefore means, in all likelihood, not 'only begotten', but 'one-of-a-kind' son (in Isaac's case, son of promise; according to Heb. 11:17, Isaac is a type [*typos*] of Christ).[7]

In both OT and Second Temple literature, the Son of David and Israel are called God's 'firstborn' or even 'only' son.[8] In a decisive step further, John applies the designation *monogenēs* to God's 'one-of-a-kind' Son par excellence, Jesus (cf. 1:18; 3:16, 18; 1 John 4:9). In keeping with the Isaac narrative and the parable of the wicked tenants, the term *monogenēs* in John 1:14 has significant soteriological implications, culminating in John's assertion in 3:16 that 'God so loved the world that he sent his one-of-a-kind Son'.

This designation also provides the basis for Jesus' claim that no one can come to the Father except through him (14:6). It is likely that 'one of a kind' in John's context refers to Jesus' uniqueness in that 'he is *both* the *human* Son of Joseph *and* the *divine* Son of God'.[9] Jesus is the 'one-of-a-kind Son' *from* [alongside] (*para*) the Father, in the sense that he was 'with' the Father (1:1); that he has come 'from' the Father (16:27; 17:8); and that he will send the Paraclete 'from' the Father (15:26).

By way of *inclusio*, the phrase 'the one-of-a-kind Son, God [in his own right]' (our paraphrase), in 1:18, provides a commentary on what

---

[6] Fitzmyer 1990–3, 2: 440; Winter 1953: 337–340; Moody 1953: 213–219, esp. 217.

[7] For an argument that the notion of Jesus as the 'only begotten' of the Father is foreign to Johannine thought and was read into the Gospel only later during the patristic period, see Pendrick 1995: 587–600. Among other pieces of evidence, Pendrick cites ancient references where *monogenēs* is applied to an only child who was not the only begotten, 'for the father might have begotten other children who died young and so the preservation of his name rests on the only surviving son' (590). In the light of the high infant mortality rate in the ancient world, Pendrick notes that 'there must have been many only children who were not the only ones begotten by their parents' (590, n. 23). See also Moody 1953: 213–219; and W. O. Walker 1994: 41, n. 37.

[8] Cf. Ps. 89:27; *4 Ezra* 6.58; *Pss Sol.* 18.4; *Jub.* 18.2, 11, 15.

[9] W. O. Walker 1994: 41, n. 37.

is meant in 1:1c where it is said that 'the Word was God'.[10] The Word was God, and so Jesus is 'unique and divine, though flesh'.[11] Rather than functioning attributively ('the one-of-a-kind God'), *monogenēs* probably is to be understood as a substantive in its own right as in 1:1 ('the one-of-a-kind Son'), with *theos* in apposition ('God [in his own right]').[12]

The phrase 'one-of-a-kind Son, God [in his own right]', which John here uses with reference to Jesus, is both striking and unusual.[13] If this is what John actually wrote, it would identify Jesus even more closely as God than the phrase 'one-of-a-kind Son'. Judaism, as we have seen, believed that there was only one God (Deut. 6:4). As John shows later in his Gospel, Jesus' claims of deity brought him into increasing conflict with the Jewish authorities. In the end, the primary charge leading to his crucifixion was blasphemy (19:7; cf. 10:33).

The phrase 'at the Father's side' (*eis ton kolpon*) refers to the unmatched intimacy of Jesus' relationship with the Father,[14] which enabled him to reveal the Father in an unprecedented way.[15] Literally, as mentioned earlier, John here says that Jesus is 'in the Father's lap', an idiom for greatest possible closeness (cf. Prov. 8:30; Hofius 1989: 164–165). This is the way the term is used in the OT, where it portrays the devoted care of a parent or caregiver).[16] The most pertinent NT parallel is the reference to 'Abraham's side' (TNIV) in Luke 16:22.

These parallels show how intimate John considered Jesus' relationship with the Father to be.[17] Access to divine revelation was also

[10] There is some question as to whether the original reading here is *monogenēs huios* (one-of-a-kind Son) or *monogenēs theos* (one-of-a-kind [Son, himself] God). With the acquisition of p[66] and p[75], both of which read *monogenēs theos*, the preponderance of the evidence now leans in the direction of the latter reading. Harris (1992: 78–80) expresses a 'strong preference' for *monogenēs theos*, for at least four reasons: (1) its superior manuscript support; (2) it represents the more difficult reading; (3) the phrase serves as a more proper climax to the entire prologue, attributing deity to the Son by way of *inclusio* with 1:1 and 14; (4) this reading seems best to account for the other variants. Most likely, then, *monogenēs huios* represents a scribal assimilation to John 3:16 and 18.

[11] Mowvley 1984: 37.

[12] Hofius 1989: 164.

[13] Note the equally clear ascriptions of deity to Jesus in 1:1 and 20:28.

[14] Wallace 1996: 360.

[15] Cf. the contrast with Moses in 1:17; Brown 1966: 36.

[16] Num. 11:12; Ruth 4:16; 2 Sam. 12:3; 1 Kgs 3:20; 17:19; Lam. 2:12; cf. *b. Yeb.* 77a; Hofius 1989: 166, nn. 19–21. Greek parallels include Aristotle, *Mir ausc.* 846b.27 and Demosthenes, *Orat.* 47.58.

[17] The evangelist later uses the same expression with regard to himself, the 'disciple Jesus loved', indicating that his closeness to Jesus during his earthly ministry made

prized in the pagan mystery religions and Jewish apocalypticism and mysticism. Yet here John claims that Jesus' access to God far exceeds not only that claimed by other religions but even that of Judaism. This is why Moses' system was inferior: under it, no one could see God.[18] By contrast, as John asserts at the conclusion of his prologue, Jesus made God known in a unique, climactic, definitive and most graphic way (*exēgeomai*).[19]

The references to Jesus as God's 'one-of-a-kind Son' in the prologue are fleshed out in the Gospel narrative in 3:16 and 18. In 3:16, the emphasis is on the greatness of God's gift[20] and the intensity of his love. The word 'gave' draws attention to the sacrifice involved for God the Father in sending his Son to save the world.[21] In the OT antecedent passage, Abraham was asked to give up his 'one-of-a-kind son', Isaac (Gen. 22). Though, unlike Jesus, Isaac was not offered up but spared when God provided a substitute.

Son of God

As mentioned, there are eight references to Jesus as the Son of God in John's Gospel, of which seven are positive (the eighth reference to Jesus as Son of God, in 19:7, is uttered by Jesus' hostile Jewish opponents before Pilate), including the initial instance by Nathanael (1:49), two references by the evangelist (3:18 and in the purpose statement of 20:31), whose second reference is anticipated by Martha (11:27), and three self-references by Jesus (5:25; 10:36; 11:4). Hence, as the following chart shows, it appears that the evangelist has carefully grouped these references to Jesus as the Son of God and is developing this theme deliberately during the progression of his narrative.

The opening reference to Jesus as Son of God by Nathanael stands by itself, as it were, sounding the opening salvo, as part of a series of elevated Christological references to Jesus. The evangelist's reference to Jesus as Son of God in 3:18 finds its complement in the concluding purpose statement in 20:31. At the centre of the

---

him the perfect person to write this Gospel (13:23). On the character of the Gospels as eyewitness testimony, see Bauckham 2006, though Bauckham falls short of appreciating the full nature of John's Gospel as *apostolic* eyewitness testimony.

[18] Morris 1995: 100.

[19] Found only here in this Gospel. Cf. Luke 24:35; Acts 10:8; 15:12, 14; 21:19.

[20] Carson 1991: 204.

[21] Witherington 1995: 101.

Table 4.2   The seven references to Jesus as Son of God in John's Gospel

Character	Major Section in John	Reference	Literary Feature
Nathanael		1:49	Opening
Evangelist	1 – 4: Cana cycle	3:18	Anticipates 20:31
Jesus		5:25	
Jesus	5 – 10: Festival cycle	10:36	*Inclusio*
Jesus		11:4	see 11:27
Martha	11 – 12: Transition	11:27	Anticipation/Purpose
Evangelist	20: Conclusion	20:31	Statement

Gospel's characterization of Jesus as Son of God are three self-references of Jesus, in 5:25 and 10:36 (an *inclusio* bracketing the festival cycle) and in 11:4 (at the beginning of the climactic sign of raising Lazarus, anticipating Jesus' own resurrection). Jesus' final self-reference in 11:4 is matched later in the narrative by Martha's confession of Jesus as Son of God in 11:27, a statement that is reproduced virtually verbatim by the evangelist at the conclusion of his Gospel in 20:31.

Seven references to Jesus as Son of God in John's Gospel may appear to be a small number of instances (though note the possible numerical symbolism). Yet when one consults the Synoptics, it becomes apparent that not once does Jesus call himself the 'Son of God' in any of these Gospels. He comes closest to doing so when answering in the affirmative the high priest's question at his Jewish trial whether or not he is the Son of God (Matt. 26:63 par. Luke 22:70). Otherwise, it is Satan or his demons (Matt. 4:3, 6 par. Luke 4:3, 9; Mark 3:11; Luke 4:41; Matt. 8:29 par. Mark 5:7 and Luke 8:28); the angel Gabriel (Luke 1:35); the Twelve (Matt. 14:33) or Peter (Matt. 16:16); the centurion (Matt. 27:54 par. Mark 15:37); or those who mock his messianic claims (Matt. 27:40, 43) who refer to Jesus as the 'Son of God'.

In John, as shown, Jesus refers to himself as 'Son of God' as early as 5:25, and later in the global reference of 10:36 plus at the outset of the raising of Lazarus in a statement addressed to his disciples in 11:4. As noted, the instances in 5:25 and 10:36 form an *inclusio* bracketing the 'festival cycle' in chapters 5–10, which begin and end with the Jews trying to stone Jesus for blasphemy. This helpfully illuminates how the high priest at Jesus' trial according to the Synoptics can arrive at the same charge of blasphemy after interrogating Jesus (19:7).[22]

'Son of God' and 'king of Israel' are both messianic designations roughly equivalent in nature,[23] though 'King of Israel' may reflect a nationalistic mentality.[24] By attaching to Jesus the label 'Son of God', Nathanael identifies him at the outset of the Gospel as the Messiah predicted in the OT (2 Sam. 7:14; Ps. 2:7; cf. 1 Sam. 26:17, 21, 25); the term 'Son [of God]' was also a current messianic title in Jesus' day (cf. 1QSa 2.11–12; *4 Ezra* 7.28–29).[25] Elsewhere in Jewish literature the Davidic king is also described as God's son (apart from the previous references, see also 4QFlor 1.6–7; *1 En.* 105.2; *4 Ezra* 13.52; 14.9; Carson 1991: 162).

The fourth evangelist's references to Jesus as God's Son in 3:16–18 and 20:31 both speak of believing and having life in the 'name' of Jesus the Son of God. This explicates the initial reference to believing in Jesus' name in the prologue (1:12) and identifies Jesus as the bearer of God's name in a weighty manner that would certainly not be lost on John's Jewish readership. The reference in 3:16–18 also harks back to, and constitutes an *inclusio* with, the evangelist's introductory statement in 2:23–25; it also corresponds to the references to Jesus as the 'one-of-a-kind Son' in 1:14–18. Notably, in 3:16–18, references to Jesus as the 'one-of-a-kind Son', as the 'Son' and as the 'Son of God' are used virtually interchangeably.

The major point made in 3:18 is that faith in Jesus as 'one-of-a-kind Son of God' will help people evade judgment, while settled unbelief will incur certain judgment. Significantly, the evangelist's explication follows Jesus' interchange with Nicodemus, the 'teacher of Israel', which indicates that the Jews are part of the world that persists in moral, sinful and culpable darkness unless and until individuals come to faith in Jesus the Messiah and Son of God. This makes Jesus' encounter with Nicodemus (one of) the paradigmatic encounter(s) of

[22] This should be set within the context of the 'interlocking patterns' between John and the Synoptics (see Carson 1991: 52–58, esp. 53, in further development of Morris 1969: 40–63).

[23] Cf. Barrett 1978: 186; cf. Ridderbos 1997: 91. 'Messiah' and 'king of Israel' are juxtaposed in Matt. 27:42 / Mark 15:32.

[24] Morris 1995: 147, n. 115. Nathanael's judgment is vindicated, and his expectation apparently fulfilled, when Jesus is hailed as 'king of Israel' at the 'triumphal entry' in 12:13 (where 'king of Israel' is added by the evangelist to his quotation of Ps. 118:25–26).

[25] On the reference to 'Son of God' and 'Son of the Most High' in 4Q246, see the discussion in Charlesworth 2006, 3: 113–114, with further bibliographical references.

the entire Gospel, which forms the basis for the evangelist's concluding purpose statement in 20:30–31.

Jesus' self-reference in 5:25, similar to 3:16–18, features 'Son of God' in parallelism to other Christological designations, in the present case 'the Son' (5:26) and 'the Son of Man' (5:27). As in 3:16–18, the focus is on Jesus' serving as the catalyst for divine judgment, depending on people's faith or unbelief in him as God's Son (cf. 1 John 5:11–12). Strikingly, Jesus words 'I tell you the truth, a time is coming *and has now come* when the dead will hear the voice of the Son of God and those who hear will live' (5:25) become a reality in John 11 when he raises Lazarus from the dead in the climactic seventh sign of the Gospel (cf. esp. 11:4 and 27), proving that Jesus is indeed the resurrection and the life (11:25; i.e. he has life in himself: 5:26).[26]

The corresponding self-reference of Jesus in 10:36 harks back to the just-discussed passage 5:25, but makes more explicit the Jews' charge of blasphemy against Jesus (cf. 10:31–33). It comes on the heels of Jesus' claim in 10:30 that he and the Father are one. In the context of the Johannine narrative, Jesus' public ministry to the Jews, for all practical purposes, ends with the encounter at the end of chapter 10 that concludes the 'festival cycle' of John 5 – 10. The Jewish rejection, sealed at 19:7, is presented as a fait accompli in the light of Jewish hardening (cf. 12:37–41). The raising of Lazarus is thus performed, like the opening sign in Cana (2:11), to reveal Jesus' glory to his own (11:4), and Martha's confession of Jesus in 11:27 stands in striking contrast to the Jewish rejection of Jesus as a blasphemer.

As mentioned in the previous chapter, Jesus' assertion in 10:30 (cf. 5:17–18), echoing the basic confession of Judaism, 'Hear, O Israel: The LORD our God, the LORD is one' (Deut. 6:4), amounts to a claim to deity. Jesus' assertion of oneness with the Father challenged narrow Jewish notions of monotheism, even though there are already hints in the OT of a plurality within the Godhead, some of which Jesus was careful to expose (e.g. Matt. 22:41–46 par.). Jesus' present pronouncement constitutes the first major climax in John's Gospel (the penultimate high point being 8:58).[27] The second, no less important, climax has Jesus cry on the cross, 'It is finished' (19:30; Hengel 1999: 319). Jesus' unity with the Father later constitutes the basis on which Jesus prays that his followers will likewise be unified (17:22; note again the neuter *hen*, 'one').

---

[26] The statement in 5:25 is reminiscent of Ezekiel's vision of the valley of dry bones in Ezek. 37. Cf. Rom. 4:17; Eph. 2:1–5.

[27] Carson 1991: 395.

The Jews' charge against Jesus in 10:33 appears to be grounded in Leviticus 24:16, which says that 'anyone who blasphemes the name of the LORD must be put to death. The entire assembly must stone him' (see also Num. 15:30–31; and Deut. 21:22). The present passage represents an *inclusio* with 5:18, which, together with 7:25, 8:59 and the present passage punctuates the current section (chs. 5–10) as part of an escalating pattern of controversy between Jesus and the Jews. Jesus' rebuttal in 10:34–38 involves an explicit quotation of Psalm 82:6.

The quotation, following on the heels of the 'Good Shepherd' discourse (10:1–18, 25–30), occurs in the context of a trial scene that focuses, seriatim, on the dual question of whether Jesus is the Christ (10:24) and the Son of God (10:33). In both cases, the Jews mount an initial charge (10:24, 33), which is rebutted by Jesus (10:25–30, 34–38), but is rejected by the Jews, who unsuccessfully attempt to stone or arrest him (10:31, 39). With its dual focus on the question of whether or not Jesus is the Christ, the Son of God, as mentioned, the present scene anticipates Martha's confession in the following chapter (11:27) and the Johannine purpose statement in 20:30–31.[28]

A similar line of investigation is found in the Synoptic portraits of Jesus' Jewish trial before the Sanhedrin (Mark 14:62; Luke 22:67, 70). However, in contrast to the Synoptic Gospels, which locate Jesus' trial at the end of his ministry, John's Gospel has Jesus on trial throughout his entire ministry. What is more, John's 'trial motif' turns the notion of trial on its head by focusing, not on Jesus' guilt, but on the Jews' culpability in rejecting their Messiah despite ample evidence to the contrary (see esp. 12:37–41; Lincoln 2000; Daly-Denton 2004: 124; and Köstenberger 2005a = 2006).

It is in response to this charge of blasphemy that Jesus cites OT Scripture: 'Is it not written in your Law, "I have said you are gods"? If it [the Law, more likely than 'he' as in the NIV; see Köstenberger 2004c: 314] called them "gods", to whom the word of God came . . .' (10:34). In its entirety, Psalm 82:6 reads:

> I said, 'You are "gods";
> you are all sons of the Most High.'

In context, Jesus' purpose in adducing this particular OT passage in response to the Jews' charge of blasphemy 'is an appeal to Scripture

---

[28] Daly-Denton 2004: 123.

to justify His claim to be *one with the Father*, and to be His Son (cf. vv. 25, 29–30)'.[29] In essence, Jesus is saying that there is OT precedent for humans being referred to as 'gods'.[30]

In what follows, Jesus cites his works as evidence for his claim of divine sonship (10:37–39). It is his hope that, when people see the kinds of works he does, namely works that stand in continuity with the works done by God the Father, they will recognize that Jesus does in fact stand in perfect communion with the Father and that he therefore rightfully claims to be God's Son. The present passage builds on previous similar encounters between Jesus and his Jewish opponents, most importantly the aftermath of Jesus' healing of the lame man in chapter 5. There Jesus, when accused of breaking the Sabbath, had claimed to do his work in continuity with the Father and was promptly charged with blasphemy (cf. 5:18–21).

Jesus' statement at the inception of the Lazarus narrative in 11:4, 'it is for God's glory so that God's Son may be glorified through it', parallels his earlier verdict regarding the man's blindness from birth (9:3; see also the possible *inclusio* with 2:11). As Carson (1991: 406; cf. Barrett 1978: 390) observes, it is not that the sickness occurred *in order* for God to be glorified, but rather that it constituted an occasion for God's glory to be revealed. Here as elsewhere in the Gospel, God's self-disclosure takes place pre-eminently in his Son (13:31; 14:13; 17:4; Carson 1991: 406; Ridderbos 1997: 387). As mentioned, Martha's almost creedlike confession of Jesus as 'the Christ, the Son of God – the one who is coming into the world' (11:27; our trans.), strikingly anticipates the purpose statement at the end of the Gospel (20:30–31).[31]

As has been seen, references to Jesus as the Son of God thus pervade John's Gospel to a much more significant degree than the Synoptic Gospels. The opening confession of Nathanael, the evangelist's identification of Jesus as the Son of God, and Jesus' self-reference to that effect already at 5:25, set the early stage for the Christological controversy, sustained through the entire first half of John's Gospel, centring on whether or not Jesus is the Son of God (cf. 10:36; 11:4, 27). The purpose statement in 20:31 answers the question in the affirmative, contrary to the Jews' assessment before Pilate (19:7).

---

[29] Johnson 1980: 28.
[30] See the treatment of the OT quote in John 10:34 in Köstenberger 2007: 464–467.
[31] See the discussion in Ridderbos 1997: 399–400; Morris 1995: 489–490; and Köstenberger 2004c: 336, n. 72.

Son of Man

Jesus' references to himself as 'Son of Man' in John's Gospel are four times as common as those involving the claim of being the 'Son of God'.[32] Close to half of these are part of a cluster of references involving the term *hypsoō* in the passive voice ('to be lifted up', a euphemism for Jesus' crucifixion; cf. 3:13–14; 8:28; 12:34). The references to Jesus as the 'Son of Man' span from 1:51 to 13:31 (the outset of the farewell discourse). Remarkably, they are absent from the farewell discourse proper and the passion narrative. Overall, the references to Jesus as the 'Son of Man' in this Gospel conform fairly closely to those found in the Synoptics.

The initial reference to Jesus as the Son of Man in 1:51 dramatically anticipates the following narrative. Against the backdrop of an 'open heaven', every Jewish apocalyptic's dream, Jesus identifies himself as the mysterious figure of Daniel 7:13 who has come as a human being from transcendent origins to complete his mission and who will return to earth in the last days to serve as the end-time judge. What Jesus claims is that he is that Son of Man prophesied in Daniel, the one who has seen God and given a full account of him (cf. 1:18), the one who was lifted up at the cross (cf. 3:14; 8:28; 12:32) and who will return in all his glory (cf. Matt. 26:64).

The picture invoked in 1:51 is drawn from Jacob's vision of the ladder 'resting on the earth, with its top reaching to heaven, and the angels of God . . . ascending and descending' (Gen. 28:12). As the angels ascended and descended on Jacob, later renamed 'Israel' (a sign of God's revelation and reaffirmation of faithfulness to his promises made to Abraham), the disciples are promised further divine confirmation of Jesus' messianic identity. Here Jesus tells his followers that he will be the place of much greater divine revelation than that given at previous occasions to Abraham, Jacob, Moses or Isaiah.

Jesus is the 'new Bethel', the place where God is revealed, where heaven and earth, God and humanity, meet. In fact, Jesus is the very culmination of all of God's revelatory expressions, Jesus is the Word (1:1; cf. 1:14, 18), providing a fullness of divine self-disclosure of which even Jacob (Israel) could only dream; and these disciples, who as of yet know little of what awaits them, will soon be witnesses to revelation that far exceeds that received by any Israelite in previous history.

---

[32] 1:51; 3:13, 14; 5:27; 6:27, 53, 62; 8:28; 9:35; 12:23, 24; 13:31.

The next reference to Jesus as the Son of Man in 3:13 is part of Jesus' dialogue with Nicodemus. Jesus here contrasts himself, the 'Son of Man' (cf. Dan. 7:13), with other human figures who allegedly entered heaven, such as Enoch (Gen. 5:24; cf. Heb. 11:5), Elijah (2 Kgs 2:1–12; cf. 2 Chr. 21:12–15), Moses (Exod. 24:9–11; 34:29–30), Isaiah (Isa. 6:1–3) or Ezekiel (Ezek. 1:10). While all these figures entered heaven, only Jesus first descended from heaven, because he is the heaven-sent Son of Man. Elsewhere in John's Gospel, the only others who are said to have descended from heaven are the Spirit (1:32–33), angels (1:51; see above) and the divine bread (6:33, 38, 41, 42, 50, 51, 58), that is, Jesus himself in fulfilment of manna symbolism.

The reference to Jesus as the Son of Man in 5:27 is unique in that the phrase reads more literally 'he is Son of Man', the only instance of this Christological title without articles before both 'Son' and 'Man' in the entire NT. This may indicate an allusion to Daniel 7:13 LXX, where the expression 'son of man' likewise does not feature the article (cf. Rev. 1:13; 14:14). The present passage attributes to Jesus the exercise of a divine attribute, namely the authority to judge (e.g. Gen. 18:25; 1 Sam. 2:10; Pss 9:8; 82:8; 94:2 etc.). This comes on the heels of the reference to Jesus being granted to have life in himself, also a divine attribute (5:26).

The references to Jesus as the Son of Man in the 'bread of life' discourse in chapter 6 all play off the giving of the manna to wilderness Israel (6:27, 53, 62). There the manna descended from heaven. Here, Jesus claims that, like the manna, he descended from heaven as the Son of Man. Unlike the manna, however, Jesus also claims that he will again ascend to heaven in the future (see esp. 6:62). This suggests that Jesus' crucifixion, his giving his flesh and blood for the life of the world (6:51), is not going to be the end of the story but that his ascension will be every bit as striking as his forceful death (cf. 1:51; 3:13–14).

The reference to the 'lifting up' of the Son of Man in 8:28 harks back to 3:13–14 and anticipates 12:32, the three 'lifted up' sayings in John's Gospel. The expression 'lifted up' (*hypsoō*) almost certainly echoes Isaianic language regarding the Servant of the Lord, who 'will be raised and lifted up and highly exalted' (Isa. 52:13: *hypsōthēsetai kai doxasthēsetai*). There is great irony in the fact that the Jews, by having Jesus crucified, are actually 'lifting' him up. John is the only NT writer to use this term in a dual sense with reference both to Jesus' crucifixion (his literal 'lifting up') and to his exaltation (metaphorical use). The reference to the glorification of the Son of Man in 12:23 is to be seen within the same purview, as is the climactic instance in 12:32.

In the latter passage, it is said that, once 'lifted up', Jesus will draw 'all people' (i.e. all *kinds* of people, Gentiles as well as Jews) to himself.[33] Now the evangelist makes it plain that the references to Jesus' 'lifting up' are to his crucifixion (12:33). Also, the crucifixion is presented as the prerequisite for Jesus' universal mission to all of humanity, including non-Jews. It is required for Jesus to be able to draw all people to himself. This is an exceedingly important truth, one that is at the heart of the message of the entire Gospel (see esp. 1:12; 3:16; 20:30–31). No longer does the Jews' salvation-historical privilege obtain, but rather faith in Jesus' name has now become the sole prerequisite for inclusion among God's new covenant people.

The Son

As mentioned, of the eighteen references to Jesus as the Son in John's Gospel, all but the first five are by Jesus himself. It may be surprising, however, that these references are not as pervasive as might be supposed. As many as eight instances of 'the Son' are found in 5:19–26. There are two additional references in the first part of the Gospel (6:40; 8:36) and two verses containing three references in the second part (14:13; 17:1 [2]). To be sure, the frequent references to God as Jesus' Father also imply his sonship, but it is still worthy of note that explicit instances of *huios* with Jesus as the referent are not as common as might be surmised. Nevertheless, when taken in conjunction with the Christological titles 'Son of God' and 'Son of Man', 'Son' language in John's Gospel proves to be the predominant Christological label applied to Jesus.[34]

Interestingly, references to Jesus as the 'Son' are not unique to John's Gospel (which enhances their claim to authenticity). Most striking is the so-called Johannine thunderbolt found in Matthew 11:27 = Luke 10:22: 'All things have been committed to me by my Father. No-one knows the Son except the Father, and no-one knows the Father except the Son and those to whom the Father chooses to reveal him.' Another Synoptic instance of 'Son' language is Matthew 24:36 = Mark 13:32: 'No-one knows about that day or hour, not even the angels in heaven, nor the Son, but only the Father.' A further noteworthy Synoptic passage is Matthew 28:19, where reference is made

---

[33] For this interpretation, and the text-critical issue involved, see Köstenberger 2004c: 384, 388; also Carson 1991: 444; and Morris 1995: 531–532 (citing Calvin).

[34] See above, table 4.1, 'Jesus as the Son in John's Gospel: overview', and below, tables 4.3 to 4.5, for a narrative survey of Jesus as Son in John's Gospel.

to baptism in the name of the Father, the Son and the Holy Spirit. While 'Son' language is thus more pronounced in John than it is in the other Gospels, it is not entirely absent from the Synoptics.

The first major cluster of 'Son' references is contributed by the fourth evangelist in 3:16–18. Interestingly, in these verses the evangelist refers to Jesus twice as 'one-of-a-kind Son' (*monogenēs huios*; 3:16, 18) and once as 'Son of God' (3:17). This shows the close interrelatedness between these terms. While God is the one who 'gave' or 'sent' his Son, the Son is unique and the Son of God; in fact, he himself is God as well (per the prologue; 1:1, 18; cf. 20:28).

The second major cluster of 'Son' references, structurally corresponding to the first such cluster in 3:16–18, is found in 3:35–36, where in the short span of two verses Jesus is identified as 'the Son' as many as three times. The Baptist witnesses regarding Jesus that the Father gave all things to the Son owing to his love for him. The important implication from this for all people is that unless they believe in the Son, resulting in eternal life, God's wrath will continue to rest on them (3:36; cf. 1 John 5:9–13).

The third and most significant major cluster of 'Son' references in John's Gospel with regard to Jesus is found in 5:19–26. In this passage, Jesus is referred to as the 'Son' a total of eight times, plus once each as 'Son of God' (5:25) and 'Son of Man' (5:27). Once again, this shows the close interrelatedness between these three Christological titles involving the term 'Son'. Jesus' words here respond to the Jews' charge of blasphemy in the aftermath of his healing of an invalid on the Sabbath (cf. 5:17–18).

In response, Jesus avers that he, while equal to God, is personally subordinate to him as a son is to his father.[35] Their relationship preserves the distinctness of Jesus' personal identity.[36] Thus, Jesus does not assert independence from God, but dependence on him; he is at once coeternal with and subordinate to the Father.[37] The illustration in 5:19–20 may reflect Jesus' own experience with his adoptive father, Joseph, from whom he learned the craftsman's trade (cf. Matt. 13:55; Mark 6:3).[38]

The latter part of 5:19 features the first of four consecutive *gar*(for)-clauses, asserting that '[i]t is impossible for the Son to take

---

[35] Morris 1995: 277; Carson 1991: 250.

[36] Carson 1991: 251.

[37] Keener 1999.

[38] On Joseph's and Jesus' trade being that of craftsman rather than carpenter, see Campbell 2005.

independent, self-determined action that would set him over against the Father as another God' (Carson 1991: 251). The second *gar*-clause states the basis for the Son's dependence: the Father loves the Son (5:20). Clauses three and four speak of the Son's delegated authority to raise the dead and to exercise judgment (5:21, 22).

The Father's love for the Son expresses itself in his free self-disclosure to the Son; the Son's love for the Father in his obedient submission to the Father's will, including death on the cross.[39] The 'greater things' (5:20), in context, refer to raising the dead and exercising judgment (5:21–23; Morris 1995: 278). The raising of Lazarus, the climactic 'sign' performed by Jesus in this Gospel, thus presents itself as proleptic of this kind of activity. The matching statement in chapters 13–21 may be the reference to believers' 'greater things' in 14:12.

According to Jesus, the Son gives life to those to whom he is pleased to give it, just as the Father raises the dead and gives them life. The OT and Second Temple literature concur that raising the dead and giving life are divine prerogatives.[40] Jesus' contemporaries therefore did not believe that the Messiah would be given authority to raise the dead.[41] This renders Jesus' claim of being able to raise the dead and to give them life at will all the more startling. While Elijah, too, raised the dead, Jesus' claim is much bolder: he will give life *to whom he is pleased to give it.*

Not only is the Son able to give life as he desires; all judgment has also been entrusted to the Son (5:22). This is a remarkable assertion, since according to the Hebrew Scriptures judgment is the exclusive prerogative of God (e.g. Gen. 18:25; cf. Judg. 11:27; though see the association of 'the LORD' with 'his Anointed One' in rule and judgment in Ps. 2:2). In Second Temple literature, too, the Messiah remains very much in the background as far as judgment is concerned, apart from carrying out God's judgment on his enemies in keeping with Jewish nationalistic expectations (e.g. *Pss Sol.* 17.21–27).[42] Rabbinic writings likewise assign judging the world to God alone.

The purpose of the Father's delegation of authority to give life and to render judgment to the Son is that people might honour the Son

---

[39] Carson 1991: 251.

[40] See Deut. 32:39; 1 Sam. 2:6; 2 Kgs 5:7; Tob. 13.2; Wis. 16.13.

[41] Cf. *b. Ta'an.* 2a (attributed to Rabbi Yohanan, c. AD 70) and the *Shemoneh 'Esreh* (c. AD 70–100, cited in Schürer 1979, 2: 455–463).

[42] The singular exception is the Son of Man (or 'Chosen One') in the *Similitudes of Enoch* (*1 En.* 37–71; esp. 49.4; 61.9; 62.2–6; 63.11).

as they do the Father.[43] Conversely, whoever fails to honour the Son also fails to honour the Father who sent him. In the OT, Moses and the prophets were considered to be God's agents and mouthpieces who acted and spoke on God's behalf. The Jewish fundamental affirmation regarding a messenger (*šālîah*) is that 'a man's agent is like the man himself' (e.g. *m. Ber.* 5.5).[44]

Jesus' role as the sent Son thus highlights both his equality with the Father in purpose (and even nature) and his obedience to the Father in carrying out his mission: 'it is a legal presumption that an agent will carry out his mission' (*b. 'Erub.* 31b–32a; cf. *b. Ketub.* 99b).[45] According to John, this is precisely what Jesus did: he came to earth, accomplished the mission entrusted to him by the Father and returned to the one who sent him (4:34; 17:4; cf. 19:30; see also 1:1, 14; cf. Isa. 55:11–12).

Jesus goes on to assert that, just as the Father has life in himself, so he has given the Son to have life in himself (cf. 5:21). The OT states repeatedly that God grants life to others (see Gen. 2:7; Job 10:12; 33:4; Ps. 36:9). But here Jesus claims that God granted him life in *himself*, a divine attribute.[46] The remaining two references to Jesus as 'the Son' come in 6:40 (similar in wording as 3:15–16), in the midst of several references to Jesus as the Son of Man, and in 8:36, where Jesus 'the Son' claims to bring true liberation from the slavery of sin.

The farewell discourse features two additional passages where Jesus is referred to as the Son. In 14:13, Jesus promises to answer prayer offered in his name 'that the Son may bring glory to the Father'. Similarly, in his final prayer in 17:1, Jesus petitions, with reference to the impending crucifixion and subsequent resurrection and exaltation, 'Father, the time has come. Glorify your Son, that your Son may glorify you.' These two final passages show that the Father–Son motif in John's Gospel culminates in the Son's 'glorification' at the cross, which, in turn, becomes the basis on which Jesus commissions his followers and sends them on their mission (20:21).[47]

---

[43] In effect, this establishes Jesus' right to be worshipped (Carson 1991: 255) and amounts to a claim to deity (Morris 1995: 279).

[44] See Rengstorf 1964, 1: 414–420.

[45] Contra Giles 2006: 117–124. We will discuss further the theological significance of this portrait of Jesus in chapter 7 below.

[46] The verse relates to the 'eternal generation of the Son' (Carson 1991: 257).

[47] See chapter 9 below.

Summary and conclusion

While it has been helpful to look at each of the Christological titles involving 'son' language individually, it is appropriate to conclude the present chapter with a synoptic view of the Johannine narrative tracing all 'son' references jointly in narrative sequence. Here is a list of all the relevant passages (M = *monogenēs*; SJ = son of Joseph; SG = Son of God; SM = Son of Man; S = Son).

Table 4.3   Prologue and Cana cycle (1:1 – 4:54)

M	SJ/SG/SM	SM/M/S/SG	S
1:14, 18	1:45, 49, 51	3:13–14, 16–18	3:35–36
Evangelist	first followers/Jesus	Jesus/evangelist	John the Baptist

Table 4.4   Festival cycle (5:1 – 10:42)

S/SG/SM	SM/S/SJ/SM	SM	S	SM	SG
5:19–27	6:27, 40, 42, 53, 62	8:28	8:36	9:35	10:36
Jesus	Jesus	Jesus	Jesus	Jesus	Jesus

Table 4.5   Final sign, farewell discourse, and passion narrative (11:1 – 20:31)

SG	SM	S	SG
11:4, 27	12:23, 34; 13:31	14:13; 17:1	19:7; 20:31
Jesus	Jesus	Jesus	Jews/evangelist

The above survey shows that apart from the fourth evangelist (1:14, 18; 3:16–18), Jesus' first followers (1:45, 49) and John the Baptist (3:35–36), it is primarily Jesus who speaks of himself as Son, variously referring to himself as 'the Son', 'the Son of Man' or even 'the Son of God' (though not as *monogenēs*). The focal point of 'Son' language in John's Gospel is Jesus' defence against the charge of blasphemy in 5:19–26, which features a total of ten instances of 'Son' language.

As we have seen in the previous three chapters dealing with the characterization of the Son (*huios*) and God (*theos*) the Father (*patēr*), the Word-made-flesh in the Son and God-the Father are both equally God; hence Jesus can say, 'I and the Father are one' (10:30), and yet sustain a relationship that can be described as that between a Son (who is 'sent') and a Father ('the one who sent' his Son). Before turning to a study of the characterization of the Spirit in John's Gospel, it may be helpful to summarize our findings thus far in the following chart:

Table 4.6   The Word/God-made-flesh / the Son and God-the-Father relationship in John's Gospel

Creation	The Word = God ↓	God ↓	Ontological Equality
Incarnation	made flesh The Son	sends the Son The Father	Functional Subordination

Chapter Five

The Spirit in John's Gospel

Introduction

As one seeks to explore the role of the Spirit in John's Gospel, one is initially struck with the way in which the Son–Father relationship between the Word-made-flesh and God-the-Father completely predominate in the first half of John's Gospel. This is not to say that the Spirit is completely absent from these chapters, as we will see; quite to the contrary. Nevertheless, it is not until the second half of the Gospel, when the Son's return to the Father is rapidly approaching, that the Spirit becomes the focal point of much of the discussion.

As we will discuss more fully in the remainder of the chapter, there is no reference to the Spirit in John's prologue, and there are only four passages in which reference to the Spirit is made in the first half of the Gospel. All of these relate to the Spirit's role in Jesus' ministry. The Spirit rests on him (1:32–33) and does so to an unlimited degree (3:34). His words are life-giving and Spirit-infused (6:63), and the Spirit is to be given only subsequent to Jesus' earthly ministry (7:39).

As intimated above, references to the Spirit in the second half of the Gospel increase dramatically in both number and prominence in keeping with the Spirit's pivotal role in the disciples' mission subsequent to Jesus' departure and his return to God the Father. The Spirit is referred to variously as the 'Spirit of truth' (14:17; 15:26; 16:13), the 'Holy Spirit' (14:26; 20:22; cf. 1:33) and by the adumbration *paraklē-tos*, or 'helping presence' (14:16, 26; 15:26; 16:7).[1]

The Book of Signs

The initial references to the Spirit in John's Gospel are in connection with Jesus' baptism by John (1:32–33). The Baptist witnesses that he saw the Spirit descend from heaven as a dove and remain on Jesus.

---

[1] For a discussion of this translation of *paraklētos*, see Köstenberger 2004c: 435–438.

The Baptist had been told (by God) that this would be the one who would baptize, not with water as John did, but with the Holy Spirit (1:33; cf. Matt. 3:11; Mark 1:8; Luke 3:16; Acts 1:5; see also John 14:26; 20:22). Hence the Spirit's first appearance in this Gospel is as confirming Jesus as the God-sent future dispenser of the Spirit.

The next possible cluster of references occurs in the context of Jesus' instruction of Nicodemus regarding the spiritual birth required for entering the kingdom of God (3:5–8). Jesus' reference to being 'born again' in 3:3 is further explained as being 'born of water and spirit' (our trans.; better than NIV's 'born of water and the Spirit'), most likely a reference to a spiritual birth entailing cleansing and renewal. As the following verse, 3:6, makes clear, however ('That which is born of flesh is flesh, and that which is born of spirit is spirit'; our trans.), the reference is probably not to the person of the Holy Spirit but to the spiritual (rather than material) nature of the birth required for entrance into God's kingdom. This is true also for the following analogy between spirit and the wind (3:8).

In 3:34, the evangelist comments subsequent to the Baptist's testimony that 'he' (most likely God; made explicit by the NIV and TNIV)[2] gives the Spirit without measure (i.e. to an unlimited extent; cf. 1:33). If, as has been argued, 3:5–8 is not to be taken as referring to the Spirit, this would be the next reference to the Spirit after 1:32–33 in this Gospel.

Our conclusion regarding the instances of *pneuma* in 4:23–24 is similar to that reached regarding 3:5–8. The anarthrous reference to 'spirit and truth' in 4:23 resembles that to 'water and spirit' in 3:5. In 4:23, too, the emphasis is on the *kind* of worship to be rendered by those who would please God, that is, worship that is spiritual and in keeping with truth rather than that which focuses on material aspects such as locations of worship.[3] Neither in Nicodemus' nor (even less likely) in the Samaritan woman's case would a reference to the Spirit have been easily intelligible to Jesus' original audience. This understanding of 4:23 is confirmed by the reference to God as *pneuma*, spirit, in 4:24, surely not a reference to the Holy Spirit.

In 6:63, in the first of *Jesus'* references to the Spirit in this Gospel, Jesus affirms that the Spirit gives life and that Jesus' words are spirit and life. The latter reference should probably be taken to mean that Jesus' words are life-giving because they are infused by the Spirit.

---

[2] Köstenberger 2004c: 155–158.
[3] See the discussion of John 4:23–24 in chapter 3 above.

After all, the Spirit rests on Jesus (1:33) to an unlimited degree (3:34).

The next reference to the Spirit is part of an aside by the evangelist, who explains that a given utterance of Jesus at the feast of Tabernacles was with reference to the Spirit (7:39). The context is Jesus' invitation, uttered on the final day of the Feast of Tabernacles, for people to come to him and drink (7:37; the present passage harks back to Jesus' interchange with the Samaritan woman in 4:7–15). The festival was celebrated in the hope of the joyful restoration of Israel and the ingathering of the nations. Jesus here presents himself as God's agent to make these end-time events a reality.

The Scripture adduced in Jesus' saying 'Whoever believes in me, as the Scripture has said, streams of living water will flow from within him' (7:38) is probably common prophetic teaching rather than one particular passage.[4] 'From within him' probably refers to the one who believes in Jesus the Messiah rather than to Jesus himself, with the first clause, 'Whoever believes in me', serving as a pendent subject.[5] The evangelist proceeds to note that Jesus' reference is to the future (from the vantage point of the narrative) giving of the Spirit (7:39; cf. 1:33). This reflects hindsight and represents an effort by the evangelist to preserve the historical perspective prior to Jesus' 'glorification', a Johannine euphemism for the cluster of events centring in the crucifixion.[6]

Since the reference in 11:33 is to *Jesus'* spirit (as also in 13:21 and 19:30), not the Holy Spirit, this concludes the fairly sparse list of references to the Spirit in the first half of the Gospel.

The Book of Glory

The Spirit rises to considerably greater prominence in the farewell discourse, whose major thrust is the preparation of Jesus' followers for the time subsequent to his departure and return to the Father. Once Jesus has been exalted, the Spirit will play a pivotal role in the mission of Jesus' followers. This is evident by the references to the Spirit as

---

[4] Suggestions of specific passages include Ps. 77:16, 20 LXX (with the epithet 'living' coming from Zech. 14:8) or Isa. 58:11 (cf. Prov. 4:23; 5:15). See Carson 1991: 325–328.

[5] So a majority of commentators, including Ridderbos 1997: 273; Carson 1991: 323–325; and others. Less likely, Jesus is presented as the source of 'streams of living water'. Other examples of pendent subjects in this Gospel include 1:12; 6:39; 15:2; and 17:2. See the discussion and references in Köstenberger 2004c: 240–241, esp. n. 59.

[6] See on this Carson 1982; and Lemcio 1991.

'Spirit of truth' (objective genitive, the Spirit as conveying truth) in 14:17; 15:26; and 16:13; as the 'Holy Spirit' in 14:26 and 20:22 (cf. 1:33); and as the *paraklētos* (helping presence) in 14:16, 26; 15:26; and 16:7.

The farewell discourse

The entire section 14:15–24 envisions the giving of the Spirit subsequent to Jesus' exaltation, at which time Jesus and the Father will make their dwelling in believers through the Spirit. Jesus' identification with the Spirit, the 'other *paraklētos*', is so strong that Jesus can say that he *himself* will return to his followers in the person of the Spirit (14:18).[7] While 'yet a little while' (our trans.) in 14:19 and 'on that day' in 14:20 may at first blush appear to refer to Jesus' resurrection appearances, Jesus' promise not to leave his disciples as orphans in 14:18 is hardly satisfied by these appearances, which were temporary in nature. More likely, reference is made to the permanent replacement of Jesus' presence with the Spirit. This is suggested also by Jesus' response to Judas' (not Iscariot's) question in 14:23 with reference to Jesus and the Father's making their dwelling in believers as further explicating 14:18.

Contrary to what the disciples thought at the time, Jesus' departure actually had several benefits for them. The most important was that Jesus would petition the Father to provide 'another helping presence' like Jesus. This prospect ought to encourage Jesus' followers who were struggling to come to terms with the implications of Jesus' upcoming departure. As the evangelist had made clear earlier in his Gospel, this giving of the Spirit would be possible only subsequent to Jesus' glorification (7:39). With this glorification now imminent (cf. 12:23; 13:1), Jesus spends his final moments with his followers, preparing them for life in the age of the Spirit.

In the first half of his Gospel, John's treatment of the Spirit has largely resembled that of the Synoptics. Like them he has included the Baptist's reference to Jesus as the one who will baptize with the Holy Spirit (1:32–33; cf. Matt. 3:11 par.) and emphasizes that the Spirit in all his fullness rested on Jesus during his earthly ministry (1:32; 3:34; cf. Luke 4:18). Moreover, John has stressed the Spirit's role in regeneration (3:5, 6, 8; cf. 1:12–13), worship (4:23–24) and the giving of life (6:63). But as in John's presentation of Jesus' followers,

---

[7] For this interpretation and a discussion of the issues involved, see Köstenberger 2004c: 439 and further below.

96

his adoption of a post-exaltation vantage point leads to a vastly enhanced portrayal of the Spirit in the farewell discourse, where he is featured primarily as 'the *paraklētos*' (14:16, 26; 15:26; 16:7) and as 'the Spirit of truth' (14:17; 15:26; 16:13), two closely related terms (see 15:26).[8]

Unsatisfactory approaches to resolving the meaning and import of the term *paraklētos* in John's Gospel are legion.[9] The expression does not occur in the LXX,[10] and elsewhere in the NT only in 1 John 2:1, there with reference to Jesus 'our Advocate' (our trans.) with God the Father.[11] Jesus' reference to the Spirit as 'another *paraklētos*' in 14:16 indicates that the Spirit's presence with the disciples will replace Jesus' encouraging and strengthening presence with them while on earth (cf. 14:17). When the Spirit comes to dwell in believers, it will be as if Jesus himself were to take up residence in them.[12] Thus Jesus is able

---

[8] For a treatment of the Spirit-Paraclete in the context of the references to the Spirit in the entire Gospel narrative, see M. Davies 1992: 139–153. For a comparison of the treatments of the Spirit in John and the Synoptics, see Köstenberger 1999a: 156. On the translation of the term, see Köstenberger 2004c: 436, n. 70.

[9] Betz (1963) unconvincingly argues for a Qumran background (the archangel Michael; cf. Shafaat 1981: 263–269, who likewise adduces DSS parallels; and Leaney 1972: 38–61, who says the Paraclete is God himself). Windisch (1968) advances the hardly more plausible hypothesis that the Paraclete is 'a kind of angel . . . in human form', be it a prophet or teacher. Johnston (1970) unsuccessfully proposes that the *paraklētos* is an active divine power that has become embodied in certain leaders of the apostolic church, such as the fourth evangelist (see the critiques by Brown 1967: 126 and 1971: 268–270, for whom the Paraclete is the 'alter ego of Jesus', 1967: 132, cited in Smalley 1996: 297; cf. Burge 1987). Bultmann (1971: 566–572) views the concept as a Johannine appropriation of his Gnostic source's figure of 'helper'. Riesenfeld (1972: 266–274) postulates a sapiential provenance, which is equally unlikely. Boring (1978: 113–123) claims the Paraclete is an angel demythologized as the 'spirit of prophecy'! Billington (1995: 90–115) appropriately stresses the Paraclete's role in mission. If the disciples are to witness to Jesus, they must understand the significance of his coming; witness to Jesus and the Paraclete's ministry are thus inseparable (15:26–27; 16:8–11; 20:21–23). For a helpful discussion of the Paraclete as part of the Fourth Gospel's lawsuit motif, esp. in 15:26 – 16:15, see Lincoln 2000: 110–123, esp. 113–114.

[10] But see Aquila's and Theodotion's use of a related noun form in Job 16:2.

[11] For a survey of all known examples from the fourth century BC to the third century AD, see Grayston 1981: 67–82, who concludes that *paraklētos* was a more general term which was sometimes (but not always) used in legal contexts, meaning 'supporter' or 'sponsor'. The closest contemporaneous usage is found in Philo, who uses the expression to convey the notion of rendering of general help, be it by giving advice or support (with the latter meaning being the more common). In later rabbinic usage, the term in its transliterated form is used alongside the transliterated term for a Greek expression meaning 'advocate' (*synēgoros*). Patristic references include *Did.* 5.2; *2 Clem.* 6.9; and Clement of Alexandria, *Quis div.* 25.7. For a study of the Johannine Paraclete in the church Fathers, see Casurella 1983.

[12] 'The Spirit is the divine presence when Jesus' physical presence is taken away from his followers' (Morris 1989: 159).

to refer to the coming of the Spirit by saying, '*I* will come to you' (14:18).[13] This relieves a primary concern for Jesus' first followers in the original setting of the farewell discourse: Jesus' departure will not leave them as orphans (cf. 14:18); just as God was present with them through Jesus, he will continue to be present with them through his Spirit.[14] The Spirit's role thus ensures the continuity between Jesus' pre- and post-glorification ministry. What is more, the coming of the Spirit will actually constitute an advance in God's operations with and through the disciples (16:7; cf. 14:12).

The initial reference to the Spirit as *paraklētos* in 14:16 is the first of five Paraclete sayings in the farewell discourse, in each case with reference to the Holy Spirit (cf. 14:26; 15:26; 16:7–11, 12–15).[15] As Jesus' emissary, the Spirit will have a variety of functions in believers' lives. He will

- bring to remembrance all that Jesus taught his disciples (14:26)
- testify regarding Jesus together with his followers (15:26)
- convict the world of sin, (un)righteousness and judgment (16:8–11)
- guide Jesus' disciples in all truth and disclose what is to come (16:13; historically, this included the formation of the NT canon as apostolic testimony to Jesus)

While initially focused on the Eleven (cf. 15:26), the Spirit, in a secondary sense, fulfils similar roles in believers today. He illuminates the spiritual meaning of Jesus' words and works both to believers and, through believers, to the unbelieving world. In all of these functions, the ministry of the Spirit remains closely linked with the person of Jesus. Just as Jesus is everywhere in John's Gospel portrayed as the

[13] Though, as Moloney (1998: 407) points out, there are differences between Jesus and the Spirit as well: the latter neither becomes flesh nor dies for our sins. Alternatively, the statement refers to Jesus' post-resurrection appearances to his followers (so Ridderbos 1997: 505; Carson 1991: 501; Morris 1995: 578–559; Beasley-Murray 1999: 258; Borchert 2002: 126). Barrett (1978: 464) says the passage refers neither to Jesus coming in the person of the Holy Spirit nor to the parousia, but is using language appropriate to both the resurrection and parousia to refer to both.

[14] As Brown (1970: 642) points out, the promise of the divine presence with Jesus' followers in 14:15–24 includes the Spirit (14:15–17), Jesus (14:18–21) and the Father (14:22–24), hence involving all three persons of the Godhead in the indwelling of believers.

[15] In 1 John, the term refers to the exalted Jesus (2:1). In secular Greek, *paraklētos* refers primarily to a 'legal assistant' or 'advocate' (though the word never became a technical term such as its Lat. equivalent *advocatus*). In John's Gospel, legal overtones are most pronounced in 16:7–11.

Sent One who is fully dependent on and obedient to the Father, the Spirit is said to be 'sent' by both the Father and Jesus (14:26; 15:26) and to focus his teaching on the illumination of the spiritual significance of God's work in Jesus (14:26; 15:26; 16:9).

Table 5.1 The God-the-Son, God-the-Father and Spirit-of-truth / Holy Spirit / other *paraklētos* relationship in John's Gospel

Creation	The Word = God		God
	↓		↓
Incarnation	made flesh		sends the Son
	The Son		The Father
		↓	
		send	
Glorification		The Holy Spirit	
		The Spirit of truth	
		The other *Paraklētos*	

The Spirit is also called 'the Spirit of truth' (cf. 15:26; 16:13). In the context of the present chapter, Jesus has just been characterized as 'the truth' (14:6) in keeping with statements already made in the prologue (1:14, 17). The concept of truth in John's Gospel encompasses several aspects:

1. Truthfulness as opposed to falsehood: 'to speak the truth' means to make a true rather than false statement, that is, to represent the facts as they actually are (cf. 8:40, 45, 46; 16:7; 'to witness to the truth': 5:33; 18:37).
2. Truth in its finality as compared to previous, preliminary expressions: this is its *eschatological* dimension (cf. esp. 1:17: 'the law was given through Moses; grace and truth came through Jesus Christ').
3. Truth is an identifiable body of knowledge with actual propositional content (e.g. 8:32: 'you will know the truth'; 16:13: 'he will guide you in[to] all truth').
4. Truth is a sphere of operation, be it for worship (4:23–24) or sanctification (17:17, 19).
5. Truth as relational fidelity (1:17; 14:6).[16]

---

[16] For the first four categories, see Swain 1998. For a recent treatment of Pilate's question in John 18:38 'What is truth?', in its Johannine context, see the first essay in Köstenberger 2005b. On the larger issue of truth in theological, philosophical and

The Spirit is involved in all five aspects: he accurately represents the truth regarding Jesus; he is the eschatological gift of God; he imparts true knowledge of God; he is operative in both worship and sanctification; and he points people to the person of Jesus.

The expression 'spirit of truth' was current in Judaism (e.g. *T. Jud.* 20.1–5). Similarly, the Qumran literature affirms that God placed within man 'two spirits so that he would walk with them until the moment of his visitation; they are the spirits of truth and of deceit' (1QS 3.18; cf. 4:23–26). Yet these parallels are in all likelihood merely those of language, not thought. For while these expressions are part of an ethical dualism in Second Temple literature (including Qumran), John's Gospel does not feature a 'spirit of error' corresponding to the Spirit of truth.[17] Rather, the Spirit of truth is the 'other helping presence' who takes the place of Jesus while on earth with his disciples. This 'other helping presence', the 'Spirit of truth', the world cannot accept,[18] because it neither sees nor knows him. Yet Jesus' followers do, because 'he lives with you and will be in you' (14:17; see 1 John 3:24; 4:13).[19]

On the other side, the fourth evangelist acknowledges the presence of 'the devil' (13:2), 'Satan' (13:27), the 'prince of this world' (12:31) or the 'evil one' (17:15), though references to demon exorcism are notably absent in John. This suggests that, in John, Satan is pitted against Jesus, and the Spirit Jesus would send subsequent to his departure, but not in the sense of two equally matched dualities of good and evil, but in the sense that Satan opposes the triune God's salvation-historical purposes centred in Jesus' God-glorifying cross-death, his 'lifting up'. This, we submit, is quite different from the Qumran theology of the two spirits, the spirit of truth and the spirit of falsehood.[20]

---

hermeneutical perspective, see the other essays in the same volume by R. A. Mohler, J. P. Moreland and K. J. Vanhoozer.

[17] But see 1 John 4:6, where 'the Spirit [or spirit] of truth and the spirit of falsehood' occur together.

[18] See at 1:10; cf. 10:26; 12:39; see also 1 Cor. 2:14.

[19] D. M. Smith (1999: 274–275) notes that 'you' here is plural, which leads him to infer that the statement does not necessarily refer to personal indwelling. In principle, this is true. The Spirit indwells the community of Jesus Christ *as* a community (cf. 1 Cor. 3:16). But the statement certainly does not rule out the indwelling of individual believers (note e.g. the singular pronoun *kakeinos* in 14:12, and compare the Pauline teaching on the Spirit's indwelling of individual believers in 1 Cor. 6:19).

[20] See the discussion in Charlesworth 2006, 3: 132 and esp. 136–137 in which the author strenuously seeks to maintain John's direct dependence on Qumran pneumatology, against Bauckham 2000, whose caution, however, is in our view well taken.

The commissioning scene

The final reference to the Spirit is found in the context of Jesus' commissioning statement, 'As the Father has sent me, I am sending you' (20:21; cf. Matt. 28:18–20; Luke 24:46–49),[21] which climaxes the characterization of Jesus as the sent Son.[22] The disciples are drawn into the unity and mission of Father and Son.[23] Succession is important both in the OT and in Second Temple literature. In the present Gospel, Jesus succeeds the Baptist and is followed by both the Spirit and the Twelve (minus Judas) who serve as representatives of the new messianic community. OT narratives involving succession feature Joshua (following Moses) and Elisha (succeeding Elijah).

The reference to Jesus breathing on his disciples while saying, 'Receive the Holy Spirit' (20:22),[24] probably represents a symbolic promise of the soon-to-be-given gift of the Spirit, not the actual giving of him fifty days later at Pentecost.[25] Against many commentators, the present pericope does not constitute the Johannine equivalent to Pentecost,[26] nor is the proposal satisfactory that at 20:22 the disciples 'were only sprinkled with His grace and not [as at Pentecost] saturated with full power'.[27] The present event does not mark the

[21] The statement harks back to 17:18, albeit without reference to the sphere of the disciples' commission (the world), indicating the emphasis in the present passage is on the disciples' authorization rather on the realm of their activity (Ridderbos 1997: 643). Compare also the general statement in 13:20, which suggests that the present passage extends beyond the original disciples also to later generations of believers (Morris 1995: 746, n. 55 et al.).

[22] Köstenberger 1998b: esp. 96–121, 180–198. The vast majority of the instances of 'sending' in John's Gospel relate to Jesus' having been sent by the Father. 'Sending' terminology also occurs with regard to God's sending of the Baptist, the Father's and the Son's sending of the Spirit, and Jesus' sending of his disciples. The present passage features two sending verbs, *pempō* and *apostellō*, with no apparent difference in meaning (as is the virtual consensus among major commentators, including Ridderbos, Morris, Carson, Barrett, Schnackenburg and Brown; see also Köstenberger 1999b: 125–143). Morris (1995: 746, n. 56) notes that this is already suggested by the use of *kathōs* linking the two verbs.

[23] Cf. 17:21–26; Ridderbos 1997: 642.

[24] The absence of the article in the expression 'Holy Spirit' may indicate a focus on 'the quality of the gift of the Holy Spirit rather than on the individuality of the Spirit' (Morris 1995: 747, n. 59).

[25] See Acts 2; Carson 1991: 649–655; cf. Witherington 1995: 340–341. The critique by Hatina 1993: 196–219 (who says the reference is to the indwelling Paraclete) fails to convince.

[26] So Brown 1970: 1038; Barrett 1978: 570, who says the present passage cannot be harmonized with Acts 2; Bultmann 1971: 691 et al.

[27] So Calvin *John*, 1: 205. Beasley-Murray 1999: 382, followed by Borchert 2002: 307–308, believes John telescoped the giving of the Spirit without concern for

actual fulfilment of these promises other than by way of anticipatory sign.[28]

On any other view of the present passage, it is hard to see how John would not be found to stand in actual conflict with Luke's Pentecost narrative in Acts 2, not to mention his own disclaimers earlier in the narrative that the Spirit would be given only subsequent to Jesus' glorification, which entailed his return to the Father.[29] The disciples' behaviour subsequent to the present incident would also be rather puzzling had they already received the Spirit.[30] The present gesture is made to the group in its entirety rather than to the separate individuals constituting it, just as the authority to forgive or retain sins is given to the church as a whole.[31]

The Greek verb *enephysēsen* means 'breathed *on*' (NIV) rather than 'breathed *into*' (TNIV). The theological antecedent is plainly Genesis 2:7, where exactly the same form is used.[32] There God breathes his Spirit into Adam at creation, which constitutes him as a 'living being'. Here, at the occasion of the commissioning of his disciples, Jesus constitutes them as the new messianic community, in anticipation of the outpouring of the Spirit subsequent to his ascension.[33] Hence the circle closes, from creation in 1:1 to new creation in 20:22.

---

chronology (citing the reference to the ascension in 20:17 as a parallel). Turner (1977: 24–42) thinks the reference is not to the Spirit at all, but to Jesus' message as Spirit and life. Schnackenburg (1990, 3: 325) surprisingly contends that the Johannine instance involves all believers, while the events in Acts 2 pertain to the apostles. If anything, one might have expected the opposite kind of reasoning, with John's account anticipating the general outpouring narrated in Acts 2.

[28] Contra Burge 2002: 558; cf. 1987: 148–149.

[29] E.g. 7:39; 14:12, 16–18, 25–26; 16:12–15; cf. 20:17. Luke's account of Pentecost hardly reads as if Acts 2 represents merely 'one of several additional empowerings of the Spirit', as Hatina (1993: 201) alleges. Talbert (1992: 252) concludes from 20:22 that Jesus must have ascended by then or, according to 7:39, he could not yet have given the Spirit. But this presupposes that the Spirit was in fact imparted at 20:22. If not, there is no need to suppose that Jesus had already ascended by then.

[30] In 20:26, the doors are still locked (as prior to 20:22 in 20:19), presumably still 'for fear of the Jewish leaders'; in 21:3, Peter decides to go fishing and is joined by six others, but they catch nothing. Hatina's (1993: 200) argument that the latter may have been 'an atypical circumstance' fails to convince, as does his claim that Peter's threefold confession of love suggests reception of the Spirit (cf. Peter's earlier offer in 13:37 to lay down his life for Jesus).

[31] Morris 1995: 747, 749.

[32] See also 1 Kgs 17:21; Ezek. 37:9; Wis. 15.11; cf. Philo, *Opif.* 135.

[33] This 'new creation' theme is noted by several commentators, including Morris 1995: 747, n. 58 (who also cites Ezek. 37:9); Barrett 1978: 570; Brown 1970: 1035, 1037; and Witherington 1995: 342. Whitacre (1999: 482) speaks of the present event as the church's 'conception', and of Pentecost as its 'birth'. See also N. T. Wright 1992: 416–417 (though we do not agree with all of Wright's conclusions there).

Summary

In the few references to the Spirit in the first half of John's Gospel, Jesus is associated with the Spirit in his present ministry and as the future dispenser of the Spirit subsequent to his exaltation to the Father. References to the Spirit increase dramatically in the second half of the Gospel, which is taken up with the anticipation of the disciples' mission subsequent to Jesus' crucifixion, resurrection and ascension (his 'glorification'). It is that Spirit, the 'Spirit of truth', the 'Holy Spirit', the 'helping presence' sent by Jesus from the Father, who will continue Jesus' ministry and empower the disciples' mission in the unbelieving world. As in the case of the Father–Son relationship, the references to the Spirit in the Fourth Gospel culminate in the commissioning passage in 20:21–22, a (proleptic) reference to the disciples' reception of the Spirit for the purpose of their mission of extending forgiveness of sins upon people's belief in Jesus.

Chapter Six

Father, Son and Spirit in John's Gospel

Introduction

Previous chapters have focused specifically on the characterization of God the Father, the Son and the Spirit. The present chapter seeks briefly to summarize and synthesize these findings in order to lay the foundation for the exploration of trinitarian themes in the next section of this volume.

Summary and synthesis

The relationships between the Father, the Son and the Spirit are presented in John's Gospel within a clearly defined relational as well as salvation-historical framework. In relational terms, it is the Father who sends the Son, not the Son the Father. Likewise, it is the Father and the Son who send the Spirit rather than vice versa. In salvation-historical terms, God the Father sends the Son as the incarnate Word to mark an event of comparable import to creation. This intersects with John the Baptist's ministry, whose purpose it is to reveal the Christ to Israel. John sees the Spirit descend and rest on Jesus. At the same time, Jesus is said to live in constant intimate fellowship with God the Father throughout his earthly ministry.

As he goes about his work, the Son everywhere affirms his unity with the Father in both his works and his words. In the context of the Sabbath controversy, Jesus affirms that the Father is still working, and so is he. Later in the Gospel, Jesus states even more plainly that he and the Father are one (not one person, but one God).[1] At the same time, Jesus can affirm that the Father is greater than he. Jesus is presented everywhere in the Fourth Gospel as equal yet obedient to God the Father.[2] The Spirit, in turn, is sent by the Father and Jesus, yet

---

[1] Bauckham 2005: 163–164.
[2] We will develop this point more fully in the next chapter.

sent in continuity to their salvific and revelatory work. Throughout the Gospel it is made clear that the Spirit will be sent only subsequent to the Son's exaltation as the next salvation-historical milestone to follow.

In John's presentation of the interface between Father, Son and Spirit, the programmatic division of the Gospel into two major parts of equal length features significantly. The first half deals with Jesus' ministry to the Jews and presents Jesus' claims in the context of a pattern of escalating controversy between him and his opponents. Jesus' repeated claims of a unique relationship with God (including calling himself the Son of God) are shown to constitute the major bone of contention between him and his opponents, which in due course issues in the main charge leading to his crucifixion. The pattern of rejection is evident both at the midway point of the first half of John's Gospel (end of ch. 6) and at the end of the first major unit (end of ch. 12).

In the second half, particularly in the farewell discourse, both the evangelist and Jesus adopt a vantage point subsequent to Jesus' exaltation with the Father (his 'glorification'). This has two important consequences. First, the unity between Father, Son and Spirit emerges all the more clearly, since Jesus' exaltation, which is now imminent, marks the point at which the Spirit will be sent by him and the Father. Jesus' followers are told about a soon-coming era during which their mission will be directed by the exalted Jesus and enabled by the indwelling Holy Spirit. Second, the disciples themselves are shown to be taken into the unity and love of the Father, Son and Spirit as they carry out their mission.

Thus not only is the ministry of the Son grounded in the love and commission of the Father, but the ministry of Jesus' followers is grounded in the love and commission of Jesus, and by virtue of Jesus' close relationship with both the Father on the one hand and the Spirit on the other, also in the unity of Father, Son and Spirit among one another. At the same time, this does not obliterate all distinctions of person and role. Just as Jesus is the Son who does the bidding of the Father who sent him, so his followers are to pursue their mission in total dependence on the Son and under the direction of the Holy Spirit. In the end, Father, Son and Spirit are shown to provide redemption and revelation to a community that is itself sent on a redemptive and revelatory mission.

On the receiving end of this mission of unity, love and redemption is a dark and dying world. Satan, the ruler of this world, inspires the

Jewish nation in particular and the world at large to unite in their rejection of the Christ. Repeatedly in the course of the Gospel narrative Father, Son and Spirit are mentioned together.[3] In 1:33–34, the Baptist says that 'the one who sent' (the Father) him told him that the Spirit would mark the one who was to come as the Son of God. The collocation of references to Father, Son and Spirit is particularly pronounced in the farewell discourse, especially in passages pertaining to the Spirit's sending by the Father or the Son or both (14:26; 15:26).

This joint characterization culminates in the commissioning reference in 20:21–22, where Jesus sends his followers as the Father sent him and (proleptically?) equips them with the Spirit.[4] Hence mission proves to be the major thrust of John's depiction of Father, Son and Spirit. In one way or another, all three persons are intimately involved in the mission of believers:[5] just as the Son represented the Father, so Jesus' followers are to represent the Son as they are indwelt and enabled by the Spirit. This unity of mission in no way overrides personal distinctions between Father, Son and Spirit. Neither does it compromise the ontological distinction between Father, Son and Spirit on the one hand and believers in the Messiah on the other.

We will return to the Johannine mission theology at the end of the present volume. With this we are ready to turn to an exploration of some of the most important trinitarian themes in John's Gospel.

---

[3] See Erickson 1995: 7.
[4] Cf. 15:26–27; 16:7–11; see also 14:16–24.
[5] Erickson 1995: 207.

Part 3: Theological Reflections

Chapter Seven

Christology in John's trinitarian perspective: Jesus' filial identity

Introduction

'Christology' is the church's answer to Jesus' question 'Who do you say that I am?' (cf. Matt. 16:13).[1] In the church's attempts to answer this question, John's Gospel has always played a pivotal role,[2] and rightly so. The Fourth Gospel presents the testimony of one who beheld Jesus' miraculous signs (2:11), reclined on Jesus' chest at the table (13:23), and witnessed his glorious death (1:14; 19:35) and resurrection (20–21). Moreover, the Fourth Gospel was written with explicitly Christological aims: 'that you may believe that Jesus is the Christ, the Son of God' (20:31).

The purpose of the present chapter is not to survey the entire land-scape of Johannine Christology but instead to provide an orientation, a *perspective*, for viewing that landscape. Our claim is this: when it comes to understanding Jesus' identity and mission ('Christology'), John urges us to perceive Jesus' identity and mission in a trinitarian light. John's Christology is a *trinitarian* Christology.

What does this mean? To say that John's Christology is a trinitar-ian Christology is not simply to repeat Richard Bauckham's argument that John's vision of Jesus is one of 'Christological monotheism', a vision where Jesus belongs and is internal to the identity of the one true God of Israel. We certainly concur with Bauckham's thesis. John ascribes to Jesus prerogatives that belong uniquely to the one true God of Israel. John's Jesus created and now governs the world (1:3; 5:17), raises the dead (5:21), judges the world (5:22) and breathes the Spirit of life (20:22), to cite but a few

---

[1] Behr 2001: 1–16.
[2] Pollard 1970; Wiles 1960: 112–157; and Edwards 2004. D. M. Smith (1995: 174) states, 'The ancient church's christological controversies look something like an exer-cise in the development of Johannine thought.'

examples. John also attributes to Jesus the 'name' of the one true God. John's 'I am' sayings, in both their absolute and predicative forms, function in this regard. Moreover, John ascribes to Jesus the right to be worshipped, a right enjoyed by Israel's God alone (see 5:23; 20:28).[3]

These Johannine patterns of identifying Jesus place him squarely within the identity of God by pointing to what he holds in common with his Father as the one and only true God. Jesus, too, performs singularly divine acts. Jesus, too, bears the unique divine name. Jesus, too, receives the worship due to God alone. Therefore Jesus belongs to the identity of Israel's one Lord God.

Nevertheless, these identifying patterns do not in themselves constitute a *trinitarian* claim about the identity of Jesus. Perceiving John's trinitarian Christology requires that we identify not only what Jesus holds *in common* with the Father but also the *distinctive personal way* in which Jesus holds what he holds in common with the Father.[4] According to John, Jesus holds the unique divine identity in common *with* the Father *as* the Son *of* the Father. Moreover, as we will see, Jesus' way of being God, his sonship, illuminates not only his deity; it illuminates the nature of his humanity and saving work as well. Perceiving Jesus' filial identity is therefore essential to grasping John's Christological claim.[5] The glory of Jesus the Messiah according to John is the glory of 'the only Son from the Father' (1:14, ESV).

---

[3] See Bauckham's discussion in 2005; also Bauckham 1998a.

[4] Andrew Louth (1996: 59) explains the difference between 'person' and 'nature' according to the 'Chalcedonian logic' of the early church: 'Person is contrasted to nature: it is concerned with the way we are (the mode, or *tropos*), not what we are . . . Whatever we share with others, we are: it belongs to our nature. But what it is to be a person is not some thing, some quality, that we do *not* share with others – as if there were an irreducible somewhat within each one of us that makes us the unique persons we are. What is unique about each one of us is what we have made of the nature that we have: our own unique mode of existence, which is a matter of our experience in the past, our hopes for the future, the way we live out the nature we have. What makes the Son of God the unique person he is is the eternal life of love in the Trinity which he shares in a filial way.'

[5] Thus, Paul Meyer, reflecting on John's Father–Son language argues 'that the reader is compelled by this language to redefine the term "Christology" itself and to recognize that in its profoundest dimension – not just in this Gospel but in all its variations throughout the diverse traditions of the New Testament – it concerns not the person of Jesus or his identity ("who he is") and the consequences of his life so much as – first, foremost, and always – his open or hidden *relationship* to God, and of God to him' (Meyer 1996: 259). The only qualification we would make to Meyer's statement is that it is precisely Jesus' '*relationship*' to God and, of God to him' that reveals to us the nature of his '*identity*' ('who he is') and of the saving '*consequences*' of his life'.

The prologue: John's initial characterization of Jesus as the Son

John 1:1–18 provides us with John's initial characterization of Jesus, identifying him with a 'paradigm of traits'[6] that will characterize his messianic identity and mission for the rest of the Gospel.[7] In 1:1, we are told that Jesus, described as 'the Word', has existed eternally 'with God' as 'God'.[8] 1:3, 4 and 5 describe this Word as the agent of God's creative work, the one in whom divine life resides and through whom God's creative light shines forth in the darkness (cf. Gen. 1:3). In 1:9–13, we learn that the Word has come into the world as light in order to accomplish a mission: giving God's people 'the right to become children of God' (1:12).[9] 1:14, the high point of the prologue, announces that the Word 'became flesh and made his dwelling among us', manifesting the fullness of God's glory, a 'glory as of the only Son from the Father' (our trans.). 1:18 rounds out the prologue's initial characterization of Jesus, describing him as one who dwells 'at the Father's side' and who is therefore fully capable of making the Father known.[10]

A striking feature of John's Gospel is that, after the prologue, Jesus is never again called 'the Word'. Instead, John prefers to describe Jesus under some denomination of sonship (e.g. Son, Son of God, Son of Man etc.).[11] The 'paradigm of traits' ascribed to Jesus in the prologue nonetheless remains constant throughout the Gospel. He enjoys perfect fellowship with the Father; he is God; he is the agent of God, sent on a mission from God; he is God in the weakness of

---

[6] According to Tolmie, who follows Chatman's model for this notion, a 'paradigm of traits' denotes 'a relatively stable or abiding quality which may unfold, disappear, or be replaced. While reading a text a reader associates a paradigm of traits with each character, and whenever a certain character appears in the text s/he sorts through the paradigm in order to account for the action performed by the character' (Tolmie 1995: 122).

[7] Culpepper 1983: 103: 'In John, the character of Jesus is static; it does not change. He only emerges more clearly as what he is from the beginning.'

[8] By attaching the Greek article to both *logos* and *theos*, the prologue establishes a personal distinction between 'the Word' and 'the God' (later identified as 'the Father' in 1:18). By predicating 'God' (anarthrous) to 'the Word', the prologue establishes the divine identity of 'the Word' with the Father (Moloney 2002: 108). The Word is not *who* God is, but he is *what* God is.

[9] Cf. 12:36, where the disciples are called 'sons of light'. John develops the ethical import of this teaching in 1 John 1:5 – 2:11.

[10] The comparison between Jesus and Moses in 1:14–18 is significant. Whereas Moses beheld God's glory and reflected it to God's people (Exod. 33:18–20; 34:5–7, 29–35), becoming a kind of typological restoration of the image and glory of God, Jesus is the incarnation of God's glory, God's true Son, the antitypical image of the Father (cf. 2 Cor. 4:4; Col. 1:15; Heb. 1:3).

[11] Stibbe 2006: 175. See chapter 4 above.

mortal human flesh;[12] he reveals God.[13] But these traits are now traits of Jesus *the Son*.[14] They are distinctly filial traits that manifest his distinctly filial glory. As we have seen, the prologue itself prepares us for this substitution in nomenclature in 1:14: the glory of the incarnate Word is the glory of 'the Son'.

Having identified the paradigm of traits ascribed to Jesus in the prologue, we are in a position to trace several Johannine Christological themes that bear special relation to these character traits of Jesus. Doing so will enable us to grasp better the filial dimension of John's Christology. We will explore two themes in particular: (1) Jesus' filial identity and divine agency; and (2) Jesus' filial identity and the nature of salvation.

Jesus' filial identity and divine agency

As we have seen, John 1:3 describes the Word as the one through whom 'all things were made' and without whom 'nothing was made that has been made'. Jesus' role as the one through whom God's work is accomplished is a central theme of Johannine Christology.

In describing the Word's role in God's creative work, John does not violate the monotheistic principle that God alone created the world without the help of anyone else (e.g. Isa. 44:24).[15] The distinction between God and the Word with respect to the act of creation is not a distinction *between* God's action and the action of an 'other' helper, perhaps a semi-divine intermediary or even a second god.[16] Rather, the distinction *between* God and the Word with respect to the act of creation is a distinction *within* the singular creative activity of the one God.[17] God exercises his own singular divine activity in creating the

---

[12] The humanity of Jesus is often underemphasized in Johannine studies. For a helpful corrective to this tendency, see M. M. Thompson 1988.

[13] Compare this list with Tolmie's: 1995: 125–126.

[14] D. M. Smith 1995: 101. This does not mean that Jesus was first the Word and later became the Son. Describing Jesus as 'the Word' connects us to the OT Scriptures (Bauckham 2005: 150–151). Describing Jesus as 'the Son' represents John's new salvation-historical revelation, one that comes as a result of the incarnation. Once revealed, however, this name is understood to represent Jesus' eternal personal identity. See John 17 and our discussion in chapter 10 below.

[15] See Bauckham 1998a: 10–13.

[16] John's Gospel thus forbids understanding the Word's work in either 'subordinationist' or 'tritheistic' directions.

[17] The ancient rule is *Opera Dei ad extra indivisa sunt* (the external works of God are undivided). We are indebted to E. F. Rogers for the concept of a 'distinction *within* one action' versus a 'distinction *between* two actions' (Rogers 2005: 11–16, 45–46, *et passim*).

world and does so *by means of* his *own* Word: 'Through him all things were made' (1:3).[18] God does not need the help of another to create the world but instead works through his own sovereign Word.[19]

The prologue's portrayal of the Word's creative agency thus establishes an important theme that will command the reader's attention for the rest of John's Gospel. While the Word is personally distinct *from* God, the work he performs is nonetheless nothing but the work *of* God. The two participate in one divine work (cf. 14:10–11).

In order to appreciate John's filial development of this theme, it is important to mention another dimension of the Word's activity according to the prologue. This dimension may be seen in the way the fourth evangelist compares and contrasts the Word's role as an agent of God with John the Baptist's role as an agent of God.

That the prologue regards both John the Baptist and the Word as personal agents of God is apparent for several reasons. First, 1:6 describes John the Baptist as 'a man who was *sent* from God'. 'Sending' is widely recognized as a key term in the Fourth Gospel's conception of 'agency'.[20] The next verse says that John, the sent one, '*came* only as a witness' to the light (1:7). Later, in 1:9 and 11, the evangelist says that the Word 'came' into the world and to his own. Arguably, then, we are to conclude that, just as John 'came' because he was first 'sent', so the Word 'came' because he was first 'sent'. 'Sending' and 'coming' apparently represent two sides of one relationship: the sender sends; the sent one comes in obedience to his commission.[21]

Second, it is important to note the contrast between the agencies of John the Baptist and the Word according to the prologue. While both are portrayed as agents of God, the prologue nonetheless paints

---

[18] God is the *efficient cause* of creation. God's Word is the *instrumental cause* of creation. See Bauckham 1998a: 39. Compare with Paul's similar statement concerning divine action in Rom. 11:36: '*from* him and *through* him and *to* him are all things'.

[19] John's teaching in this regard is foundational for Irenaeus' trinitarian theology. See Bingham 2005.

[20] See esp. Köstenberger 1998b: 115–121.

[21] For other places in John's Gospel where 'sending' and 'coming' stand in such a relationship, see 7:29; 8:42; and 17:8. That both the Word and John the Baptist are to be understood as agents of God is further confirmed when we consider the most likely background for John's description of Jesus as 'the Word'. As we saw in chapter 2 above, John's description of Jesus as the Word of God is an allusion not only to certain OT creation texts, but also to Isa. 55:10–11, where God's 'word' is said to go forth from his mouth to accomplish the purpose for which he '*sent* it'.

a contrasting picture in terms of the status or rank of the two. John came 'as a witness to testify concerning that light' (1:7). The Word *is* the light (1:4–5; cf. 1:8: 'He himself [John the Baptist] was *not* the light'). The Baptist himself highlights the contrast in 1:15: 'He who *comes* after me ranks before me, because he *existed* before me' (our trans.; see also 1:30). John the Baptist, as he later tells us in the Gospel, is the 'friend who attends the bridegroom' who 'belongs to the earth' and speaks in an earthly way (3:29–31). Jesus is 'the bridegroom' who 'comes from above' and who speaks according to 'what he has seen and heard' from above (3:29–32).[22]

The present point is very important to note. The contrast between John the Baptist and the Word is not that one is an agent of God whereas the other is not. Both are agents of God. Both come because both (implicitly) have been sent on a mission. The contrast between John the Baptist and the Word concerns, then, their *status* as agents. One is earthly, merely human. The other is divine (and *also* human: see 1:14).

According to the prologue, then, the Word is an agent sent from God to accomplish a mission. But, in contrast to John the Baptist whose mission is to bear witness to the works of God, the Word's mission is to perform the very works of God (see 4:34; 5:36; 9:4; 10:25, 32, 37, 38; 14:10–11; 17:4). He is able to do so because he *is* God (1:1).

Having considered the prologue's portrait of the Word as God's agent, we are now in a position to appreciate the way John develops this theme in a *filial* direction. In John 5, at the beginning of the Gospel's 'festival cycle' (5:1), Jesus heals a man who 'had been an invalid for thirty-eight years' (5:5). And he does so on the Sabbath (5:9). In response to this miraculous sign performed on the Sabbath, John says 'the Jews persecuted [Jesus]' (5:16).

Jesus responds to this opposition by declaring that he is simply engaging in the family business: 'My Father is working until now, and I myself am working' (5:17 NASB). Jesus' response incites further opposition: 'For this reason the Jews tried all the harder to kill him; not only was he breaking the Sabbath, but he was even calling God his own Father, making himself equal with God' (5:18).

Jesus then begins a discourse concerning the nature of his agency as 'the Son' of 'the Father' (5:19–47), several features of which are relevant to the present theme. First, Jesus claims the right to perform

---

[22] Cf. Dunn 1996: 244–245.

the distinctly divine action of raising the dead. 'The Son', Jesus declares, has the authority to give 'life to whom he is pleased to give it' (5:21).[23]

As any biblical monotheist would know, only Yahweh has the authority to 'put to death' and to 'bring to life' (Deut. 32:39). Indeed, this authority is what demonstrates Yahweh's unique and unrivalled power over against all other would-be gods:

> See now that I myself am He!
> There is no god besides me.
> I put to death and I bring to life,
> I have wounded and I will heal,
> and no-one can deliver out of my hand.
> (Deut. 32:39)

Thus, Jesus' claim that he possesses the power to 'give life' is a claim to the title of the one Lord God of Israel.[24]

The point is further established when Jesus claims the prerogative to execute eschatological judgment (5:22, 27–29). Jesus' authority to judge the world is not so much a second divine prerogative alongside the power to give life. It is simply another way of indicating Jesus' authority over life and death, for according to the OT, Yahweh exercises his power to 'put to death' and to 'bring to life' in his office as 'Judge' of the earth.[25]

Nevertheless, while Jesus claims the power to perform the distinctly divine work of raising the dead and thus claims to be 'equal with God' (cf. 5:18), he also explains that 'his work is entirely derivative'.[26]

[23] Thus Bauckham 2005: 152.

[24] The fact that certain OT prophets (e.g. Elijah, Elisha) raised the dead does not count against the present argument that Jesus' power to raise the dead exhibits his deity. Others, by God's power, have raised the dead. But Jesus has this power 'in himself' (5:26) to exercise on behalf of whomever he is pleased to exercise it (5:21). Thus M. M. Thompson (2001: 52) states, 'By making Jesus not only the one who exercises these prerogatives, such as the power to give life and to judge, but who also *has* them *'in himself'* (5:26–27), John places Jesus in a different category from all other figures who might be thought worthy or capable of exercising similar prerogatives.'

[25] Note the surrounding context of Deut. 32:39 (particularly vv. 34–43, which speak of Yahweh's coming both to judge Israel's Gentile oppressors and to vindicate his people). See also Isa. 26, where Israel is said to wait 'in the way [path] of' Yahweh's 'judgments' (26:8) in hope that Yahweh will 'punish the people [inhabitants] of the earth for their iniquity' (26:21) and cause *his* dead (his people) to 'live; their bodies' being raised from 'the dust' (26:19). See M. M. Thompson 2001: 118–119; Lincoln 2000: 210; Ridderbos 1997: 201.

[26] Barrett 1982: 24.

'The Son can do nothing of himself; he can do only what he sees the Father doing, because whatever the Father does the Son also does' (5:19, NIV altered). The Son judges because the Father 'has entrusted all judgment to the Son' (5:22). The Son gives life to whomever he wishes because the Father 'has granted the Son to have life in himself' (5:26). The Son performs the works of the one true God as God. But he performs them as a son who is absolutely dependent upon his father in every respect.

Jesus' absolute filial dependence upon the Father characterizes all of his activity in the Gospel of John. According to the Fourth Gospel, the Son lives in absolute dependence upon the Father at every moment. Jesus depends upon the Father for his life (5:16), power (5:19), knowledge (8:16), message (7:16), mission (7:28), instruction (14:31), authority (17:2), glory (17:24) and love (10:17).[27]

Reconciling Jesus' equality *with* God to his dependence *upon* God constitutes a perennial challenge to Johannine interpreters.[28] Contemporary scholars sometimes appeal to the *šālîaḥ* figure and its attending notion of 'agency' discussed in rabbinic Judaism to explain Jesus' relationship of dependence upon God.[29] According to this conception of agency, 'a man's agent is like the man himself' (e.g. *m. Ber.* 5.5) and thus equal to the man in some respects.[30] Moreover, according to this conception of agency, the agent is subordinate to his sender in some respects: 'it is a legal presumption that an agent will carry out his mission' (*b. 'Erub.* 31b–32a; cf. *b. Ketub.* 99b).[31]

There is little agreement, however, concerning how far this concept will go toward reconciling Jesus' dependence upon the Father to his equality with the Father. Marianne Meye Thompson, in her fine work on John's doctrine of God, concludes that the *šālîaḥ* figure is of 'limited usefulness' for explaining Jesus' relationship to God 'in light of assertions' that indicate Jesus' equality with God. 'The *shaliach* figure', she concludes, 'serves poorly to account for the heavenly origins assumed in the assertions of the prologue regarding the pre-existence and incarnation of the Word.'[32] For this reason, Thompson contends, Second Temple speculation on 'Wisdom's' role in the world

---

[27] This list is taken almost directly from Barrett (ibid. 22), who follows that of Davey 1958.

[28] Meyer 1996: 261.

[29] M. M. Thompson 2001: 126.

[30] See Rengstorf 1964, 1: 414–420.

[31] See the discussion in chapter 4 above.

[32] M. M. Thompson 2001: 126–127.

suggests 'a more satisfactory explanatory model' for grasping the shape of Jesus' distinctly divine action in the Gospel of John.[33]

There is some degree of truth in Thompson's appeal to Wisdom speculation. As we have seen, John initially characterizes Jesus as 'the Word', the one through whom God created the world and whom God sent into the world to accomplish a mission. This role is sometimes assigned to Wisdom in Second Temple literature. However, John provides another 'explanatory model' in addition to that of Wisdom to account for Jesus' equality with and dependence upon the Father, a model that transfigures the šālîaḥ concept in its own way. That model is the father–son relationship.[34]

Thompson's own work is instructive at this point. According to Thompson, the father–son relationship bears a distinctive character and shape in the OT social order. The role of 'father' is characterized primarily by three aspects: '(1) Above all, the father is the source or origin of a family or clan, who as the founding father provides an inheritance to his children. (2) A father protects and provides for his children. (3) Obedience and honor are due to the father, and, hence, when children disobey or go astray, they are corrected or disciplined.'[35] Corresponding to this role of 'father' there is the role of 'son', who is (1) 'begotten' of his father and therefore an 'heir' to the family inheritance; (2) beloved and cared for by his father; and (3) called to obey his father's instruction (see Exod. 20:12, where the principle is generalized to include the obedience of 'children' to their fathers *and* mothers).[36] What Thompson's work on the father–son relationship in the OT suggests is that there exists a biblical model for conceiving a relationship at once characterized by *equality* and *obedience*, the relationship that exists between a father and a son.[37] In biblical anthropology, a son is at once 'like' his father as his 'image' (Gen. 5:3) and 'heir'; but a son is also called to submit to his father's will.[38]

That this model is indeed helpful for conceiving Jesus' *distinctly personal, divine* activity is confirmed by two texts, one from within John's Gospel and one from without. As we have already seen, the prologue portrays the Word as God's agent, sent to accomplish

---

[33] Ibid. 128.

[34] See the similar analysis of Dunn 1996: 244–245.

[35] M. M. Thompson 2000: 39.

[36] See her discussion in ibid. 39–55, which highlights the corresponding role of a 'son' that goes with the described role of a 'father'.

[37] Unfortunately, Thompson minimizes the significance of this model in her discussion of the fatherhood of God in John's Gospel. See ibid. 133–154. Cf. Stibbe 2006: 179.

[38] So Ware 2005: 138.

God's purpose in the world. Moreover, the Word is able to accomplish his particular mission because he is himself God. What is fascinating with respect to our present discussion concerns the *way* in which the prologue contrasts the agency of the Word with the agency of John the Baptist. Both missions no doubt imply some sort of order between sent one and sender (see Isa. 55:10–11). Nevertheless, the two agents belong to qualitatively different classes: the Word is *God* (1:3), whereas John the Baptist is 'a *man* who was sent from God' (1:6; see also 1:15, 30). We will comment on the significance of this point after we discuss our second confirmatory text, the parable of the wicked tenants, found in Mark 12:1–12 and pars.[39]

The parable tells the story of a man who plants a vineyard and hires out tenants to keep it. When the season for bearing fruit comes, the owner sends a servant on a mission: to gather from the tenants 'some of the fruit of the vineyard' (Mark 12:2). However, the tenants take the servant and 'beat him' and send him 'away empty-handed' (Mark 12:3). So the owner sends a series of other servants, some of whom the tenants beat, others of whom they kill (Mark 12:4–5). 'Last of all', the parable states, the owner sends 'a beloved son' (NASB), hoping that the tenants will respect his status as heir of the vineyard (Mark 12:6). But instead, recognizing the beloved son's status as 'the heir', it is precisely this status that motivates the tenants to kill him, as they conclude that, with the heir out of the way, the vineyard will be theirs (Mark 12:7–8).

It is unnecessary for our present purposes to discuss whether or not the contrast between the 'beloved son' and the many 'servants' in the parable represents a contrast between God's *human* servants, the prophets, and God's *divine* Son, Jesus (though this may indeed be the intention of the Synoptic evangelists). The only point necessary to note for our present purposes is this: the notion of 'being sent' does not necessarily imply that the sent one is of a *lesser class* than the sender, *even though it implies a relationship of order and obedience*. In fact, in both John's prologue and the parable of the wicked tenants, the contrast in class or status lies between the two different *sorts* of agents, the Word and John the Baptist on the one hand, and the 'beloved son' and the 'servants' on the other. As John the Baptist

---

[39] Our assumption is that the Synoptic Gospels provide a reliable account of Jesus' teaching and therefore may function to confirm an interpretation of John's Gospel, which itself claims to be a reliable account of Jesus' teaching. See Bauckham 2006.

declares in the prologue, 'He who comes after me ranks before me, because he existed before me' (1:15, our trans.).

What is the significance of this observation for understanding John's conception of Jesus' agency? It is that there is a *kind* of ordered, obedient agency that presupposes an *equal class or status* between sender and sent one (the Word is *God*; the beloved son is *heir* of his father's vineyard), even as there is a *kind* of ordered, obedient agency that presupposes an *unequal class or status* between sender and sent one (John the Baptist is 'a *man* who was sent from God' [1:6]; the servants do *not* own the vineyard).[40] What John makes explicit everywhere is that the *kind* of ordered, obedient agency that presupposes an *equal status* between sender and sent one is the kind that obtains pre-eminently between a father and a son, between *the* Father and *the* Son. *The kind of agency exhibited by Jesus in John's Gospel is a distinctly divine-filial agency.*[41]

This filial conception of Jesus' agency, with its particular configuration of equality and order that exists between sender and sent one, explains several textual phenomena relevant to Johannine Christology. Space permits commenting on only two of those phenomena.

First, as Barrett notes, the situation in John's Gospel is not that we have certain texts that stress Jesus' equality with the Father while we have other texts that stress his dependence and obedience such that the challenge facing interpreters concerns how to reconcile these different sets of texts. In fact, the case is just the opposite:

> [T]hose notable Johannine passages that seem at first sight to proclaim most unambiguously the unity and equality of the Son with the Father are often set in contexts which if they do not deny at least qualify this theme, and place alongside it the theme of dependence, and indeed of subordination.[42]

We might conclude from this phenomenon that John is apt to making inconsistent assertions about Jesus in the same contexts without realizing the contradiction. But this is highly improbable, especially when there exists 'a more satisfactory explanatory model'

---

[40] Interestingly, Jesus contrasts a 'son' with a 'servant' in John 8:31–36 with respect to their standing/status in a father's 'house' – one is free, the other is not. See also Heb. 3:1–6.

[41] For further dogmatic discussion, see Barth IV/1: 192–210.

[42] Barrett 1982: 23.

for reconciling the apparent 'tensions' in the text.[43] John's Gospel suggests another way of 'configuring' the paradoxical identity of Jesus as the sent one.[44] When sender and sent one are father and son, we are no longer dealing with a relationship between a superior and an inferior, where, among other things, the will of the former is imposed upon the latter. When sender and sent one are father and son (at least in the case of the triune life) we are dealing with a relationship between equals, between those sharing the same ontological status. Thus, when sender and sent one are father and son we are dealing with a relationship where the action to be undertaken involves not the imposition of the will of the one upon the other, but where the action to be undertaken must be understood as a common cause, and a common cause because it is family business.

Nevertheless, inasmuch as the analogy holds, equality and engagement in a common cause in no way rule out the relationship of command and obedience that holds between a father and a son, biblically conceived.[45] This explains, for example, why Jesus can say in John 10:18 that, on the one hand, he has received a 'charge' from his Father that, on the other hand, consists in having the 'authority' to lay down his life on his own accord (freely, as Lord) and to take it up again. The Son's obedience to the Father's charge does not compromise the Son's authority to act but rather establishes it.[46] He is the free Lord of all – including his own death – *as* the Son who obeys the Father.

Jesus' filial relationship to the Father also explains the enigmatic statement 'the Father is greater than I' (14:28), a statement that bears similarities to Paul's teaching in 1 Corinthians 15:27–28:

[43] We dislike the language of 'tension' (e.g. Dunn 1996: 250; Cowan 2006: 115) on this theme, not because this conception of agency has no room for mystery (how does one explain a situation where *two agents* perform *one undivided activity*?). We dislike the language of 'tension' because it represents a stall in the interpretative process, one that fails to take into account indicators provided by the Gospel itself for illuminating its own apparently inconsistent phenomena.

[44] The allusion recalls Paul Ricoeur's discussion of 'narrative identity'. According to Ricoeur, narrative possesses the capacity for 'configuring' events, relationships and actions in ways otherwise unimaginable. See especially Ricoeur 1992: 141–143. Torrance similarly argues that we must interpret the father–son analogy 'according to the sense given' it 'by the Scriptures and within the whole scope and framework of the biblical narrative and message' (Torrance 1995: 120).

[45] Contra M. M. Thompson 2000: 150.

[46] Commenting on Matt. 8:5–13, O'Donovan notes that being '*in* authority' presupposes being '*under*' authority' (1996: 90). The significance for our present discussion is this: the Son possesses *equal* authority to the Father (*homoousios*) as the Son *of* the Father, i.e. the one who *receives* full, divine authority from the Father (cf. Matt. 28:18).

For he 'has put everything under his feet'. Now when it says that 'everything' has been put under him, it is clear that this does not include God himself, who put everything under Christ. When he has done this, then the Son himself will be made subject to him who put everything under him, so that God may be all in all.[47]

The Father enjoys *personal* priority in the *taxis* (order) of the triune life, not ontological superiority, for the Father and the Son hold all things in common: one divine name (17:11), one divine power (5:19, 21–22), one divine identity (10:30).[48]

The balance between the unity of being and purpose prevailing between Father and Son (e.g. 10:30) and the affirmation of the Son's filial submission to the Father (e.g. 14:28), so carefully maintained by the fourth evangelist and other biblical writers such as Paul, suggests that the resolution of the apparent tension between these two aspects of biblical teaching must not be found by pitting one against the other, affirming one aspect while denying the other, but by probing more deeply, and seeking to understand more fully, both dimensions of the Father–Son relationship.[49]

In the light of the present discussion, it is clear that Giles poses a false dilemma on this point. According to Giles, *either* one member of a relationship stands in authority over another and 'prevails' over that other, who is 'under compulsion' to do as commanded,[50] *or* both members share a relationship of equal standing where one may, if he or she wills, 'dispose' him or herself or 'defer' to the other.[51] However, understanding John requires that we consider another alternative. The Father commands; the Son obeys. But the

---

[47] Cf. Ps. 8:6. Note the 'Son' language in Paul here, which closely resembles Johannine terminology. See also the description of God's purpose in Christ in Eph. 1:10 (NIV): 'to bring all things in heaven and on earth together under one head, even Christ' (cf. Eph. 1:3–14).

[48] See further discussion in chapter 10 below.

[49] Giles (esp. 2002) has brought a great deal of confusion to contemporary trinitarian studies due to his misapplication of the term 'subordinationism'. Subordinationism is the heretical teaching that the Son is not God but is instead a creature of God, albeit a highly exalted one. Giles, however, does not sufficiently distinguish 'subordinationism' from 'subordination'. The latter term may be applied appropriately to the way that the consubstantial Son relates to his Father. As the consubstantial Son *of* the Father, the Son submits *to* his Father in all things. As the present study demonstrates, there is a personal order and subordination in the Godhead (*taxis*) that does not vitiate the essential equality of the persons.

[50] Giles 2006: 121.

[51] Ibid. 123, 171.

Son does not obey because he is inferior to the Father or 'under compulsion' to do so. He obeys the Father because the Father's will *is* his will (*homoousios*) and because obedience to the Father is the truest *personal* expression of his *filial* unity with the Father. In this sense, the Son is *equal* in authority *to* the Father as the Son *of* the Father, whose will is always to obey the Father's will.[52]

Along similar lines, it should be noted that a construal of the Father–son relationship which focuses primarily on the Father's *rule* inadequately considers the fact that, properly understood, the Jewish notion of the father's place in the family focused not so much on patri-archy (father-rule; though this notion is certainly not absent) but on patri-centrism (the father's central role in the life of the family in terms of nurturing the life of, and providing for the needs of, the extended household under his care).[53] This 'configuration' further seems to mitigate Giles's concern that a rigid understanding of authority and submission provides an improper model for male–female relationships.

John's 'I am' sayings represent a second textual phenomenon illuminated by a filial notion of Jesus' agency. John's Gospel contains two sets of 'I am' sayings, each set comprising seven pronouncements made by Jesus concerning his own identity. One set consists of Jesus stating, 'I am' followed by a *predicate* that highlights Jesus' saving significance for the world: 'I am the bread of life' (6:35, 41, 48); 'I am the light of the world' (8:12); 'I am the gate for the sheep' (10:7, 9); 'I am the good shepherd' (10:11, 14); 'I am the resurrection and the life' (11:25); 'I am the way and the truth and the life' (14:6); 'I am the true

---

[52] Giles's charge that evangelicals who teach the Son's eternal obedience to the Father are 'heading off on their own' is unfounded. Not only is such teaching thoroughly Johannine; it also finds ecumenical support in the theologies of Karl Barth (Protestant), Boris Bobrinskoy (Orthodox) and Hans Urs von Balthasar (Roman Catholic), to name but three examples (see also Adam's comments [2005: 43–44]). Furthermore, the combination of *personal order* and *essential unity/equality* is built into pro-Nicene discussions of the *homoousion* itself. This combination of personal order/essential equality is seen, for example, in that the Son and the Spirit are said to be consubstantial with the Father, whereas the Father is not said to be consubstantial with the Son and the Spirit. The Father retains his personal priority even as the Son and the Spirit share fully in all that the Father is and has as God. For this line of thought in Gregory of Nazianzus, see McGuckin 2001: 294–296; on the broader pro-Nicene tradition, see Behr 2004. For further critique of Giles, see Letham 2004: 489–496; and Adam 2005: 35–50.

[53] See the discussion of the work of D. I. Block in chapter 3 above. Similarly, see M. M. Thompson 2000: 133–154. Cf. the slightly different emphasis of Ware 2005: 21, 137–138.

vine' (15:1).[54] The other set consists of seven absolute 'I am' sayings, where Jesus announces that 'I am he' or 'I am' with *no predicate* (4:26; 6:20; 8:24, 28, 58; 13:19; 18:5–8).[55] These pronouncements constitute clear allusions to Yahweh's own sevenfold self-declaration of unique and unrivalled divinity that occurs in the OT.[56] John's point is clear: Jesus is Yahweh.[57]

The 'I am' saying found in John 8:28 is especially interesting in the light of our present discussion. There, in the midst of a paternity dispute with the Jews, Jesus declares, 'When you have lifted up the Son of Man, then you will know that I am he, and that I do nothing on my own authority but speak just what the Father has taught me' (NIV altered). Jesus' being 'lifted up' is a reference to his crucifixion. The language is derived from Isaiah's discussion of Yahweh's true Servant, who will appear at the end of the age to accomplish Yahweh's will and bring him glory where Israel had previously failed to do so (Isa. 42:18–25; 49:1–3). As a consequence of the Servant's obedience, Yahweh promises that the Servant will be 'lifted up', that is, exalted before the eyes of the nations (Isa. 52:13–15).[58] Jesus' claim in John 8:28 is that when he is 'lifted up' on a shameful cross, this event will constitute at once his 'exaltation' as God's true Servant *and* his self-revelation as the one true God and Saviour of the world.[59]

A filial understanding of Jesus' agency illuminates the nature of Jesus' claim. When Jesus is raised up on the cross, he says that the Jews will know two things: (1) 'that I am he'; *and* (2) 'that I do nothing on my own authority, but speak just what the Father has taught me'. The cross reveals Jesus' *divine* identity. He is 'I am'. More specifically, the cross reveals Jesus' *filial-divine* identity. He is the 'I am' *who does and says all that he does and says on the basis of his Father's authority and teaching*. The cross, in other words, reveals Jesus' *divine sonship* because it is the culminating revelation of the relationship between the teaching Father and the obeying Son.[60] The cross is therefore the culminating revelation of John's *trinitarian* monotheism.

Jesus' identity as the divine Son also suggests how his 'lifting up' on the cross can constitute the fulfilment of his *human* vocation to

[54] Bauckham 2005: 153–154.
[55] Bauckham 1998a: 65, n. 14. Bauckham suggests that the last saying in John 18 is repeated twice to echo the same phenomenon in the OT canon (2005: 159).
[56] See Bauckham 2005: 153–163.
[57] See chapter 1 above.
[58] See Bauckham 1998a: 63–68.
[59] Ibid. 65–66.
[60] So Ware 2005: 73–75.

suffer as 'the Servant of the Lord' (Isa. 52:13 – 53:12). As Barrett observes, whatever one may think of John's 'alleged docetism', there is no doubt that 'the Johannine Jesus shares with mankind the human property of dying'.[61] The crucifixion is the moment when Jesus suffers the all-too-human fate of death. Ironically enough, far from hiding his divinity, Jesus' death becomes the supreme moment for unveiling the unique divine glory he shares with his Father. The glory of God's Son is manifest in and through his flesh, which withers like the grass (1:14; cf. Isa. 40:6–8). A *trinitarian* understanding of the incarnation indicates how this can be the case.[62] Jesus' crucifixion can constitute at once the culmination of his human vocation unto death and the manifestation of his divine glory because of *who* he uniquely is.[63] Because he is the Son of God in the flesh (whose personal way of being God includes his filial obedience to the Father) his death can constitute the moment where he fulfils at once the roles of sovereign Lord *and* humble, obedient human Servant.[64] As Bobrinskoy observes, 'The obedience of Jesus is the hinge of his double relation to the Father: as eternal Son, and suffering Servant.'[65]

In the light of this discussion, we may summarize John's understanding of the Son's agency as follows: Jesus performs the singular divine actions of Israel's Lord God, but he does so *as* God the Son, who depends upon, obeys and thereby fulfils the one will and work

[61] Barrett 1982: 11.

[62] Here we must note, 'indication' is much more modest than 'explanation'. Who can explain the suffering of the incarnate Son of God?

[63] A trinitarian understanding of divine agency and more specifically of the incarnation accounts for the mystery of Jesus' suffering on the cross better than modern theories of divine passibility. The divine Son suffers a *human* (as opposed to a divine) death and he does so because he is the *divine Son* in the flesh, whose personal character it is to obey and accomplish the Father's will. Ironically (in the light of modern passibilist theology), it is the fact that the Son shares the Father's unswerving (impassible!) love and commitment to saving the world that grounds his willingness to suffer a human death for the world's sake (3:16; 13:1; 15:13). It may be added that only a trinitarian theology like that of John makes sense of the patristic slogan 'the Impassible suffers!' See Gavrilyuk 2004.

[64] To the perennial dogmatic question 'Could any person of the Trinity have become incarnate?' John's Gospel says 'No!': that is, *if* the incarnation entails fulfilling the role of 'Servant of Yahweh' at the climax of Israel's history. Only *the Son* could do that.

[65] Bobrinskoy 1999: 118. Here again, we may identify where Giles's proposal (2006) fails. Giles can account only for Jesus' *equality with* and *distinction from* the Father, and the latter only abstractly considered. Giles cannot account for Jesus' *personal identity*, i.e. his distinctive, filial *way* of being God. Letham (2004: 491–492) concurs: 'Giles has a strong and emphatic grasp of the consubstantiality of the Son and the Spirit with the Father, of that there is no doubt. However, while paying lip service to the order, he does not give anywhere near corresponding stress to the distinctions of the three persons.'

of God the Father. Moreover, as a consequence of the incarnation (1:14), the Son fulfils the one will and work of God the Father in 'the form of a servant': the form of *the* Servant, whose vocation reaches its climax in his death on a cross (cf. Phil. 2:7–8). One divine action is executed on the stage of the Fourth Gospel, the singular action *of* the Father *through* his obedient, incarnate Son (see also 1:3; 10:37–38; 14:10–11) in the power of the Spirit.[66]

Jesus' filial identity and the nature of salvation

A second major theme concerns the Son's role in God's saving plan for the world. Here, too, the filial dimension of John's Christology is illuminating.

According to John 1:12, the Word was sent by God to deliver a gift: 'the right to become children of God'.[67] The Word is particularly suited to deliver such a gift, for he is 'the only Son from the Father' (1:14; our trans.). Surprisingly,[68] John's Gospel makes hardly any mention[69] of the gift of sonship again until 20:17, where the risen Lord commissions Mary: 'Go instead to my brothers and tell them, "I am returning to my Father and your Father, to my God and your God."'

The reason for the relative silence between 1:12 and 20:17 may be explained in the light of the overarching shape of Jesus' mission. Broadly considered, Jesus' mission follows a descent–ascent pattern.[70] The Son first 'descended'/'came down' from heaven to do the will of his Father (3:13; 6:38). Having completed his Father's will, the Son 'ascends'/'leaves'/'goes' back to heaven, the place he was before (3:13; 6:62; 7:33; 16:28). According to the sequence of John's narrative as well as the logic of John's soteriology, the right to sonship can come to Jesus' disciples only *after* his earthly mission is 'finished' on the cross (19:30; cf. 13:36).[71] Once his work on the cross has been

---

[66] Putting the same point in a slightly different way, it is Jesus' *personal identity* as the Second Person of the Trinity that determines the way he acts. His *'natures'*, to borrow later dogmatic terminology, provide the capacities within which he acts: the man Jesus can raise the dead because he is God; the Lord can die because he is 'flesh'. But he performs *both* sorts of actions in a filial manner because he is *the Son of God* in the flesh.

[67] Culpepper 1983: 88.

[68] So N. T. Wright 2003: 666–667.

[69] Except for Jesus' 'final word to the crowd' in John 12:36 (Ridderbos 1997: 442).

[70] See Köstenberger 1998b: 126–130 *et passim*; Nicholson 1983.

[71] It is also worth noting that Jesus' mother is given to be the Beloved Disciple's mother at the foot of the cross, thus making Jesus and the Beloved Disciple 'brothers' (see 19:26–27).

accomplished, the risen and ascending Jesus can deliver to his 'brothers' the glad tidings of their reception into the Father's household (20:17; cf. 14:2–3).

Why must this be the case? John 3:16–17 provides an initial clue. According to John, God 'saves' the world by 'giving' his own beloved Son.

In order to understand the significance of this gift, we must consider the influence of Genesis 22 upon John 3:16, and more broadly upon John's view of salvation. The reference to Jesus as 'the only Son' in John 3:16 is undoubtedly an allusion to Genesis 22:2, where Abraham is commanded to offer his 'only son' Isaac on Mount Moriah.[72] Though Isaac is ultimately spared, Abraham's willingness to sacrifice his beloved son reveals the true measure of his reverence for God (Gen. 22:12). Abraham so trusted and revered God that he did not withhold his most treasured possession, but instead offered him freely in obedience to God. Similarly, the Father's gift of the Son reveals the true measure of his love for the world.[73] God's Son-sacrificing love is the fountainhead of the world's salvation.

To grasp the full significance of this point, we must step back and survey the broader landscape of John 1 – 3. In John 1, John the Baptist identified Jesus as 'the Lamb of God, who takes away the sin of the world' (1:29, 36). This description probably represents another allusion to Genesis 22. In Genesis 22:8, Abraham expresses his confidence to Isaac that 'God himself will provide the lamb for the burnt offering'. God answers Abraham's confidence by providing a ram in the thicket, a ram that Abraham promptly offers 'instead of his son' (Gen. 22:13). Consequently, the patriarch names the mountain 'The LORD Will Provide' (Gen. 22:14). This further clarifies the meaning of John 3:16. The Father's gift of the Son constitutes not only the *measure* of his love for the world, but also the *means* by which he saves the world. The Father so loved sinners that he did not withhold his own beloved Son, the Second Person of the Trinity, but 'gave him up for us all' (Rom. 8:32) as a substitutionary sacrifice. *Unus ex Trinitate passus est* (One of the Trinity suffered).[74]

Jesus' crucifixion during the feast of the Passover (13:1; 19:14) confirms this interpretation. The feast of Passover commemorated God's deliverance of his 'firstborn son' Israel (Exod. 4:22) from

---

[72] Levenson 1993: 223–225.
[73] Cf. Watson's similar analysis of Rom. 8:32 (2000: 107–108).
[74] See Studer 1993: 112, 156, 223, 226–228, 237–238, 243.

slavery by providing a sacrificial lamb in Israel's place (Exod. 12 – 13). In John's Gospel, the feast occasions God's eschatological provision of 'the Lamb of God' (1:29) to liberate those enslaved to sin and death (8:34–35) that they might enjoy the freedom of sonship in God's household. 'If the Son sets you free, you will be free indeed' (8:36). Read in this light, the substitutionary, sacrificial death of Jesus constitutes the turning point of the new exodus. The Father gives his own beloved Son to suffer as the eschatological Passover Lamb in order to deliver his enslaved people into the freedom of being God's children.[75] As a result of the Son's redeeming, substitutionary death, God becomes our Father and we become his children (cf. Gal. 4:4–7).[76]

It is not only Jesus' death that makes the disciples' adoption possible. His resurrection also plays a significant role. In order to understand John's teaching regarding adoption, we must therefore discuss Jesus' resurrection as well.

According to John, both Jesus and his contemporaries held to the inherited Jewish doctrine of a general resurrection of the dead at the end of history.[77] Jesus speaks about an 'hour' of judgment when some will be raised to life and some will be raised to condemnation (5:28–29; cf. Dan. 12:2). Similarly, Martha assures Jesus that she believes in the resurrection 'at the last day' (11:24). What Jesus' disciples did not fully grasp was Jesus' identity as 'the resurrection and the life' (11:25) and how this identity assured their adoption as children of God.

A brief glance at John 16:21 and 20:22 will reveal the connection. In John 16:21, Jesus tells his disciples that they will experience sorrow and then joy as a result of his death and resurrection. He compares their experience with labour and childbirth: 'A woman giving birth to a child has pain because her time has come; but when her baby is born she forgets the anguish because of her joy that a child is born into the world.' The comparison draws upon common human experience. It also draws upon OT imagery, particularly that of Isaiah 26:16–21.[78]

---

[75] We should note in this context that for John, the Lamb is not merely a passive victim but is himself the active deliverer of his people. He '*takes away* the sin of the world' (1:29; Michaels 2004: 107–108). Jesus' sacrificial death thus fulfils the Passover event in a twofold way: providing a substitutionary death for sin *and* executing judgment upon the ruler of this world (12:31; 16:11; cf. Exod. 12:12). For this dual aspect of Jesus' cross work, see also Rev. 5:5–6; 12:1–11.

[76] Contra Loader 1989: 226, who fails to appreciate the sacrificial, substitutionary dimensions of John's Christology.

[77] On this doctrine, see N. T. Wright 2003: 85–206.

[78] Carson 1991: 544.

In those verses, Israel's experience of God's covenant curses is likened to the travail of a woman in labour who 'writhes and cries out in her pain' (Isa. 26:17). According to Isaiah's prophecy, following the birth pangs of God's judgment, 'the earth will give birth to her dead', the 'dead will live; / their bodies will rise'. As a result, those who rise will 'shout for joy' (Isa. 26:19). This text provides one of the OT's clearest references to a literal, bodily resurrection.[79] John's allusion to Isaiah 26:16–21 suggests that the prophesied eschatological birth pangs of divine judgment, as well as the accompanying birth of bodily resurrection from the dead, find their fulfilment in *Jesus'* death and resurrection.[80]

This interpretation is confirmed by Jesus' action in John 20:22. In John 20, the risen Lord appears to his disciples and turns their sorrow into joy (20:20), just as he had promised (16:20–22). Jesus then 'breathes on' the disciples and says, 'Receive the Holy Spirit' (20:22). As mentioned in chapter 5 above, Jesus' action here is reminiscent of two OT texts, Genesis 2:7 and Ezekiel 37:9, where the same verb translated 'breathed on' in 20:22 (NIV) is used. In Genesis 2:7, the Lord 'breathed into' Adam's nostrils, making him a 'living being'. In Ezekiel 37:9, the Lord commands Ezekiel to summon 'the breath' to 'breathe into' the slain of Israel that they might live. Just as the Lord breathed life into Adam, making him a living being, so the Lord promises through Ezekiel to breathe into exiled Israel, reconstituting them a living and breathing people in his presence.

In the light of 16:21 and 20:22, the connection between Jesus' resurrection and the disciples' adoption becomes clear. Through his death, God's beloved Son bore the eschatological birth pangs of divine judgment. Through his resurrection 'on the first day of the week' (20:1),[81] God's Son inaugurated the eschatological rebirth of Israel. Jesus is the firstborn Son of Israel's dead, the first fruits of the new creation (cf. Col. 1:18; 1 Cor. 15:20, 23).[82] As such, Jesus breathes new life into his disciples, reconstituting eschatological Israel around himself in those who have been born his 'brothers' (20:17; cf. 1 Cor. 15:45). God's purpose for creation and redemption

[79] N. T. Wright 2003: 117. With respect to Isa. 26:19's teaching on bodily resurrection, J. A. Motyer (1993: 219) states, 'Within the progressive revelation of the Old Testament only Daniel 12:2 is comparable.'

[80] Carson 1991: 544.

[81] See N. T. Wright's comments (2003: 667) related to Jesus' resurrection 'on the first day of the week' (20:1). John's soteriology is one of 'new creation', not of an escape from creation, contra every form of Gnosticism, ancient and modern.

[82] See the discussion below on Jesus' 'representative' role.

will now be fulfilled in the community of Jesus' Spirit-infused brothers.[83]

The preceding discussion suggests that, for John, the 'new birth' is a redemptive-historical phenomenon. The new birth does not merely concern the subjective conversion of the sinner to faith, though this is certainly part of John's teaching (see 1:12–13; 3:3–7). More foundationally, the new birth concerns an objective turning point in redemptive history, the turning point that came with the death and resurrection of God's incarnate Son.[84] The resurrection of the Son of God on the first day of the week is the first instalment of the general resurrection[85] and therefore the *basis* of hope for the resurrection in the hearts of believers, a hope birthed by the sovereign work of the Holy Spirit (1:12–13; 3:3–7).[86] 1 Peter 1:3 thus provides an apt summary of John's teaching in this regard: God the Father 'has given us new birth into a living hope through the resurrection of Jesus Christ from the dead'.[87]

Jesus' filial identity thus enables us to understand the significance of both his cross *and* resurrection in God's plan to give his people 'the right to become children of God' (1:12). God the Father sacrificed his own beloved Son that he might bear God's eschatological wrath on behalf of God's people. God subsequently raised his Son that he might be 'the firstborn among many brothers' (Rom. 8:29).

The significance of Jesus' divine sonship for soteriology does not end there, however. Jesus' identity as God's only Son also determines

---

[83] Pryor 1992: 89. As in the case of *the* Son, the *right* to sonship entails the *responsibility* of mission: 'As the Father has sent me, I am sending you' (20:21).

[84] Put differently, the new birth does not merely concern the *ordo salutis*: the subjective *application* of Christ's redemptive benefits to believers. It also, and even primarily, concerns the *historia salutis*: the objective *accomplishment* of redemption in the history of Jesus' incarnation, death, resurrection and ascension.

[85] For reflections upon this theme in Paul, see Gaffin 1987.

[86] The question is often asked, were OT saints 'born again'? The present discussion provides a helpful biblical theological framework for addressing this question. If the 'new birth' primarily signifies the resurrection / hope in the resurrection, a birth accomplished by the Holy Spirit, then we must say that OT saints were born again to the extent that they hoped for the resurrection (cf. Isa. 26:19; John 11:24). Nevertheless, the resurrection of Christ marks the dawning of a new day with respect to this hope. The hope has not changed. But the *object* and *basis* of this hope has been fully and finally realized in the incarnate Son of God, the firstborn of the dead.

[87] The present interpretation sheds light upon the relationship between John 20:22 and Luke's account of Pentecost. John 20:22 recounts the *birth* of the eschatological community of God's children, a community born in the presence of the risen Lord and Son of God. Luke 1 – 2 recounts the *empowerment* of that community to bear witness to the ascended Lord.

the *destiny* of God's children. This destiny is revealed in John's teaching on Jesus' ascension.

Jesus' death and resurrection mark the beginning of his ascent to the Father (12:23; 13:32–33), his return to the place from which he came (6:62; 16:28). In his final prayer in the Gospel, Jesus describes this destination as the place where he enjoyed the Father's glory before the world existed (17:3) and where he basked in the Father's eternal love (17:24). To use the language of the prologue, God's Son is returning to 'the Father's lap' (1:18; our trans.).

The striking claim of John's Gospel is that, whereas the Son must necessarily travel the way of the cross alone ('you cannot follow [me] now'),[88] his entrance into the Father's presence assures the arrival of the rest of God's children as well: 'you will follow me afterward' (13:36; our trans.). The grain of wheat that dies alone becomes fruitful (12:24) in bringing many sons to glory (12:26; 14:1–3; cf. Heb. 2:10). The Son's place in the Father's house will be the place of Jesus' 'brothers' as well (14:2–3).[89]

It is significant to mention here the close association between Jesus' ascent and the Son of Man title (see 3:13–15; 6:62; 12:34; 13:31–36). The Son of Man in biblical theology functions as an 'inclusive representative' of God's people.[90] As it goes for the Son of Man, so it goes for God's people. Consequently, it is Jesus' exaltation as the Son of Man that guarantees the exaltation of his brothers as well.

In the light of this fact we may summarize John's Christology as follows: the Son of God became incarnate to suffer as 'the Servant of the Lord' and 'the Lamb of God' on behalf of his people. He ascends as the risen and glorified 'Son of Man', the inclusive representative of his brothers and guarantor of their full and final exaltation.[91] John's doctrine of Jesus' person and work must therefore be viewed as a trinitarian theology of 'the wonderful exchange'.[92] The Son became

[88] Ridderbos 1997: 478, n. 95.

[89] Ridderbos (ibid. 492) speaks of John's Christological 'reinterpretation' of apocalyptic expectations. In John, apocalyptic speculation regarding the destiny of God's people is reinterpreted in trinitarian terms of the believer's enjoyment of the eternal love of the Father for the Son by the indwelling of the Holy Spirit. See chapter 10 below.

[90] Pryor 1992: 125–128, following Dodd 1953 and Burney 1922. According to Morris (1995: 151), John uses the Son of Man title 'because of its societary implications. The Son of Man implies the redeemed people of God.'

[91] Similarly, Ridderbos 1997: 138, n. 108; also 429. The structure of John's Christology in this regard parallels that of the Synoptics. See Ridderbos 1962: 462–467.

[92] On the influence of John's Gospel on the Greek Fathers' teaching regarding 'the wonderful exchange', see Wiles 1960: 148.

flesh to deliver his people from the snare of sin and death into 'the Father's lap' (1:18). The Son became a man that, in and with him, men and women might become sons and daughters of the living God.[93]

Conclusion

John's Christology is a trinitarian Christology. Jesus' person and work can be understood only in the light of his filial relationship to the one he called 'Father'. Of course, in order to establish fully the claim that John's is a trinitarian Christology, and not merely a binitarian one, we must also consider Jesus' relationship to the Holy Spirit. This relationship is the subject of the next chapter.

[93] In John, there remains a distinction between the sonship of Jesus and that of his brothers. Jesus is the 'One and Only' Son (1:14; 3:16, 18); his brothers are 'children of God' (1:12). Jesus is 'Lord' (20:28), who shares all things pertaining to deity with his Father; his brothers are 'slaves' and 'friends' (13:16; 15:15, 20) who bow in worship to him. He eternally participates in the intra-trinitarian glory of God; his brothers are invited to behold and enjoy that glory on a creaturely plane of existence. Cyril of Alexandria well summarizes John's theology at this point: 'The Son gives what belongs properly to him alone and exists by nature within him as a right. . . . We, therefore, ascend to a dignity that transcends our nature on account of Christ, but we shall not also be sons of God ourselves in exactly the same way as he is, only in relation to him through grace by imitation' (*Jo.* 1.9 [Russell 2000: 100–101]). See also D. M. Smith 1995: 145–146.

Chapter Eight

The Spirit who rests and remains on God's Son and his brothers

Introduction

In the previous chapter, we argued that John's Christology is best understood as a trinitarian Christology. Jesus' filial identity as 'the only Son of the Father' determines the 'glory' of both his person and his saving mission. Nevertheless, the claim that John's is a trinitarian Christology has not yet been fully established. To establish the point we must consider Jesus' relationship not only to the Father but also to the Spirit.

According to John, the Spirit holds all things in common with the Father and the Son (16:15) and thus shares with the Father and the Son the unique divine identity of Israel's one Lord God. As we have seen in the case of the Son, the Spirit's divine identity is revealed primarily through his performance of distinctly divine actions: the Spirit is sovereign in his activity (3:8); he rules 'from above', not from below (3:3, 12; cf. Ps. 11:4). The Spirit gives life (6:63): a distinctly divine prerogative according to John.[1] The Spirit comes to dwell in the midst of God's people (14:17; cf. Lev. 26:12; Isa. 63:11). The Spirit reveals the future (16:13).[2] The Spirit ushers in the new creation (20:22; cf. Gen. 2:7; Ezek. 37:9). According to John, the Spirit *of* God *is* God.[3]

Nevertheless, as in the case of the Son, the Spirit's *personal* identity is revealed not in the divine activities he holds *in common* with the Father and the Son. The Spirit's personal identity is revealed in *the distinctive, characteristic ways in which he relates to the Father and the*

---

[1] See John 5:25–29 and our discussion of these verses in relation to Jesus in the previous chapter.

[2] In Isaiah (e.g. 41:22–23; 44:7), declaring things that are to come distinguishes the one true God from false gods (Lincoln 2000: 122).

[3] Though John does not 'say' the Spirit is God, he certainly 'shows' that the Spirit is God. Contra Crump 2006: 408.

Son.[4] As we will discover, the Spirit's way of relating to the Father and the Son follows a complex but consistent pattern: *the Spirit descends from the Father to rest and remain upon the Son so that, through the Son, he may come to rest and remain upon Jesus' disciples as well*.[5] This relationship determines the full significance of Jesus' identity as 'the Christ, the Son of God' (20:31). Jesus is 'the Christ / Anointed One' in so far as he bears and bestows the Spirit of the Father.

We will trace this pattern in two steps. First, we will trace John's initial characterization of the Spirit's relationship to Jesus in the 'Book of Signs'. According to John, the Spirit descends from the Father upon the Son in order to empower him for his mission (1:32–33; 3:34), a mission that reaches its climax when Jesus baptizes his 'brothers' (20:17) with the same Spirit (1:33; 7:37–39). This pattern is set with the Spirit's first appearance in John's Gospel at the baptism of Jesus.[6] The pattern is confirmed throughout the Book of Signs as Jesus declares himself to be the surpassing fulfilment of every previous divine/spiritual dwelling place and therefore the source of eschatological life and light in the Spirit.

Second, we will trace John's fuller characterization of the Spirit in relationship to Jesus' disciples in the 'Book of Glory'.[7] According to John, the Spirit is given by the Father to the disciples at Jesus' request in order to empower them for their mission and to abide with them forever (14:16–17; 15:26–27). This pattern is developed most fully in the promises of 'the farewell discourse' and finds its initial fulfilment in Jesus' resurrection appearances to his disciples.

John's initial characterization of the Spirit in relation to Jesus: Book of Signs

The first week of Jesus' public ministry (1:19 – 2:11)[8] begins with Jesus' baptism by John[9] and his public 'revelation' to Israel (1:31). In

---

[4] Recall Meyer's comments regarding John's Christology (1996: 259) and Louth's discussion of the distinction between 'person' and 'nature' (1996: 59).

[5] John of Damascus, *Fid. orth.* 1.8; see also Bobrinskoy 1999: 103.

[6] Jesus' reception of the Spirit at his baptism is a public display of his status as 'the Christ' (see 1:31, where John the Baptist says his mission is to 'reveal' the Son of God to Israel). As we will see in chapter 10, Jesus' baptism does not constitute the *beginning* of his relationship to the Holy Spirit. The Son eternally receives the Spirit from the Father.

[7] See also Tolmie 1995: 134.

[8] See Köstenberger 2004c: 55–56; see also the discussions in Carson 1991: 167–168 (drawing new creation parallels) and Keener 2003: 496–498 (suggesting a possible link with Jesus' resurrection on the 'third day', cf. 2:19–20).

[9] Though not explicitly recorded, John probably presupposes that his readers will

this context, the fourth evangelist picks up the comparison between Jesus and John the Baptist that he began in the prologue (1:6–8, 15). He develops the comparison by contrasting John and Jesus in two ways.

First, the evangelist contrasts their identities. John the Baptist is by his own admission 'not the Christ' (1:20). He is instead 'the voice of one calling in the desert' sent to prepare 'the way for the Lord [Yahweh]' (1:23; cf. Isa. 40:3). Jesus, however, is the Christ, the recipient of the Spirit's anointing in fulfilment of Isaianic prophecy (e.g. Isa. 11:1; 42:1; 66:1). The Spirit's anointing also signals Jesus' filial relationship to the Father. Thus John confesses, 'this is the Son of God' (1:34; or 'the Chosen One of God'; cf. 20:31).

Second, the evangelist contrasts John and Jesus in terms of their respective missions. Whereas John's ministry consisted in a baptism with water (1:26, 33), the ministry of 'the Christ' will consist in a baptism 'with the Holy Spirit' (1:33).

The descent of the Spirit upon and through Jesus represents the dawning of the eschatological age.[10] Jesus assumes the role of the long-awaited 'Anointed One', God's special servant who bears God's Spirit in full measure (John 3:34; cf. also Isa. 11:1; 42:1; 66:1; *1 En.* 49.3; *Pss Sol.* 17.37; *T. Levi* 18.2–14; *T. Jud.* 24.2–3).[11] He also assumes the role of Yahweh. As the one who 'baptize[s] with the Holy Spirit' (1:33), Jesus will keep Yahweh's own promise concerning the latter days: Jesus will bestow God's Spirit upon God's people, thereby bringing eschatological forgiveness and renewal (Isa. 32:15; 44:3; Ezek. 36:25–27; Joel 2:28–32; cf. *Jub.* 1.23; *2 Esdr.* [*4 Ezra*] 6.26; *T. Jud.* 24.3; 1 QS 4.20–21). As we have seen in the previous chapter, Jesus is particularly suited to fill the role of one who at once *receives* and *dispenses* divine blessing because he is 'the Son of God'.[12]

A further feature of the Spirit's coming is important to note. The Spirit who descends upon Jesus 'remains' with Jesus (1:32–33).[13] This claim is striking. According to some Second Temple texts, the Spirit

---

be familiar with some account of Jesus' baptism as rendered, for example, in the Synoptic Gospels. Contra Lincoln, who argues that the evangelist 'suppresses' Jesus' baptism by John 'to avoid any suggestion that Jesus could be considered subordinate to John in some sense' (2005: 114).

[10] Carson 1991: 152.
[11] Kruse 2003: 72.
[12] So Badcock 1997: 30–31.
[13] On the significance of 'remaining' in John, see Burge 1987: 54–56.

had departed from Israel.[14] Indeed, in John's presentation, 'the permanence of Jesus' anointing is directly stressed in contrast to the transitoriness of every other prophetic inspiration in Israel's history'.[15] Just as the dove after the flood tried many times before finding a permanent place to rest (Gen. 8:6–12), so now at last, at the climax of Israel's history, the Spirit of God has found a permanent place to rest and remain in the Son of God incarnate (1:32).[16]

The permanence that marks Jesus' bearing of the Spirit will later mark his bestowal of the Spirit. In the farewell discourse, Jesus promises his disciples that the Spirit will remain with them forever (14:16–17). In and through Jesus, the fullness of God's eschatological blessing in the person of the Holy Spirit has come. And he has come to stay.

The remaining chapters of the Book of Signs confirm and develop this portrait of the Spirit in relation to Jesus. John unpacks the theological significance of this portrait by displaying Jesus as the fulfilment and replacement of tabernacle and temple, God's former dwelling places in the midst of his people (Exod. 29:45–46; 1 Kgs 8:27; Ps. 78:60; Isa. 63:11 etc.).[17]

In 2:1 – 4:54, Jesus travels from Cana to Jerusalem and back to Cana again.[18] Through a series of enigmatic words and deeds,[19] the evangelist develops his portrait of Jesus as the fulfilment and replacement of God's previous dwelling places. The incarnate Son is the new Bethel, where the gateway of heaven is opened and upon whom the angels of God ascend and descend (1:51). His body is a 'temple' that must first undergo destruction before it is raised in eschatological splendour (2:19–21; cf. Mic. 3:12 – 4:5). He is the source of 'living water' promised by Ezekiel (4:10, 13–14; cf. Ezek. 47:1–11), whose coming supplants all previous houses of worship, both Jew and Gentile, and inaugurates the full and final worship of the messianic age, worship 'in spirit and in truth' (4:21, 23–26). In each instance,

[14] See Du Rand 2005: 46.

[15] Burge 1987: 54.

[16] For an explicit link between Noah's flood and baptism, see 1 Pet. 3:21.

[17] On this theme, see Kerr 2002; Coloe 2001; Beale 2004; Köstenberger 2005a = 2006; and Hoskins 2007. Moloney summarizes the point: 'embodied in the Son of God they can find the perfection of what was done in the Jewish Temple in signs and shadows' (Moloney 1996: 207). On the import and function of the temple in Jesus' day, see N. T. Wright 1996: 405–428.

[18] For a discussion of this structure and its attending themes, see Köstenberger 2004c: 51–52, 89–90; Ridderbos 1997: 97–99; and Moloney 1980.

[19] See Stibbe 1991: 19–38.

Jesus' striking claims are not empty, for he bears the Spirit 'without limit' (3:34).

In John 5 – 10, the stakes are raised as Jesus takes his enigmatic words and deeds to the epicentre of Jewish worship, the Jerusalem temple, and attends a series of major Jewish festivals. Jesus continues to present himself as the true dwelling place of God among men, the site of God's presence and source of God's blessing. Only now he makes this self-presentation *in competition with the contemporary forms of divine presence and blessing in the Jewish temple and festivals.* His behaviour in this regard 'initiates a process that promises to be fatal'.[20] Jesus' words and actions at the feasts of Passover (John 6) and Booths (John 7) are particularly relevant to the present discussion.

At Passover Jesus feeds five thousand followers, which causes the crowd to identify him as the 'Prophet' like Moses 'who is to come into the world' (6:14).[21] Jesus then goes on to explain that, whereas in former days God provided 'bread from heaven to eat' (6:31, citing Neh. 9:15 LXX?),[22] God now provides 'the true bread from heaven' (6:32), the consumption of which guarantees eternal life (6:35, 50–51, 53–57).[23] This true bread is the flesh of the one who 'came down from heaven' (6:51).

Jesus' 'hard teaching' causes many to turn back (6:60). Knowing that his disciples, too, are offended, Jesus calls for a spiritual (rather than 'carnal') understanding of his teaching (6:63).[24] He is not inviting cannibalism. Jesus' words must be understood in the light of his true identity and mission (a mission, at any rate, that culminates in his *ascension* [6:62], and hence a time when he will no longer be physically present to his disciples). Faith may feed[25] on Jesus' body

---

[20] Moloney 1996: 29.

[21] See Deut. 18:18. Boismard 1993: 63.

[22] Schlatter 1948: 172–173. As the quotation of Neh. 9:15 indicates, Jesus' actions during the feast of Passover recalled for his audience the great gifts of God associated with the exodus, including the gifts of bread from heaven, water from the rock, and, pre-eminently, the Law of Moses. Interestingly, all three gifts are associated with the gift of God's 'good Spirit' in Neh. 9:20 (Moloney 1996: 46–47).

[23] The contrast between the bread remembered at Passover and the 'true bread' is not between *false* bread and *true* bread. Indeed, Jesus' comparison rests on the assumption that ordinary bread/manna is 'truly' edible and life-sustaining (see 6:55: 'my flesh is real food and my blood is real drink'). The contrast is between bread that was *provisional* ('Your forefathers ate the manna in the desert, yet they died' [6:49]) and bread that is *eschatologically full and final*: 'food that endures to eternal life' (6:27). On this aspect of John's usage of 'real', see Vos 1980b: 343–351; and Swain 1998.

[24] Ridderbos 1997: 246–248.

[25] John's theology here may be summed up as follows: 'eating is believing' (compare 6:54 with 6:40). So Carson 1991: 297, following Augustine.

and receive eternal life because of who he is and what he came to do: he is *the Son of God sent from heaven and made flesh that he might give his life for the world* (1:14; 3:16–17; 6:33, 51); he is *the one who bears and bestows the Spirit who 'gives life'* (3:34; 6:63). Faith recognizes and receives the incarnate Christ as sustenance for the soul and in so doing receives the Spirit of the incarnate Christ, 'the Lord and Giver of Life'.[26]

The festival cycle continues in John 7, where Jesus travels to the feast of Booths (7:2).[27] This feast, originally instituted through Moses (Lev. 23:34–36; Deut. 31:9–13), had become 'associated with eschatological and messianic expectations' by Jesus' day under the influence of Zechariah 14 and other Jewish literature.[28] The festival included a water-libation ceremony. For many present, the pouring of water on the altar symbolized the outflow of living water from Ezekiel's eschatological temple (Ezek. 47:1–12).[29] On this occasion, celebrants sang Psalms 113 – 118 and read Isaiah 12:3:

> With joy you will draw water
> from the wells of salvation.[30]

'On the last and greatest day of the Feast', just when the events of the feast and their attendant symbolism were beginning to sink into people's minds, Jesus announced, 'If anyone is thirsty, let him come to me and drink. Whoever believes in me, as the Scripture has said, streams of living water will flow from within him' (7:37–38).[31] As on previous occasions, Jesus claims to fulfil Jewish expectations related to the temple in the very presence of the temple itself. He is the substance of every prophecy associated with the feast.[32] He is the true source of 'living water'.

---

[26] The Nicene Creed. Space forbids a full discussion of the theological and sacramental issues raised by this text, including the important issue of *how* faith feeds on the risen Jesus through the Spirit. For a helpful if only introductory discussion, see Calvin *John*, 1: 174–175.

[27] For a discussion of this feast in its historical context, see Moloney 1996: 66–70.

[28] Moloney 1996: 68–70; Köstenberger 2004c: 229; and Beale 2004: 197.

[29] See Moloney's discussion in 1996: 67; also Köstenberger 2004c: 239–240; and Beale 2004: 197.

[30] Congar 1997, 1: 50; Moloney 1996: 67.

[31] John 7:38 is notoriously difficult to interpret. The issue concerns whose 'inmost being' is in view, Jesus' or the believer's. See for opposing interpretations Burge 1987: 88–93; and Carson 1991: 321–328. Either way, the present point remains the same.

[32] Congar 1997, 1: 51; Köstenberger 2004c: 240, following Calvin.

Jesus has mentioned this gift of 'living water' before in the Gospel (4:10). Now John explains the significance of this gift: 'By this he meant the Spirit, whom those who believed in him were later to receive' (7:39a). John goes on to indicate the timing of this gift: 'Up to that time the Spirit had not been given, since Jesus had not yet been glorified' (7:39b). Jesus will pour out the Spirit of life upon God's people only after his glorification (death, resurrection and ascension).

Initial summary: Jesus and the Spirit in the Book of Signs

Our survey of the Spirit's relationship to Jesus in the Book of Signs is now complete. According to John's testimony, the incarnate Son of God is the surpassing fulfilment of every previous divine/spiritual dwelling place and therefore the source of eschatological life in the Spirit. Before moving on to John's fuller characterization of the Spirit in the Book of Glory, it will be helpful to draw three points from the preceding discussion.

First, John's Christology is sometimes characterized as a 'temple Christology'.[33] This description is true so far as it goes. In the light of the present discussion, however, it is probably better to say that John's is not so much a 'temple Christology' as it is a trinitarian Christology, in which all the blessings once associated with tabernacle and temple have now found their full and final embodiment in the Word made flesh, the only Son of the Father (cf. 1:14). Indeed, all of Jesus' enigmatic words and deeds in the presence of the temple are but *'figures'* (cf. John 16:25) of the eschatological, trinitarian *reality* (truth)[34] that has dawned in the person of Jesus Christ. The incarnate Son, not the temple, is the substance prefigured in every OT sign and shadow because the Spirit of the Father rests on and remains in him and flows from him to everyone who believes.[35]

Second, for all the misunderstanding associated with Jesus' enigmatic words and deeds surrounding the temple and its feasts, the Jewish authorities were right about one thing: if they allowed this supplanter to continue his ministry, it would mean the end of the

---

[33] See e.g. D. A. Lee 2004: 284.
[34] Vos 1980b; Swain 1998.
[35] See also Moloney 1996: *passim*; and Coloe 2001.

temple, the loss of their 'place' (11:48).[36] Of course, the Jewish authorities cannot accept this situation and thus plot Jesus' destruction (11:49–50; cf. 2:19). Jesus' competition with the Jewish temple and its feasts thus proves to be fatal.[37] It is precisely at this point that we encounter one of John's rich ironies.[38] Far from undermining his claim to be the new point of contact between God and humanity, Jesus' death marks the *fulfilment* of such a claim (12:38–40).[39] His death causes the fountain of blood and water to flow for eschatological cleansing and renewal (19:30, 34).[40] Jesus' death marks the climactic manifestation of his temple's 'glory' (1:14; 12:27–28; 13:31; 17:1), opening through his flesh a new and living way into the Father's presence (14:6; cf. Heb. 10:20).

Third, John 7:39 provides at once the last mention of the Spirit in the Book of Signs and an important clue regarding the role of the Spirit in relation to Jesus.[41] As we have learned from John's presentation, Jesus is 'the Christ' in so far as he bears and bestows the Spirit of God (1:29–34). The teaching of John 7:39 concerning the *timing* of this bestowal enables us to grasp better the shape of the Spirit's ministry in relation to Jesus. If Jesus is 'the Christ' in so far as he bears and bestows the Spirit, it is the 'glorification' of the Christ through his death, resurrection and ascension that is the great hinge upon which his messianic work turns. The Spirit will flow to all who believe in Jesus only *after* he is glorified. The cross, resurrection and ascension constitute the great turning point of redemptive history. After these events are fulfilled, the age of the Spirit will dawn (cf. 4:23).

---

[36] According to Carson (1991: 420), the mention of 'our place' in 11:48 is 'almost certainly a reference to the temple: cf. 2 Ezra 14:7 [LXX; cf. Neh. 4:7]; Je. 7:14; Acts 6:14)'.

[37] Moloney 1996: 29.

[38] Lincoln 2000: 17–21.

[39] Evans (2000: 78) shows that John follows a fairly consistent pattern in the way he cites Scripture in the two halves of his Gospel. In the first half of the Gospel, John commonly employs the word 'written' to introduce OT citations (1:23; 2:17; 6:31, 45; 7:38, 42; 8:17; 10:34; 12:14). Such citations 'demonstrate that Jesus conducted his ministry in keeping with scriptural expectation ("as it is written")'. In the second half of the Gospel, John commonly employs the phrase 'in order that it be fulfilled' to introduce OT citations (12:38, 39–40; 13:18; 15:25; 19:24, 28, 36, 37). Such citations are meant to demonstrate that 'It is not until Jesus is rejected, despite his signs, that the Scriptures are said to be "fulfilled". It is in Jesus' rejection and crucifixion that the Scriptures find their ultimate fulfilment.'

[40] See Vanhoozer 2002: 300–302; Carson 1991: 623–625; and Köstenberger 2004c: 552–554.

[41] John 7:39 forms an *inclusio* with 1:33 in this regard.

John's fuller characterization of the Spirit in relation to Jesus and the disciples: Book of Glory

The second half of John's Gospel provides the fullest characterization of the Holy Spirit in the four Gospels, indeed in the entire NT. Here the focus shifts from the Spirit's relation to Jesus during his earthly ministry to Jesus' teaching about the Spirit's relation to his disciples. According to Jesus, the disciples' relationship with the Spirit will enter a new stage after Jesus returns to his Father by way of the cross, resurrection and ascension.[42]

The announcement of Jesus' departure deeply troubles the disciples (13:36 – 14:1). Up to this point, the disciples have enjoyed Jesus' physical presence 'tabernacling' in their very midst (1:14); 'they have been able to see his glory with their own eyes and touch it (as it were) with their own hands' (cf. 1 John 1:1).[43] They have concluded that he has 'the words of eternal life' and that there is nowhere else for them to go to enjoy this life (6:68). They suppose therefore that Jesus' departure can only be bad news for them.

However, Jesus instructs them that his departure is 'a reason for joy'.[44] His departure will not constitute an absence on his part. Nor will it mean the end of his life-giving ministry. Jesus' fellowship with his disciples and his life-giving ministry will continue, only now in a different mode.[45] According to Jesus, when he departs to the Father he will send the Holy Spirit. The coming of the Spirit will guarantee the disciples' new mode of fellowship with Jesus and enable the continuation of Jesus' mission through the disciples (14:12; 16:7).[46]

In John 14, Jesus explains why his departure does not constitute abandonment and assures them that he will not leave them as 'orphans' (14:18). He has already explained that the disciples will one day follow him (13:36). Now he explains why he must go ahead of them: he goes to prepare a place for them (14:2–3).[47] As we saw in

[42] Tolmie 1995: 144.

[43] Ridderbos 1997: 475.

[44] Ibid. 487.

[45] Ibid. 482, 498–499.

[46] D. M. Smith 1995: 141–146. On the relationship between the earthly, historical mission of Jesus and that of his appointed eyewitnesses (the apostles), see Bauckham 2006: 387–411.

[47] Jesus' provision of a place seems to be patterned after Deuteronomy, where God is said to have gone ahead and to have prepared a place for his people in the Promised Land (e.g. 1:29–33; see P. W. L. Walker 1996: 186–190, esp. 188). Elsewhere in the NT, in the book of Hebrews, Jesus is depicted as our 'forerunner'

the previous chapter, the 'place' that Jesus prepares for the disciples is *his* filial place in the presence of the Father, the place where he has eternally basked in the Father's love (1:1, 18; 14:3; 17:5, 24–26).

Nevertheless, Jesus promises that the disciples' enjoyment of the Father's 'house' and presence (14:2) is not reserved strictly for the future. Jesus promises to send another 'helping presence' in the interim, the Spirit of truth, who will take up residence in their midst and remain with them forever (14:16–17). Moreover, when the Spirit comes, he will not come alone. The Father and the Son will also come to make their 'home' with those who abide in Jesus' teaching (14:23). Even now, in the time between Jesus' first and second comings, the Spirit will enable the disciples to enjoy the ultimate covenant blessing: the indwelling presence of the triune God (cf. Lev. 26:12; 2 Cor. 6:16–18; 1 John 3:24; 4:13; Rev. 21:3, 7).[48]

The Spirit's arrival will not only guarantee Jesus' ongoing communion with the disciples; the Spirit's arrival will also empower them to continue Jesus' mission in the world. As John's Gospel makes clear, the Spirit's assistance in this regard was severely needed.[49] Despite the fact that the disciples had been with Jesus from the beginning of his ministry (15:27; 16:4), they continually failed to understand (and sometimes took offence at) Jesus' enigmatic words and deeds (see e.g. 6:61; 14:5 etc.). Indeed, in the great hour of Jesus' trial before the world his disciples deny (13:38) and desert him (16:32). When the Spirit comes, this will change.[50]

The Holy Spirit is 'the Spirit of truth' (14:17; 15:26; 16:13). As the Spirit *of* truth, he will 'guide' (16:13) the disciples *in* (or *into*) the way of truth revealed in Jesus (14:6).[51] He will enable them both to remember Jesus' enigmatic revelation (14:26; cf. 2:22) and to understand 'plainly' (16:25) the full import and meaning of that revelation (14:26; 16:12–15).[52] The Spirit is especially equipped to play this

---

(NASB), who has finished the course and entered heaven (6:20; 12:2). In the same book, mention is made of a 'heavenly country' or 'city' prepared for the saints (11:16).

[48] Chennattu 2006: 106. According to Lincoln, 'the coming of Jesus and the Father and the sending of the Paraclete are mutually interpretative . . . The Spirit is the mediator of the presence of Jesus and God to believers' (Lincoln 2005: 396).

[49] Kellum 2004: 152.

[50] Burge 2006: 248–250.

[51] Congar 1997, 1: 57.

[52] Porsch (1974: 296) sees in John 16:25 a pattern common to apocalyptic literature, where first comes the phase of actual revelation followed by a second phase, where that revelation is interpreted. In this case, 'Jesus ist der Vermittler der Offenbarung . . . der Geist, deren Interpreter' (Jesus is the agent of the revelation . . . the Spirit, the interpreter).

interpretative role vis-à-vis the disciples because he too is a 'hearer' of the Father's revelation through the Son (16:13), albeit an especially privileged one, who enjoys full access to divine truth: 'He will bring glory to me by taking from what is mine and making it known to you. All that belongs to the Father is mine. That is why I said the Spirit will take from what is mine and make it known to you' (16:14–15; cf. 1 John 2:27; 1 Cor. 2:10–13).[53]

With the help of the Holy Spirit, the truth of Jesus will thus continue to go forth into the world through the witness of the disciples (15:26–27).[54] But, Jesus warns, the world will not receive this Spirit-empowered witness, because it neither 'sees' nor 'knows' the Spirit of truth (14:17). Consequently, the Spirit-Paraclete will convict[55] the world concerning sin, because it refuses to believe in Jesus (16:9). In the absence of the vindicated and ascended Lord, the Spirit will convince the world that Jesus was indeed in the right (16:10). Conversely, he will convict the world of judgment, because the ruler of the world has been judged on the cross; and as the ruler of the world goes, so goes the world (16:11; cf. 12:31).[56] The forensic activity of the Spirit is not entirely negative. The book of Acts demonstrates that the Paraclete's convicting work through the witness of the disciples also produces salutary effects (Acts 2:37–41).[57]

In spite of Jesus' teaching on the topic, the disciples still do not understand the full significance of the Spirit's work (cf. 16:29–32). That understanding will dawn on Easter morning and continue to grow after Jesus ascends to the Father and baptizes them with the Holy Spirit (1:33; cf. Acts 1 – 2). 'On that day'[58] the disciples will begin to understand the nature of their indwelling unity with Jesus and the Father as Jesus continues to 'disclose' (NASB) himself to

[53] Poythress 2006: 97–98; cf. Burge 2006: 249.

[54] Bauckham 2006: 388–390.

[55] Michel Gourgues's thesis (2005) that John's two designations for the Holy Spirit, 'the Spirit of truth' and 'the Paraclete', signify two different functions, a didactic function and a forensic function, is probably a bit too tidy. As Lincoln has demonstrated, both designations belong to the forensic realm. The Spirit's witness to the truth has a 'dual impact': it *convicts* the world, which rejects the truth, and *comforts* the disciples, who receive the truth (2000: 113). See also Isa. 40 – 55.

[56] For this interpretation of 16:8–11, see Lincoln 2000: 117–120; for an alternative interpretation, see Carson 1991: 534–539.

[57] Ferguson 1996: 69–70.

[58] For the view that 'on that day' refers to Easter morning, see Ridderbos 1997: 506; for the view that it represents a more generalized reference to the future, see Köstenberger 2004c: 479.

them via the Spirit's presence (14:20–21).[59] On that day, they will be constituted as Jesus' authorized emissaries, charged and empowered by the Spirit to take the good news of the risen Lord to the world with the promise of forgiveness to all who believe (20:21–23).

The Spirit who rests and remains on God's Son and his brothers

Tracing the Spirit's relation to Jesus' disciples reveals an illuminating pattern with respect to his distinctive personal character: the *role the Spirit plays in relation to the disciples is analogous to the role he played in relation to Jesus during his earthly ministry*. The Spirit, along with the Father, remained with/indwelled[60] Jesus (1:32–33; 10:38; 14:10–11); the Spirit, along with the Father and Jesus, remains with/indwells the disciples (14:16–17, 20–23). The Spirit empowered Jesus to speak the words of God (3:34; 6:63); the Spirit empowers the disciples to speak the words of God revealed in Jesus (15:26–27; 16:12–15). The Father gave the Spirit to Jesus because he loves him (3:34–35); the Father will give the disciples the Spirit because he loves them, too (14:21, 23).

The *reason* for this analogous relationship is clear. The Spirit relates to the disciples as he relates to Jesus because of their vital union with him (14:15–16, 23; 15:1–17; 17:23–26) and because of his saving work on their behalf.[61] The Spirit rests and remains upon the Son *and* upon those who, by receiving and abiding in the Son, have become 'children of God' and 'brothers' of Jesus (1:12; 20:17). Jesus' God has become their God, Jesus' Father, their Father (20:17), Jesus' Spirit, their Spirit. Indeed, viewed in this light, we may see the Son's reception of the Spirit at his baptism as an anticipation of his brothers' reception of the same Spirit (1:32–33; 7:39; 20:22). This is the great blessing that Jesus the anointed Son of God brings – *a share in*

[59] Ridderbos 1997: 507.

[60] 'Remaining' and 'indwelling' probably should be viewed as complementary rather than sharply distinct ways of describing the Spirit's work (cf. 14:10, where both terms are used to describe the Father's indwelling relationship to the Son). So Burge 1987: 54–55; contra Crump 2006: 403.

[61] The benefit of sharing in Jesus' relationship to the Father by the Spirit does not come on the basis of the disciples' fidelity (see 13:38; 16:31–32) but on the basis of Jesus' costly obedience to the Father (14:31). See Ridderbos's profound comments in this regard (1997: 478, esp. n. 95).

his filial relationship with the Father by the indwelling of the Holy Spirit.[62]

Identifying the Spirit's relationship to Jesus and his disciples enables us to detect the Spirit's distinctive personal activity even in places where he remains otherwise unnamed.[63] The principle is this: when you see an analogy between the Son and his brothers, assume that the Spirit is the author of the analogy. Because we are familiar with his characteristic ways, we may hear the rustling of his effects even when his comings and goings are not explicitly mentioned (cf. 3:8). Three examples are particularly interesting:

1. Just as the Father has glorified himself in the Son by answering his prayers (12:27–28), so he will continue to glorify himself in the Son by answering the disciples' prayers in Jesus' name (14:12–14; 15:16; 16:23–24, 26).
2. Just as the Son glorifies the Father by bearing fruit (12:23–24), so the disciples will glorify the Father by bearing fruit (15:8).
3. Just as the world has hated and persecuted Jesus (15:18, 20), so the world will hate and persecute Jesus' disciples (15:18–21); in each instance, the world's hatred reveals that it knows neither the Father nor the Son (15:23–24; 16:2–3).

That each of these analogous situations indeed signifies that the Spirit's 'anonymous' work in God's 'children' is confirmed not only by the fact that Jesus' teaching on these three subjects accompanies his teaching about the Spirit's (14 – 16), but also by the fact that, according to the rest of the NT, the three aforementioned blessings are distinctive signs of the Spirit's presence in God's children. Thus, believers call upon God in prayer as 'Abba! Father!' because the Spirit of God's Son has been sent into their hearts (Gal. 4:6). Believers bear 'fruit' because the eschatological age has dawned and the Spirit has been poured out upon them (Isa. 32:15; Gal. 5:22–23).[64] Even the

---

[62] To be sure, there is a striking *contra analogy* in this relationship as well. Jesus is 'the true vine' (15:1) and 'one-of-a-kind Son' (1:14; 3:16). His disciples are 'the branches' (15:5) and 'children'/'brothers' (1:12; 20:17). The incarnate Son is the *source* of their life in relation to the Father through the Spirit. The disciples are entirely *dependent* upon the fruitfulness of the vine (15:4). Again, see D. M. Smith 1995: 144–146.

[63] On the Spirit's characteristic 'anonymity', see Bobrinskoy 1999: 96; and Rogers 2005: 46.

[64] Indeed, the permanent 'peace' (14:27), 'love' (15:9) and 'joy' (15:11; 16:20–24) that abide with the disciples abide with them because of the Spirit's indwelling presence (cf. Gal. 5:22–23).

suffering of believers at the hand of the world signifies that 'the Spirit of glory and of God rests' upon them (1 Pet. 4:14).

Conclusion

Our survey of the Spirit's distinctive personal way of relating to Jesus and the disciples is now complete. Who, then, is the Spirit according to John? He is the one who descends from the Father upon the Son that he might flow through the Son to all who believe, bringing forgiveness and renewal, life and light. His coming signals the replacement of God's former dwelling in tabernacle and temple with the triune indwelling of the children of God. His role is to confirm believers' interest in the Son, and thus in the Father as well, and to continue the mission given by the Father to the Son through the church in the world. The Spirit effects all these things 'that the Father may be glorified in the Son' (14:13 NASB).

In the next chapter, we will discuss the shape of this triune mission in greater depth.

Chapter Nine

'As the Father has sent me, so I am sending you': Toward a trinitarian mission theology

'For God so loved the world that he gave his one and only Son, that whoever believes in him shall not perish but have eternal life' (3:16). John's entire Gospel is pervaded by this divine mission: God the Father in his love sending Jesus, his Son, to save all those who believe in him for eternal life. The Spirit, too, is shown to play an important part in Jesus' mission as well as in the mission of his followers, jointly witnessing with them (15:26–27) and empowering the community's proclamation of forgiveness and salvation in Jesus (20:22–23).

The present chapter[1] seeks to demonstrate the following dual thesis: (1) John's mission theology is an integral part of his presentation of Father, Son and Spirit; and (2) rather than John's mission theology being a function of his trinitarian theology, the converse is in fact the case: John's presentation of Father, Son and Spirit is a function of his mission theology.[2] After a brief summary of John's references to *theos*, God, and his presentations of Father, Son and Spirit, with particular attention to their role in mission, we will discuss the way in which John's trinitarian theology culminates toward the end of the Gospel in several strategic references to mission involving the persons of the triune Godhead. Hence, it will be shown that Father, Son and Spirit all contribute to God's mission to the world. We will then discuss the implications of John's presentation of the triune mission for the mission of the church.

---

[1] The present study builds on ch. 8 in Köstenberger and O'Brien 2001. The following sections draw on and summarize the findings in chapters 2–6 above.
[2] The point pertains to the order of knowing, not to the order of being. The triune identity is *revealed* through the triune missions. But the triune missions flow *from, through and to* the eternal Trinity. See chapter 10 below.

God (*theos*)

Apart from three major references to Jesus as *theos* in John 1:1, 18 and 20:28, the usual referent of *theos* is God the Father. On the whole, God as a character remains in the background; references to God's actions are limited to his loving the world (3:16) and sending (3:17) and approving of his Son (6:27); to his hearing righteous prayer (9:31; 11:22); and to his glorifying the Son (13:32).

References to God's nature or essential attributes, stating that God is eternal (1:1, 2), invisible (1:18), true (3:33; 17:3), spirit (4:24) and the only God (5:44; 17:3) accentuate God's difference or otherness. Overall, God is the great Given, Known, Accepted and constant Assumed in the controversy concerning Jesus whose support is sought and invoked by both sides in the escalating debate.

As mentioned, in three exceptional instances the referent of *theos* in John's Gospel is not the Father, but Jesus. While various Christological titles (including 'Son of God') are applied to Jesus by his followers, the most striking designation for Jesus in the Gospel is the term *theos*, which occurs in the opening and closing verses of the prologue and in the final pericope of the Gospel proper (20:28). This literary *inclusio*, whereby Jesus is affirmed to be God at the beginning and at the end of the Gospel (and nowhere else in those terms) is startling in that it takes a designation, *theos*, which is universally applied to the God of the Hebrew Scriptures in the entire body of the Gospel, and changes the referent to Jesus.

Remarkably, this is done without any sustained attempt at adjudicating the issue of how the God of the Hebrew Scriptures and Jesus can both be called *theos*.[3] The major exception is found at the inception of the Gospel, where the Word, himself *theos*, and *theos* are said to have existed eternally in close fellowship with one another.

At the same time, even the risen Jesus still refers to the God of the Hebrew Scriptures as 'my God' in 20:17 and earlier in the Gospel affirms that the Father is greater than he (14:28). This hints at a resolution of an apparent ditheism: while there is more than one referent of *theos* in this Gospel, these two persons sustain a complementary relationship most frequently described in the Johannine narrative as that of 'Father' and 'Son'.

---

[3] See the discussion in chapter 1 above.

The Father

While the notion of God as Father is not common in the Hebrew Scriptures, in John's Gospel 'Father–Son' is the dominant, controlling metaphor for Jesus' relationship with God. The two persons of God the Father and the Son are thoroughly and inextricably intertwined. Jesus derives his mission from the Father and is fully dependent on him in carrying it out. The imagery of 'father' and 'son' plainly draws on Jewish cultural expectations related to father–son relationships, especially those pertaining to only sons.[4]

The emphasis on the Father as the one who sent Jesus and who witnesses to him portrays him as the Authorizer and Authenticator of Jesus. Emphatically, it is Jesus himself who refers to God as 'the' Father and in close to twenty instances even as 'his' Father. 'The Father' is Jesus' natural, almost unselfconscious, way of referring to God.

The Son

The identification of Jesus as the 'Son' is at the very heart of John's Christology. While the term *logos* (the Word) is limited to the prologue, and Jesus is repeatedly addressed as *kyrios* ('sir' or 'Lord') and *rabbi* (teacher), it is the term 'Son' (*huios*) that pervades the Gospel, both absolutely and in combination with various Christological titles applied to Jesus. This includes references to Jesus as God's 'one-of-a-kind Son' (3:16, 18; cf. 1:14, 18) or as the 'Son of God' (1:34?; 1:49; 3:18; 5:25; 10:36; 11:4, 27; 19:7; 20:31). It also encompasses Jesus' self-references as the 'Son of Man'.[5] Finally, there are eighteen references to Jesus as 'the Son', virtually always in relation to God 'the Father'.[6]

When compared with 'Father' language in John's Gospel, references to God as Father are more frequent than references to Jesus as the Son. Strikingly, Jesus affirms his unity with God the Father in purpose, mission and divinity (10:30). In the context of the remainder of the Gospel, this unity is said to form the basis for the unity of Jesus' followers in their mission to the world, whose purpose, in turn, is said to be the world's coming to recognize and believe that the Father sent Jesus (17:11, 21–23; cf. 20:21). This firmly establishes the

---

[4] See esp. Köstenberger 1998b: 96–121.
[5] 1:51; 3:13, 14; 5:27; 6:27, 53, 62; 8:28; 9:35; 12:23, 34 (2); 13:31.
[6] 3:17, 35, 36 (2); 5:19 (2), 20, 21, 22, 23 (2), 26; 6:40; 8:36; 14:13; 17:1 (2).

thesis of this chapter that Jesus' relationship with the Father is presented within the larger purview of mission.

As developed at length elsewhere,[7] John represents Jesus' mission in three distinct yet related ways: (1) Jesus as the sent Son; (2) Jesus as the eschatological shepherd-teacher. (3) Jesus as the one who comes into the world and returns to the Father (descent–ascent). Jesus' work in the Fourth Gospel is described in terms of 'signs' performed as part of his ministry to 'the Jews' (John 1 – 12) and of 'works' performed 'from the Father'. Everything Jesus says and does is presented under the rubric of revelation of God and of his glory, including even the cross itself.

With regard to the first aspect of his mission, Jesus' mission as the sent Son significantly entails the gathering of the new messianic community and its commissioning for its mission to the world (20:21). As mentioned, in this respect Jesus' union with the Father forms the basis for believers' union in their mission, which places the Father–son relationship under the rubric of mission as well. Especially in the farewell discourse, it becomes clear that the disciples are taken into the love and unity of the persons of the Godhead as responsible agents and representatives of Jesus the sent Son.

With regard to the second aspect of Jesus' mission, Jesus as the eschatological shepherd-teacher, this accentuates his role as the messianic shepherd and teacher who gathers the new messianic community, cleanses it (viz. the footwashing and removal of Judas the betrayer in 13:1–30) and prepares it for its mission. This aspect is evident especially in Jesus' 'Good Shepherd' discourse (ch. 10) and in his commissioning of Peter at the end of the Gospel (ch. 21). Against the backdrop of an entire set of OT messianic images and expectations, Jesus' mission is presented as part of an eschatological framework that shows him as inaugurating the messianic age at which 'all' will 'be taught by God' (6:45; cf. Isa. 54:13). Jesus' mission of gathering God's children into 'one' community (11:52) continues after his ascension as the new messianic community, indwelt by Father, Son and Holy Spirit is formed into a community whose love is a magnetic force to a watching world (13:35; 17:20–23).

With regard to the third aspect of Jesus' mission, Jesus as the one who comes into the world and returns to the Father (descent–ascent), this marks out Jesus as uniquely being the Word coming

---

[7] Köstenberger 1998b.

into the world (the incarnation, 1:14) and being sent by God on a mission, accomplishing this earthly mission and as returning to his sender (e.g. 13:3; 16:28; 17:4; cf. Isa. 55:11–12). While the first aspect, the mission of the sent Son, focuses more on the horizontal dimension, the third, Jesus as coming into the world and as returning to the Father, lays more stress on the vertical dimension of Jesus' descent and ascent.[8]

There is no need to trace the narrative outworking of these motifs here. Since 'Father' and 'Son' language are inextricably intertwined in John's Gospel, this has already been done in the respective chapters on the 'Father' and the 'Son' above. Suffice it to say that Father, Son and Spirit are shown to be united in the messianic mission of the Son, distinct in personhood yet one in purpose, actively collaborating to bring about the new people of God whose identity is centred on faith in Jesus as Messiah and Son of God. This new people of God, in turn, on the basis of their identification with Jesus and their commission from him, are sent on a mission to the world overseen by the exalted Jesus and empowered by the Spirit.

The Spirit

As mentioned in the chapter on the Spirit in John's Gospel above, undisputed references to the Spirit in the first half of John's Gospel are relatively few. In every case where the Spirit is clearly in view, the reference relates to the Spirit's role in Jesus' ministry. The Spirit rests on him (1:32–33) and does so to an unlimited degree (3:34). His words are life-giving and Spirit-infused (6:63), and the Spirit is to be given only subsequent to Jesus' earthly ministry (7:39). This sets up the pattern, demonstrated above, of the Spirit's resting and remaining on Jesus, which in the second half of the Gospel is transferred to believers in Jesus.

While thus John's treatment of the Spirit in the first half of the Gospel largely resembles that of the Synoptics, his adoption of a post-exaltation vantage point leads to a vastly enhanced portrayal of the Spirit in the farewell discourse. As discussed in chapter 5 above, references to the Spirit in the second half of John's Gospel increase dramatically in both number and prominence in keeping with the Spirit's pivotal role in the disciples' mission subsequent to

---

[8] Cf. e.g. the 'bread of life' in ch. 6 or the 'Son of Man' in the lifted-up sayings, 3:13; 8:28; 13:32.

Jesus' departure and return to God the Father. Specifically, the Spirit is referred to as the Spirit of truth (14:17; 15:26; 16:13) and as the Holy Spirit (14:26; 20:22; cf. 1:33) as well as by the adumbration *paraklētos* or 'helping presence' (14:16, 26; 15:26; 16:7).

Significantly, reference to the Spirit is repeatedly part of a trinitarian pattern that presents God the Father, Jesus and the Spirit jointly (or in relationship to one another) at work in the lives of believers. Jesus' reference to the Spirit as 'another *paraklētos*' in 14:16, for example, indicates that the Spirit's presence with the disciples will replace Jesus' encouraging and strengthening presence with them while on earth (cf. 14:17). When the Spirit comes to dwell in believers, it is as if Jesus himself takes up residence in them (14:18). This relieves a primary concern for Jesus' first followers in the original setting of the farewell discourse: Jesus' departure will not leave them as orphans; just as God was with them through Jesus, he will continue to be with them through the Spirit. The Spirit's role thus ensures continuity between Jesus' pre- and post-glorification ministry.

Once sent by Jesus, the Spirit will have several important roles in the lives of believers. These include reminding them of all that Jesus taught his followers (14:26); bearing witness to Jesus together with believers (15:26); convicting the world of sin, (un)righteousness and judgment (16:8–11); and guiding believers in(to) all truth and revealing what is yet to come (16:13).

In all of these functions, the ministry of the Spirit remains closely linked with the person of Jesus. Just as Jesus is the Sent One who is fully dependent on and obedient to the Father, the Spirit is sent by both the Father and Jesus (14:26; 15:26) and focuses his teaching on illuminating the spiritual significance of God's work in Jesus (14:26; 15:26; 16:9).

Particularly significant for John's trinitarian mission theology is the final reference to the Spirit at Jesus' commissioning of his followers (20:21; cf. Matt. 28:18–20; Luke 24:46–49), which climaxes the characterization of Jesus as the sent Son. Here the disciples are shown to be drawn into the unity and mission of Father and Son. In a clear allusion to Genesis 2:7, where God breathes his Spirit into Adam at creation, constituting him as a living being, at his commissioning of his disciples Jesus constitutes them as the new messianic community in anticipation of the outpouring of the Spirit subsequent to his ascension (20:22).

Father, Son and Spirit: The three persons of the Godhead united in one mission

As mentioned in chapter 6 above, in his Gospel John presents the relationships between the Father, the Son and the Spirit with a view toward their role in salvation history. Thus it is always the Father who is the sender of the Son, never vice versa, and it is the Father and the Son sending the Spirit, never the Spirit sending the Father or the Son. The sending of the Spirit, in turn, occurs by salvation-historical necessity only after the Son's return to the Father. This shows that the roles exercised by the three persons of the Trinity are not interchangeable.

The two-part format of the Gospel with chapters 1–12 presenting the earthly mission of Jesus and chapters 13–21 anticipating the mission of the exalted Jesus subsequent to his departure back to his pre-existent heavenly glory also carries an important theological, trinitarian message. In the first part, Jesus is shown to claim a unique relationship, and, in fact, equality, with God (e.g. 5:18). The second part moves beyond the vindication of Jesus' claim through the resurrection and shows the unity of the triune Godhead in their mission to the world, extended through Jesus' followers (chs. 17; 20:21–22).

In this way, the Gospel's presentation of the Father as the one who sent Jesus as well as of John's Christology and pneumatology can be shown to issue ultimately in missiology. Thus, rightly understood, theologically speaking John's presentation of the Trinity is not a mere exercise in ontology as an end in itself but is made subservient to mission: the Spirit-enabled demonstration to the world that the Father sent the Son, offering the world forgiveness of sins and eternal life upon faith in the Messiah.

The Trinity and the church's mission

The study of the portrayal of the Father, the Son and the Spirit in John's Gospel has demonstrated that the three persons of the Godhead are involved in one great mission, the revelation of God to humanity and the redemption of humanity for God. Not only are the three persons of the Godhead united in this mission, the presentation of Father, Son and Spirit in John's Gospel (John's trinitarian theology) is clearly missiologically constrained. Rather than being one of several aspects or implications of John's trinitarian theology, mission was shown to be the nexus and focal point of John's presentation of the Father, the Son and the Spirit, individually and in relation to one another. Hence it can truly be said, not only that John's mission theology is trinitarian (which in and of itself is a very significant statement), but that his trinitarian teaching is part of his mission theology: a truly revolutionary insight.

The insight is revolutionary, because, if heeded, it calls the church to focus its major energies on *acting on and acting out her Lord's commission*, 'As the Father has sent me, I am sending you' (20:21), in the power of the Spirit, rather than merely engaging in the study of God or cultivating personal holiness (as important as this may be within the larger framework presented here). The insight is revolutionary also because a proper understanding of John's trinitarian mission theology ought to lead the church to *understand its mission in trinitarian terms*, that is, as originating in and initiated by the Father (the 'one who sent' Jesus), as redemptively grounded and divinely mediated by Jesus the Son (the 'Sent One' turned sender, 20:21), and as continued and empowered by the Spirit, the 'other helping presence', the Spirit of truth.

What is more, not only is John's mission theology trinitarian in nature; it is universal in scope. A comparison with Luke's two-volume work, the Gospel of Luke and the book of Acts, may prove instructive at this point. In essence, Luke, in his first volume, provides an account of the saving mission of Jesus culminating in his substitutionary cross-death and his resurrection. Yet, as Luke is careful to show, this is only the beginning. In his second volume, Luke consequently narrates the coming of the Spirit (in fulfilment of Jesus' promise; cf. Luke 24:48–49; Acts 1:4–5) and the church's Spirit-empowered witness 'to the ends of the earth' (Acts 1:8).

It is our contention that John's salvation-historical outlook is much the same as Luke's, but that John accomplishes in one volume what Luke does in two.[9] This lends John's Gospel a virtually unparalleled theological compactness and coherence. In John's presentation, the Son is the focal point of the *missio Dei* in that he is the sent Son from God the Father, himself God, who also, together with the Father, becomes the sender of the Holy Spirit, who thus empowers Jesus' followers for their universal witness. The universal scope of this witness is underscored by several means:

---

[9] Though note the elegant and skilful way in which Luke uses the ascension as a unifying theological and literary element between his two volumes: Luke 9:51; 24:50–51; Acts 1:9–11.

1. Believing in Jesus is made the sole requirement for inclusion in Jesus' new messianic community (1:12; 3:16; 20:30–31 *et passim*).[10]

2. The pattern of Jesus' mission is shown to anticipate the (through Acts) familiar pattern of the early church's mission, from Jerusalem and Judea (John 3) to Samaria (John 4:1–42) to the Gentile world (John 4:43–54).[11]

3. The division of John's Gospel into major halves, John 1 – 12 narrating Jesus' earthly mission to the Jews and John 13 – 21 presenting the exalted Jesus' mission to the world through his followers. While John 13 – 21 still takes place during the final days of Jesus' earthly mission, he is shown to anticipate the time subsequent to his 'departure' (one of the Johannine euphemisms for the crucifixion) in the farewell discourse and at the commissioning toward the end of the book.

4. The transcending of OT Israel's salvation-historical privilege (still acknowledged in 4:22) and the extension of the salvific scope of Jesus' mission to the Gentiles (cf. e.g. 4:34–38; 10:16; 11:51–52; 12:20–36; 15:8). By being the 'true vine' representing Israel (15:1), Jesus becomes the centre of God's salvific purposes and the channel through which salvation, subsequent to the cross and the resurrection, can be freely extended to 'whoever' believes in Jesus, the Christ, the Son of God, whether Jew or Gentile.

5. In this way, John manages at the same time to be true to the historical vantage point of his Gospel prior to Jesus' crucifixion, resurrection and ascension while at the same time showing the seeds and anticipatory signs of the universalization of the *missio Dei* in and through Jesus that would ensue subsequent to the cross and the sending of the Spirit, something that, of course, had long taken place by the time of writing of John's Gospel.

Coupled with the emphatic presentation of Jesus as sharing the identity of Yahweh, the one and only true God, the compelling message of John's Gospel is that there is no other god besides the One who is 'the way and the truth and the life', the one who unequivocally stated that 'no-one comes to the Father except through me' (14:6). John's Gospel thus follows Isaiah's teaching that because there is only one God there can be only one Saviour (Isa. 43:11; 45:21). Anyone, therefore, who has not believed in Jesus the Christ and Son of God

---

[10] See Croteau 2002.
[11] Cf. Köstenberger 2004c: 141.

must urgently be implored to place his or her faith in Jesus, for there is no other way of salvation, and God's wrath continues to rest on those who refuse to believe (3:36) and prefer their own moral darkness over the 'light of the world' (3:19–21). John (the Baptist's) witness still rings true today: 'Whoever believes in the Son has eternal life, but whoever rejects the Son will not see life, for God's wrath remains on him' (3:36; cf. 6–9, 1:15).

The question arises, then, 'How is the church to engage in its mission, particularly (for our present purposes) in Johannine terms?'[12] Several answers may be given.

1. *Mission is spiritual warfare.* As John makes clear, believers are not to 'engage' the world but rather must 'overcome' both the evil one (1 John 2:13–14) and the world (16:33; 1 John 4:4–5). Although the whole world lies under the power of the evil one (1 John 5:19), this world order is merely temporary and will pass away (1 John 2:17). It is already 'the last hour' (1 John 2:18). Judgment upon the spirit of the antichrist, who is at work in false teachers, has already been secured (12:31; 1 John 2:18; 4:1–6; 2 John 7; cf. Rev. 12).

Believers' victory in this spiritual contest is assured because Jesus 'the true light' has overcome the darkness and opposition of the world (1:9; 1 John 2:8) through his death on the cross (12:31; 16:33) and through his resurrection on 'the first day of the week' (20:1), the day that now marks the dawn of the new creation. Believers, by virtue of their spiritual birth, have thus become 'sons of light' (12:36) and heirs of the promise that 'everyone born of God overcomes the world' (1 John 5:4; cf. 1 John 2:12–14). Consequently, as they pursue their mission (which is really the exalted Jesus' mission carried on under the auspices of the Holy Spirit [John 14:15–18; 15:26–27; cf. Matt. 28:20; Acts 1:1]), believers must be mindful that they are children of God who are born of God (John 1:12–3; 3:3, 5; 8:31–59; 11:52; 1 John 3:1–2, 9–10; 4:4, 6; 5:18–19); that they possess the Holy Spirit (1 John 2:20, 27); that their sins have been forgiven in Christ (John 20:22; 1 John 1:9; 2:1); and that they have eternal life and their salvation is eternally secure (John 3:16–17; 5:24; 20:30–31 etc.; 1 John 5:11–12).

Moreover, as they proclaim God's love for the unbelieving world in Christ (John 3:16), believers must not love 'the world' as a domain

---

[12] Some of the following material is adapted from Köstenberger 1995a: 124–127. See also on 128–136 the comments on the missiological import of the book of Revelation.

currently controlled by Satan (1 John 2:15–17; 5:19). They also must keep themselves from idols (1 John 5:21).[13]

2. *Mission aims at the redemption of creation.* As the preceding point suggests, the church's spiritual conflict is not with creation per se, but with 'the prince of this world' (12:31; 14:30; 16:11) and his anti-trinitarian system (16:1–3; 1 John 2:22) that tyrannizes the world through 'the lust of the flesh, and the lust of the eyes, and the pride of life' (1 John 2:16 AV; cf. 1 John 3:8b). Creation itself is the object of the triune mission of salvation (3:16–17; 12:47; 1 John 4:14). The Father sent his Son because he loved the world that he had made (1:3, 10; 3:16).[14] He gave his Son 'authority over all people [lit. "flesh"]' (17:2) because he wished to redeem the fallen, physical creation from its bondage to darkness and death into the light and life of the trinitarian kingdom (1:5; 5:21–29; 10:10; 17:3; cf. Rev. 11:15).[15] Even in his dying hour, Jesus displays his concern to preserve the orders of creation as he commits his mother to the care of her new son, the Beloved Disciple (19:26–27; cf. 1 Tim. 5:8). The point to be emphasized is this: John is no proto-Gnostic who lacks concern for things like 'flesh' and 'family'. He is instead 'a theologian of creation';[16] better: a theologian of the trinitarian renewal of creation. The church's mission should reflect this concern as well.[17]

3. *Mission proceeds in word and deed.* In the light of the preceding discussion, the church's missionary proclamation must be characterized, first, by the announcement that Jesus, the eternal Son of the Father, has come in the flesh (1:14; 1 John 1:7; 4:2; 2 John 7). The Son did not assume a mere phantom spiritual existence as the Docetists held. God's Son became flesh to redeem and renew God's fallen creation through the power of the Holy Spirit. The church's missionary proclamation must, second, include the good news that Jesus made atonement for the sins of 'the whole world' (1 John 2:2; cf. 1 John 4:10). Contrary to those who conceived of religious experience merely in terms of esoteric divine revelation, the assertions of Christ's full

---

[13] For further development of John's 'mission as warfare' theme, see Rev. 7. See also Bauckham's discussion of this theme in the book of Revelation in 1993: 66–108; and the study by Bandy 2007.

[14] Carson classifies this love as 'God's salvific stance towards his fallen world' in distinction from 'God's particular, effective, selecting love toward his elect'. See Carson 2000: 17–18.

[15] Indeed, as is commonly noted, 'life' signifies for John what the Synoptic Gospels refer to as 'the kingdom'.

[16] N. T. Wright 2003: 667.

[17] For further reflections on this theme, see C. J. H. Wright 2006, esp. part 4.

humanity and his sacrificial atonement provide an effective counter to the notion that the gospel might merely mediate a higher knowledge of the divine or a more profound spiritual union with God. The gospel concerns God's plan to deal with sin, the world's deepest problem, by providing salvation and forgiveness through his Son's propitiatory death (cf. John 20:23; 1 John 1:9; 2:1). The assertions of Christ's full humanity and sacrificial atonement also reinforce the previous point, that the triune mission field is not simply the renewed intellect or the sanctified heart but is instead the entire cosmos (3:16; 17:2). According to John, the scope of creation and redemption is the same: '*all things*' (1:3; 3:35). A fully fledged, trinitarian theology of creation and redemption, centred in the incarnate Son's saving mission, is thus indispensable to the church's faithful proclamation of the gospel.

According to John, God's love is to be proclaimed not only in word but also in *deed*. Following a more general Johannine pattern, John's teaching regarding deeds of mercy focuses almost exclusively on believers' love for fellow-believers (see 1 John 3:16–18).[18] This focus has an important missional dimension of its own. Jesus promises that, as believers learn to share the sacrificial love of God with one another, the world will come to know that the Father sent the Son (13:35; 17:21, 23).[19] Nevertheless, the impetus of John 20:21, built as it is upon the analogy of Jesus' mission from the Father, must include loving 'the world' through deeds of mercy as well (cf. 3:16). Action in the face of neighbourly need, whether that neighbour lies in or outside the household of faith, is one of the true marks of God's indwelling love (1 John 3:16–18; cf. Luke 10:25–37). The rest of the NT confirms this teaching (e.g. Matt. 5:43–47; Rom. 12:17–21; 1 Pet. 3:9–12).[20]

4. *The shape of Jesus' mission determines the shape of the church's mission.* Because the church's mission is an extension and continuation of Jesus' mission, the particular shape of Jesus' mission is relevant to the present discussion. The first aspect of Jesus' mission, that he is sent *from* the Father *to* the world, teaches us that there is a *centrifugal* dimension to mission. The church's mission proceeds *from*

---

[18] Carson (2002: 58–64) provides a very helpful discussion of the Johannine focus upon believers' love for fellow-believers.

[19] Consider the powerful gospel witness of the Anglican Church of Rwanda, where families of those murdered in that country's terrible genocide sit reconciled in the same pews with many of the murderers.

[20] See Carson 2002: 46–57.

the sending Son *to* the world in the power of the Spirit. The second aspect of Jesus' mission, Jesus' role as the eschatological shepherd-teacher, teaches us that there is a *centripetal* dimension to mission. Jesus gathers his sheep *from* the world *into* his fold through the witness of his Spirit-empowered church (cf. 6:35–65). The third aspect of Jesus' mission, that he comes into the world and returns to the Father (descent–ascent), emphasizes the transcendent origin and power of the church's mission. Whereas the first two aspects of Jesus' mission find analogies in the church's mission, the last aspect does not. This reminds us that the church's mission to spread the gospel to the ends of the earth and to draw all peoples into the triune fellowship is wholly dependent upon the unique mission of the Son who descended to die and ascended to reign that he might baptize his people with the Holy Spirit (1:33).

Keeping all three aspects of Jesus' mission in mind will protect the church from various forms of reductionism with respect to its missionary endeavour. First, the community that focuses too exclusively on the centrifugal dimension of mission and ignores the centripetal dimension, which includes building a community characterized by worship, sound doctrine and loving fellowship, will not ultimately have an alternative way of life to offer the world (cf. 13:35). Second, the community that focuses too exclusively on the centripetal dimension of mission at the expense of the centrifugal dimension, which includes John's expansive trinitarian vision for the transformation of the entire cosmos, will eventually domesticate the gospel to the service of its own private or local ends. Third, the community that ceases, in both its centrifugal and centripetal dimensions, to depend wholly upon the spiritual power of the incarnate and ascended Son will quickly become a community that, when it comes to matters of eternal consequence, 'can do nothing' (15:5). Jesus gave his disciples spiritual authority to execute their mission (20:22), thereby authorizing them to forgive and retain sins (20:23), shepherd Christ's flock (21:15–17) and bear witness to his person and work (20:21). The church thus continues the apostolic mission through analogous activities[21] under the power of the same Spirit, not that of the

---

[21] The church's mission is only 'analogous' to that of the apostles because the apostolic mission was in many ways unique and foundational. Consider Bauckham's comments on the missions of Peter and the Beloved Disciple according to John 21:15–25: 'Although both can serve from time to time in the narrative as representative disciples, models for all Christians, the overwhelming emphasis is on the special roles which their personal discipleship of Jesus enables them to play in the church. In the Beloved Disciple's case, this is his witness as author of the Gospel' (2006: 400).

sword.[22] This does not limit the scope of the church's mission,[23] which is universal, but it does limit the means of the church's mission, which are spiritual.

5. *Pneumatology must not override Christology in the church's missiology.* In its effort to remain faithful to the full, trinitarian thrust of the Bible's (including John's) teaching on its mission as an extension of the *missio Dei* consisting of Father, Son and Spirit, properly related, the church must take care to maintain a proper understanding of the *taxis* (order) and intra-trinitarian balance between the persons of the Godhead. That is, God the Father must be understood as the Creator and sovereign Ruler of the universe, who in his love initiated the Son's redemptive mission, a mission carried out by the Son in his perfect obedience and continued in the sending and witnessing activity of the Spirit.

Some, such as the Pentecostal theologian Amos Yong, have problematically elevated pneumatology over Christology.[24] In the conviction that the inclusion of the *filioque* clause[25] in the Nicene Creed has caused the Western Church to unduly subordinate the Spirit to the Son, Yong contends that a diminishment of the Spirit has improperly weakened the recognition of the Spirit's work in non-Christian faiths. Invoking Irenaeus' metaphorical depiction of the Son and the Spirit as the two hands of the Father, Yong sets out to explore how the Spirit's 'hand' might be discerned in non-Christian religions.

How, then, is one to discern this movement of the Spirit? According to Yong, this is to be done on the basis of a threefold criterion: discerning divine presence, divine absence and divine activity. Yet as writings such as John's Gospel or 1 John, to go no further, make clear (e.g. John 14:6; 1 John 4:1–3), it is only Christology that provides a proper criterion for evaluating proper truth claims. Jesus is 'the truth' (14:6). The Holy Spirit is the Spirit '*of* truth', the one who bears witness to

---

[22] Cf. Jesus' encounter with Pilate in 18:33–38. Jesus' point is not so much that his kingdom is *located* in heaven and not upon the earth (cf. 17:2) but that his kingdom *originates* from heaven ('My kingdom is not *of* this world') and therefore that his kingdom does not operate according to the ways of the world (cf. 2 Cor. 10:4–5). See Ridderbos 1997: 594–595.

[23] On the Gospel's relationship to 'spiritual' and 'political' spheres, together with implications for the church's mission, see the illuminating discussion of O'Donovan 1996: 82–119, 211–242.

[24] See the helpful and appropriately critical reviews by Tennent 2003, 2004; and Womack (with Horrell) 2005.

[25] We will discuss the 'dual procession' of the Holy Spirit in the next chapter.

and confirms the truth of Jesus (16:13–15). Indeed, the Spirit has no other message (cf. Gal. 1:6–9; 3:2, 5–6).

For this reason it is inadequate, even fallacious, for Yong to demand that the particularity of the 'Word made flesh' in Jesus (John 1:14) be balanced by the universality of the 'Spirit poured out on all flesh' per Acts 2:17, for this dichotomous way of putting things wrongly severs the salvation-historical connection between the Spirit being given on the basis, and only on the basis, of Jesus dying on the cross and rising from the dead (as is the thrust of Peter's message at Pentecost; Acts 2). As Vanhoozer states, 'The Spirit may blow where, but not *what*, he wills.'[26] Without a particular, crucified and risen Jesus, there is no outpouring of the Spirit, and as the book of Acts makes clear, reception of the Spirit was contingent on reception of the saving message of the crucifixion and resurrection of Jesus Christ. In fact, as John states, 'the world cannot accept' the Spirit (John 14:17), and 'every spirit that does not acknowledge Jesus is not from God' (1 John 4:3).

In the end, Yong does not advance 'beyond the impasse' between exclusivist, inclusivist and pluralist paradigms but himself remains firmly as holding an inclusivist perspective. His work serves as an important reminder that the church's missiological thinking must be deeply grounded in a careful understanding of the trinitarian teaching of Scripture. This means more than merely to affirm that there are three persons in the Godhead; it also entails apprehending the intra-trinitarian relationships in proper balance to each other, so that one person of the Godhead (in Yong's case, the Spirit) is not unduly pitted against, and elevated over, the other.[27] If so, the results can be disastrous and heretical in that they rob Jesus of his glory as the Father's 'one-of-a-kind Son' apart from whom no one comes to the Father (1:14, 18; 3:16, 18; 14:6).

6. *The Triune God is the Alpha and the Omega of the church's mission.* Just as the triune mission flows from the triune love (3:16–17), so every missional manifestation of the church's love for the world emerges from the 'deeper, more fundamental reality' of God's

[26] Vanhoozer 2002: 233. Cf. Yong 2003: 192.

[27] As Chandler (2005: 195) rightly notes, Scripture 'does not subordinate the Son's mission to that of the Spirit but, instead, gives the Spirit to the world in order that the Father and Son might be glorified and may be made known (John 15:26)'. Chandler also observes, correctly in our opinion, that Yong's proposal lacks adequate criteria for distinguishing between the Holy Spirit and the work of demons in non-Christian religions (ibid.).

love (cf. 1 John 4:7–21).[28] In order to accomplish their mission, Christians must therefore continue to grow in their knowledge, trust and adoration of the triune God. 'Love comes from God' (1 John 4:7) and only those who abide in the love of the triune God will be able to take his love to the world.

The church's mission not only flows from and through the love of the triune God; it also flows *to* the love of the triune God. The Father, after all, seeks *worshippers* (4:23). The Father sent the Son to make his great and holy name known to his people (1:18; 17:6). The church's mission therefore ultimately consists in reaping a worldwide harvest of worshippers (4:35–38) gathered by the Son, through the Spirit, to serve and adore the 'Holy Father' (17:11; cf. Isa. 6:3; 66:19–21; Rev. 22:3–4).

One day the church's mission will be consummated in trinitarian worship (Rev. 22:1–5). This means that, even now, as the church engages in the worship of the Holy Trinity, she engages not simply in the *means* of her mission, but in the very *end* of her mission: the *gloria Dei*.[29]

Conclusion

As we have sought to demonstrate in this chapter, John's trinitarian teaching has not merely important theological implications; it also has great practical relevance for the way in which the church goes about fulfilling its missionary task. Belief in the Trinity is not merely needed on the intellectual, cognitive level as part of subscribing to an orthodox Christian creed; it is that very triune God who is rightly the ground, energizing force, and goal undergirding the Christian mission. The love and power of the triune God at once send us out and draw us in. Perhaps it is at the end of this volume on the Trinity and John's Gospel that we are able to read the concluding commissioning statement in John's Gospel within its proper, full trinitarian, context encapsulating the Johannine mission theology: 'As the Father has sent me, I am sending you. . . . Receive the Holy Spirit.'

---

[28] Carson 2000: 39.
[29] For further reflections on the 'means' and 'end' of the church's mission, see Piper 2003: 17–43, esp. 21–22.

Chapter Ten

The Trinity and John's Gospel

Introduction

The Trinity is the Alpha and Omega of John's Gospel. John's account of Jesus' identity and mission is literally trinitarian from beginning to end. The Trinity explains how the world began (1:1–3), where the (redeemed) world is heading (17:24–26) and how it will get there (3:16–17; 20:21–23 etc.). Nowhere is John's breathtaking trinitarian vision more pronounced than in chapter 17, Jesus' 'high-priestly prayer'.[1] Indeed, according to Walter Kasper, 'The high-priestly prayer contains the entire doctrine of the Trinity in basic form and in a nutshell.'[2]

Taking Kasper's statement as our cue, the purpose of the present chapter is to provide a summary of John's trinitarian vision, allowing his own synopsis of that vision in Jesus' high-priestly prayer to control our discussion. Such a summary will provide not only a helpful recapitulation of many of the Johannine issues and themes discussed to this point; it will also allow John to speak to a host of perennial issues related to the church's trinitarian confession. Our conviction is that John's is an abiding, ever fresh witness to the reality of the triune God,[3] a witness by which the incarnate Word himself continually enables the church to know and enjoy the Father by the Spirit. The church's trinitarian reflection thus proceeds under the promise of John 17:26, 'I have made you known to them, and will continue to make you known in order that the love you have for me may be in them and that I myself may be in them.'

---

[1] Although the label 'high-priestly prayer' does not adequately capture John's presentation here (see Köstenberger 2004c: 482, n. 1), we retain the familiar label for the sake of identification.

[2] Kasper 1984: 303. Cf. Lincoln 2005: 440.

[3] On this point, see Vanhoozer 2002: 257–274; and Bauckham 2006: 367–368; see also 387–388, 396–402.

John 17: Jesus' high-priestly prayer

Many proposals have been made regarding the structure of Jesus' prayer in John 17.[4] The most sober of these structures the prayer according to Jesus' three overarching petitions: *verses 1–5*, where Jesus prays for himself; *verses 6–19*, where Jesus prays for his disciples; and *verses 20–26*, where Jesus prays for those who will believe through the disciples' testimony.[5] As we will discover, this structure 'plots',[6] in seminal form, three great moments of redemptive history. According to this scheme, redemptive history *begins* 'before the world began' in the intra-trinitarian plan, a plan concerning the Son's descent from and ascent to the Father (17:1–5); *continues* through the apostolic mission as the Father 'keeps' and 'sanctifies' the apostles in the truth revealed to them by the Son (17:6–19); and reaches its *consummation* as those who receive the apostolic message come to participate in the eternal, glorious love of the Father for the Son (17:20–26).

This redemptive-historical plot unfolds according to the logic of a great chain of 'gifting'. The Father has 'given'[7] the Son 'authority over all flesh' (17:2 ESV); a people 'out of the world' (17:2, 6, 9, 24); a 'work' to do on earth (17:4); 'everything' (17:7); his 'words' (17:8); his 'name' (17:11, 12); and 'glory' (17:22, 24; cf. 1–5). Moreover, the Father has gifted the Son that the Son might in turn 'give' to his disciples and his church 'eternal life' (17:2); his Father's 'words'/'word' (17:8, 14); and, ultimately, a participation in his own 'glory' (17:22, 24). According to John, redemptive history is the unfolding story of 'the gifting God',[8] Father, Son and Holy Spirit.[9]

One further feature should be noted by way of introduction. Jesus' ministry up to this point has been characterized by prayer. In chapter 11, as Jesus approaches Lazarus' mourners, he is 'deeply moved in spirit and troubled' (11:33, 38). He reassures Mary that she will see

---

[4] See Köstenberger 2004c: 483, n. 7; see also Ridderbos's comments regarding structure (1997: 547).

[5] Carson 1991: 553.

[6] Jesus' prayer 'plots' redemptive history in two senses. It reveals the intra-trinitarian plan of redemption, 'plotted' in eternity past and played out in history. But it also 'plots' the story of redemptive history, which has, as every story must, a beginning, middle and end.

[7] In each instance, John uses some form of the verb *didōmi*, which means 'to give, to bestow, or to grant'.

[8] This is the title of Webb 1996.

[9] That this chain of gifting is indeed *tri*une, involving Father, Son *and* Holy Spirit, we hope to demonstrate shortly.

'the glory of God' (11:40), then lifts up his eyes and prays, 'Father, I thank you that you have heard me. I knew that you always hear me, but I said this for the benefit of the people standing here, that they may believe that you sent me' (11:41–42). Later, as the hour of his crucifixion draws near, Jesus is again 'troubled' (12:27), and once again he prays. Having asked, 'What shall I say? "Father, save me from this hour"?', Jesus replies, 'No, it was for this very reason I came to this hour.' Father, glorify your name!' (12:27–28). The Father responds, promising to do so (12:28). Jesus then adds, 'This voice was for your benefit, not mine' (12:30).

Several elements common to these earlier petitions appear in Jesus' high-priestly prayer. First, Jesus' prayer reaches its greatest intensity as he faces the 'hour' for which he was sent (12:27; so 17:1).[10] Second, Jesus uses his characteristic address 'Father' when calling upon God (11:41; 12:27–28; so 17:1, 5, 11, 21, 24, 25). When Jesus cries out to the Father from the depths of his human experience (see 11:33, 35, 38; 12:27), he does so as the Father's 'only Son' (1:14). With the very human Jesus at prayer, we are nevertheless dealing with the intra-trinitarian communion and communication of God. Third, Jesus' prayer concerns the mutual glorification of the Father and the Son (11:40; 12:28; so 17:1, 4, 5, 10, 22, 24). Fourth, and related to the previous point, Jesus asks in John 11:42 that the result of his prayer will be that the crowds 'believe that you sent me' (so 17:3, 8, 18, 21, 23, 25). Fifth, Jesus characteristically prays not for his benefit, but for the benefit of others (11:42; 12:30; so 17:9, 19, 20–26).

As the sent Son approaches the moment when his mission will be accomplished, when the misery of his fleshly existence (cf. 1:14) will reach its highest pitch, he draws upon his special relationship to the Father, together with all the rights and powers this relationship entails. Even to the depths of Jesus' human misery, we are dealing with the person and work of 'the only Son from the Father' (1:14 ESV). Even to the depths of his human misery, Jesus' constant concern for the benefit of his people reveals the glorious 'fullness' of his filial 'grace' (1:16).

Verses 1–5

In the first part of his prayer, Jesus prays for his eschatological glorification (17:1). As his Father's true Son and Servant (3:14; 8:28;

---

[10] Jesus' awareness of the approaching 'hour' is evident in ch. 11 as well (see 11:9: 'Are there not twelve hours of daylight?'). The raising of Lazarus represents Jesus' last public sign before his crucifixion.

12:32),[11] Jesus approaches 'the hour' (17:1) that marks the completion of the 'work' given to him by the Father (17:4),[12] a work that includes revealing the Father's 'name' to his disciples (17:6) and dedicating himself as a sacrifice (17:19).[13] As a consequence of his completed earthly mission, Jesus asks for divine vindication: 'glorify me' (17:5).[14]

Jesus' request for vindication is 'not an end in itself'.[15] He prays, 'Glorify your Son, *that your Son may glorify you*' (17:1). In seeking the Father's glory as the chief end of his prayer, Jesus expresses the ultimate purpose of his vocation as God's true Servant: the Servant is the one in whom Yahweh 'will be glorified' (Isa. 49:3 ESV). The nature of this glorification transcends that of any ordinary servant, however.[16] Jesus prays that the eschatological glorification of the Son by the Father and of the Father by the Son will match the protological glory he enjoyed in the Father's presence 'before the world began' (17:5).[17] This is the prayer of the eternal Son of God who came from God and is now returning to God (16:28).

Jesus refers to his pretemporal fellowship with the Father not only as the standard for the eschatological glory he requests, but also grounds his request for glorification in something given to him by the Father before the creation of the world: 'glorify your Son . . . *just as*[18] you have given him authority over all flesh' (17:1–2 ESV altered; cf. Eph. 1:4). Jesus' request for glory *now* is somehow in keeping with the authority given to him by the Father *in eternity*.[19]

---

[11] On the connection between Jesus' being 'lifted up' and his role as Isaiah's Servant, see Bauckham 1998a: 63–68; see also the discussion in chapter 7 above.

[12] For this proleptic interpretation of 17:4, see Carson 1991: 556–557; and Köstenberger 2004c: 489.

[13] As Chennattu (2006: 133–134) observes, 'to sanctify' in the LXX means to '"set apart" a person for a sacred duty and is thus used for the consecration of priests (e.g. Aaron and his sons, Exod 28:41)'. It also means '"to dedicate as a sacrifice" (Exod 13:2; Deut 15:19)'. Christ's earthly work includes both making and being a priestly offering for sin. He is, after all, 'the Lamb of God' (1:29, 36).

[14] Significantly, Isaiah's Servant is promised exaltation as a consequence of his faithful, suffering service. See Isa. 49:5–12; 52:13.

[15] Carson 1991: 554.

[16] Cf. Isa. 52:13 in the light of Isa. 6:1.

[17] Gruenler 1986: 124.

[18] For this interpretation, see Carson 1991: 554–555.

[19] Thus Morris 1995: 636; Carson 1991: 555. Ridderbos states, 'It is in the function and power of the figure of the eschatological Son of man that the Son of God came down from heaven, in order thus (cf. 3:13), from heaven, to exercise that power in an unrestricted sense (cf. 7:39), an exercise to which he was predestined by the Father and for which he now prays' (1997: 548).

Previously in the Gospel, Jesus has traced the origin of his mission to the Father's eternal 'sanctifying' and 'sending' activity, describing himself as 'the one whom the Father set apart as his very own and sent into the world' (10:36).[20] He is the Word of God, who was with God 'in the beginning' (1:1), and who was sent from 'the Father's side' (1:18) 'into the world' (1:9). Jesus now describes the origin of this mission in terms of an 'eternal grant' given to him by the Father,[21] specifically, a grant to exercise authority over all flesh 'with the express purpose of conferring eternal life'[22] upon all that the Father has given him (17:2).[23]

Jesus thus grounds his prayer for glorification in what Reformed dogmatics calls the *pactum salutis*.[24] Briefly stated,[25] the *pactum salutis* concerns the saving mission given by the Father to the Son before the foundation of the world, a mission in which the Son acts representatively on behalf of those the Father has given him, together with the Father's promise that the Son will be gloriously vindicated upon the completion of his mission.[26] Jesus now petitions the Father to glorify him because he believes the Father is 'true' (3:33) and 'righteous' (17:25). He believes that the Father will keep his promise to glorify the Son (cf. 12:28) because the Son has fully and faithfully accomplished on earth the mission given to him by the Father before the world began (17:2, 4; cf. 19:30).

Karl Barth regards the *pactum salutis* as 'mythology',[27] but it may not be easily dismissed. Indeed, the elements of this doctrine, properly understood, are present both implicitly and explicitly in Jesus' high-priestly prayer and elsewhere in John's Gospel: the Son comes into the world on a mission he received from the Father 'before'[28] he came into the world (3:19; 6:38; 10:36; 17:2, 4 etc.); the Son acts representatively on behalf of the people given him by the Father (10:11;

---

[20] See earlier comments on the meaning of the verb 'to sanctify' as 'consecration to a sacred duty'.

[21] Carson 1991: 554–555.

[22] Morris 1995: 636.

[23] For a discussion of election in John's Gospel, see Yarbrough 1995.

[24] This relationship is also called 'the Covenant of Redemption'.

[25] For standard treatments of this notion, see Witsius 1990 (1822): 165–280; and Bavinck 2006 (1906–11): 212–216. See also Muller 2003: 266–267.

[26] For a critique of more speculative, less exegetically defensible, formulations of the *pactum salutis* plus a summary of the doctrine that parallels the one provided here, see Bavinck 2006 (1906–11): 213–214. We will discuss the Spirit's role in the covenant of redemption later.

[27] See Barth *CD* IV/1: 65–66.

[28] See below on what *pretemporal* might mean.

15:1–17; 17:1–26 etc.);[29] the Son has received from the Father the promise of eschatological glory and vindication upon the completion of his mission (1:33; 12:28; 17:2–5, 24–26 etc.).[30] Moreover, while the doctrine is sometimes regarded as overly speculative, it does not assume humanity's capacity to rend the veil of time and history so that we might perceive the eternal, hidden counsels of God. It assumes only that the one who makes petitions to the Father in John 17 is none other than the Son of God incarnate,[31] and that everything he does is a true revelation of the life of love, promise and fidelity he eternally shares with the Father in the Spirit. It only assumes that John's Gospel narrates 'the interior life of the triune God visible (to the eyes of faith) in our history'.[32]

In other words, the *pactum salutis* teaches us that the story which unfolds on the stage of history is the story of an intra-trinitarian fellowship of salvation, a fellowship that reaches back 'before the world began' (17:5) and that continues even to 'the hour' of Jesus' cross, resurrection and ascension (17:1). In this regard, the claim that the *pactum salutis* is eternal is not so much a claim about 'eternity past'[33]

---

[29] Consider also John's characterization of Jesus as 'Servant' and 'Son of Man' (on the lips of Jesus). Both are *representative* roles. See chapter 7 above.

[30] It should be noted here that the Son's promised glorification *includes* the successful mission of his disciples (17:16–19) and the future enjoyment of his glory by the church (17:20–26). His glorification as representative is full of promise for his people as well (13:36; 14:1–3).

[31] Barth's ultimate objection to the *pactum salutis* (see *CD* IV/1: 66) is that it abstracts the covenant from the historical God–human relationship. But this objection, too, is ultimately unfounded. Though it is true that the covenant grant is given to the Son before the foundation of the world (17:2), it is not given without reference to his fully human incarnation, ministry, death, resurrection and ascension. Rather, it is given to the Son *as* the one who will become incarnate to represent his people as the Suffering Servant and who will consequently be exalted with 'all authority' (Matt. 28:18) as the Son of Man. Moreover, while the covenant originates before the foundation of the world, its fulfilment occurs only *upon* the Son's completion of his very human work in history on behalf of his disciples and the church (17:4). In other words, the *pactum salutis* concerns the Son *incarnate*, both prospectively (before the foundation of the world) and actually (in history). From the depths of the intra-trinitarian counsel, therefore, we are dealing only with the God 'who wills to be the God of man and to make man and have man as his man' (Barth *CD* IV/1: 66).

[32] McCabe 1987: 51. McCabe's statement concerns the whole Bible. But it is especially apt as a description of John's Gospel.

[33] 'Eternity past' is an infelicitous phrase to describe the way in which the eternal Trinity 'precedes' the creation of the world and redemptive history (see Helm 1997: 31–32). Eternity is not a time before time, for time itself is a creature (cf. 1:3). Eternity is the way the one who created and governs time *is* (cf. 8:58). In this regard, it is probably best to say that the *pactum salutis* 'precedes' history, not by coming 'before' history temporally, but by coming 'before' history as the intra-trinitarian plan of the God who is the author, governor and consummator of that history and who, as such, is present

as about eternal *persons*,[34] persons whose fellowship remains unbroken throughout the course of redemption and thus guarantees that redemption,[35] which leads to our next point.

Jesus is granted authority that he might give 'eternal life' to God's people (17:2).[36] The substance of this gift consists in knowing 'the only true God' and 'Jesus Christ' whom he has 'sent' (17:3).

The greatest privilege of the New Covenant as of the Old is a knowledge of the one true God (cf. 4:22; also Deut. 4:32–35). Here John's monotheism shines at its brightest. Moreover, John's monotheism once again reveals itself to be a fully *trinitarian* monotheism. Knowledge of 'the only true God' comes through and with the knowledge of the Messiah he has 'sent'.[37] As we have seen throughout John's Gospel, knowledge of the Father who sends is intrinsically tied to knowledge of the Son who is sent (see 4:43; 5:36–37; 6:38–39, 44, 57; 7:28–29; 8:16, 18, 26 etc.). One cannot know or honour the Father apart from knowing and honouring the Son (1:18; 5:23; 1 John 2:22–24; 2 John 1:9). One therefore cannot enjoy the eternal life granted by the Father unless one knows the sent Son, the Son who shares the Father's self-existent life (17:3; cf. 5:24, 26–29; cf. 1 John 1:1–3).[38]

Here we may recall a point made in the previous chapter on mission. John's doctrine of the Trinity is in a very real sense a function of his doctrine of mission. It is in the Father's sending of the Son (as well as in the Father and the Son's sending of the Spirit) that the three persons of the Godhead are revealed in their personal distinctions and unified purpose. We have also seen that there is a theological reason why John's trinitarian theology is embedded in his theology of mission: John no doubt wishes to provide a trinitarian

---

to history as its Lord and sustainer and who enters *into* history as the Word made flesh. Understood in this sense, the *pactum salutis* concerns the intra-trinitarian fellowship that founds, governs and consummates history. For further reflections on the relationship between a timeless Trinity and the incarnation, see McCabe 1987: 48–51; and Helm 1997:45–46.

[34] Vos 1980a: 251.

[35] Bavinck 2006 (1906–11): 215.

[36] Morris 1995: 636.

[37] According to John, the knowledge of the Father through the Son is accompanied and enabled by the Spirit. The Spirit first appears at the Son's public 'revelation' to Israel (1:31–34) and continues to reveal to the disciples and the church all that the Father has made known through the Son (16:12–15).

[38] This principle is enunciated in both 'the Johannine thunderbolt' (see chapter 4 above) of the Synoptics (e.g. Matt. 11:27; Luke 10:22) as well as in the church's dogmatic tradition (e.g. the *Symbolum quicunque*).

warrant, model and means for the apostolic mission (thus 17:18; 20:21), a mission that continues in the church.

There are at least two further reasons why Trinity and mission are so closely related in John, reasons picked up in the Augustinian tradition of reflection upon the Trinity.[39] First, it is precisely the two sendings (of the Son by the Father, and of the Spirit by the Father and the Son) that reveal the fact that within the unity of the one God there are indeed three distinct persons. In other words, the fact that Jesus Christ is the sent one reveals something about the identity of 'the only true God' (17:3). The logic of this principle is as follows: 'Sending is not a reflexive act';[40] a person cannot send himself or herself. Therefore, because the Father sends the Son, we must distinguish the Father from the Son personally.[41] Moreover, because the Spirit is sent by the Father and the Son, he too must be personally distinct from the Father and the Son. The triune *missions* presuppose and reveal the triune *persons*.

Second, the triune missions reveal not only *that* there are three distinct persons; they also reveal *how* those three distinct persons relate to one another *as persons*. John's Gospel does not recount the generic 'sendings' of 'persons' but instead tells the story of *the Father's* sending, commanding and authorizing of *his Son*, of the Son's coming, obeying and executing his Father's will, and of *the Spirit of the Father who descends and rests upon the Son* that he might ultimately be sent by the Father and the Son to indwell God's children. In other words, the missions reveal the *sorts* of persons that subsist in the one God: Father, Son and Holy Spirit.

Read in the context of the Gospel as a whole, John 17:3 therefore suggests an important principle concerning the relationship between the triune mission and the triune identity. We will have opportunity later to apply this principle to certain perennial issues in trinitarian theology. For now, the principle may be stated as follows: *the triune God is characteristically himself in his saving missions because the reliable revelation of his true identity is internal to those saving missions.*[42] If the goal of sending Son and Spirit is to tell the story of who God truly is

---

[39] See Augustine's foundational discussion of this principle in *Trin.* 152–177.

[40] B. D. Marshall 2000: 39.

[41] Ibid. 38–40.

[42] As Moltmann states, 'God cannot contradict himself. . . . If God cannot contradict himself, then he remains true to himself precisely and especially in his economy of salvation, *for it is that which reveals him himself, and offers access to him*' (Moltmann 1981: 166; italics added). See also Barth *CD* I/1: 479.

(1:18; 16:14–15),[43] then for the missions *not* to reveal the triune identity reliably would constitute the *failure* of those missions. Put differently, while the *opera Dei ad intra* (e.g. 1:1) are one thing and the *opera Dei ad extra* (e.g. 1:14) are another, there is only one way that Father, Son and Holy Spirit relate to each other *ad intra* and *ad extra*.[44] That 'way' has been revealed in the story of Jesus Christ, the incarnate and anointed Son of God (1:18; 14:6; cf. Exod. 33:13; 34:5–7).

Verses 6–19

Having prayed for his own glorification in view of his completed mission, Jesus then prays that the Father will keep and consecrate his disciples in their mission. As with the first petition, Jesus grounds the second petition in the fact of his finished work. Jesus has revealed the Father's 'name' to those whom the Father gave him out of the world (17:6). As a result of this revealing work, the disciples have received the Father's word and have acknowledged Jesus' identity as the sent Son, the one who has received all things from his Father (17:7–8). Jesus therefore prays that the Father will 'keep' (ESV) the disciples in his name, the name revealed to them by Jesus (17:11, 15).

Jesus continues to develop the theme of the inter-relationship between the triune mission and the triune identity by means of a discussion of the Father's 'name' (17:6, 11, 12). In the OT, the 'name' of the Lord functions as a summary description of his person, character and reputation; it is a sign of the Lord's presence, encapsulating in itself his characteristic way of relating to the world and his people (Exod. 6:1–8; 34:5–7; 2 Sam. 22:50; 1 Kgs 3:2; Pss 8:1; 102:15; Ezek. 36:22 etc.).[45] This understanding of the name is certainly in view in Jesus' claim to have revealed the Father's name to his disciples. Jesus is the final exposition of God's character and the climactic embodiment of his presence (1:14–18).

In asking the Father to keep the disciples in his name (17:11), Jesus also draws upon another OT theme related to 'the name'. Because the name of the Lord represents God's identity as almighty sovereign of heaven and earth, that name is the source of security and protection for all who trust in it (Prov. 18:10; cf. Ps. 125) and the means whereby God's people may gain victory over their oppressors (Ps. 118:10–12). It is in this sense that Jesus prays 'protect them by the power of your name' (17:11).

---

[43] Moloney 2002; Stibbe 2006.
[44] Hart 2003: 159.
[45] Ross 1997: 147–151.

The name to which Jesus entrusts his disciples in his prayer is the same name by which he has protected the disciples throughout the course of his earthly ministry: 'While I was with them, I protected them and kept them safe by that name you gave me' (17:12). This is a striking claim. Jesus claims to have exercised during his earthly ministry the same divine sovereignty that he now petitions the Father to exercise after his departure from the world.[46] Once again, the sovereign power Jesus has exercised is a power he has *received* from the Father (cf. 5:19). Jesus bears the name of the Lord. But he bears it *as* the Son who has received his Father's name.[47]

Significantly, of all the things that the Son has received from the Father, things that he will in turn 'give' to the disciples, the 'name' is not one of them. Jesus 'reveals' the Father's name to the disciples (17:6). He does not 'give' it to them. The theological significance of this fact later comes to light in John's account of the resurrection. When the risen Jesus appears to his 'brothers', he gives them 'the right to become children of God' (1:12), announcing, 'I am returning to my Father and your Father, to my God and your God' (20:17). Jesus' Father has become their Father as a consequence of his saving work. Nevertheless, for all the analogy that exists between Jesus and his brothers, a profound difference remains. Jesus *alone* is worthy of the worship that accompanies the divine name. And so Thomas proclaims, 'My Lord and my God!' (20:28), a clear echo of the Shema (Deut. 6:4). Jesus is related to his disciples as their brother *and* as the Lord their God. His name he will not give to another (Isa. 42:8). He alone, with the Father, retains the glory of this singular name.

There is a profound trinitarian grammar at work here. The Father and the Son are clearly distinct persons. One gives; the other receives. Nevertheless, they share one divine name, one divine power and one divine identity (cf. Matt. 28:19; also John 10:30).[48]

---

[46] Gruenler 1986: 126.

[47] Whereas Jesus is said in Phil. 2:9 to receive the divine name upon his exaltation, John brings out the complementary point that Jesus *has* received the divine name from 'before the world began'.

[48] For a discussion of how this grammar works more broadly in the NT, see Yeago 1994; and Rowe 2002. 'Social trinitarian' interpretations like those of Gruenler (1986), Plantinga (1991) and, more recently, Horrell (2004) do not adequately account for John's strict monotheism, i.e., the substantial unity of the Godhead in being, will and action. As O'Collins states, 'A threefold subsistence does not entail three consciousnesses and three wills, as if three persons, each with their own separate characteristics, constituted a kind of divine committee. One consciousness subsists in a threefold way and is shared by all three persons, albeit by each of them distinctively . . . Unless we accept that all the divine essential or natural properties (like knowing, willing, and

Jesus does not 'give' the divine name to his disciples, but he does pray that they will participate in its pre-eminent attribute, namely unity. Jesus prays that the Father will keep the disciples in his name 'so that they may be one as we are one' (17:11; cf. 21–23). The chief predicate of the name of the Lord is its oneness: 'Hear, O Israel: the LORD our God, the LORD is one' (Deut. 6:4; cf. John 10:30). As we have already seen, Jesus is not praying that the disciples will become the Lord God. That name belongs only to Father, Son and Holy Spirit. In keeping with other Jewish writings (e.g. 2 Sam. 7:22–23) and the rest of the NT (e.g. 1 Cor. 12:13; Eph. 4:4–5),[49] Jesus is praying 'that his disciples might be a single community corresponding to the uniqueness of the one God, in which he and the Father are united'.[50]

However, the disciples' gift of unity will not go unthreatened, as Jesus' prayer for protection has already implied. The disciples, like Jesus, have been sent 'into the world' to accomplish a mission (17:18). In the course of fulfilling their mission, they can expect the world to treat them as it treated Jesus (15:18–21), for they, like Jesus, 'are not of the world' (17:14). It is for these reasons that Jesus prays, 'Holy Father, . . . protect them from the evil one' (17:11, 15), so that they might accomplish their mission.

Closely related to the preceding point is Jesus' prayer that his 'Holy Father' will 'sanctify' his disciples (17:17). In John's Gospel, mission and 'sanctification' are closely related.[51] Just as Jesus was 'sanctified' by the Father and sent into the world (10:36 AV), so, too, the disciples have been sanctified and sent into the world (17:18–19). Moreover, Jesus' mission serves as the sanctifying basis for their mission. The means by which the disciples are consecrated to the Father's mission are twofold. (1) They are sanctified by 'the truth' (17:17), the full revelation of the Father through the Son; and (2) by Jesus' own self-offering on their behalf (17:19) as 'the Lamb of God, who takes away the sin of the world' (1:29). By means of his revealing and redeeming work, Jesus has set the disciples apart from the world for the service of the Father. And so Jesus prays that the Father will continue to apply the benefits of his finished work (cf. 17:4) to the disciples that they might be kept from the evil one for their mission.

---

acting) are identical and shared in common by the three persons of the Trinity, it is very difficult to see how we can salvage monotheism' (1999: 178). For a full critique of social trinitarianism, see Leftow 2002.

[49] See Bauckham 2004: 227–228; 2005: 164.

[50] Bauckham 2005: 164.

[51] Carson 1991: 566.

Verses 20–26

As in the case of their Lord, the disciples' mission is not an end in itself. Jesus thus prays not only for his disciples but also 'for those who will believe . . . through their message' (17:20). He prays that the disciples' mission in the world will accomplish the same end as that of his mission: that those who come to believe will participate in the one community that corresponds to the unity of the Father and the Son (17:21).

The revelation of the Father's name (17:11), word (17:20–21) and glory (17:22) in the Son is the means to accomplishing this end of unity. The model for this unity is found in the Father and the Son, specifically, their mutual indwelling or *perichoresis* (17:21, 23, 26).[52] Just as the unity of the Father and the Son is manifest in their mutual indwelling (14:10–11), so Jesus asks that the unity of the apostolic community will be manifest as they come to experience the mutual indwelling of the Father and the Son (cf. 14:17, 23). The effect of this new perichoretic communion will be that the world will 'know that you sent me and have loved them even as you have loved me' (17:23).

The perichoretic unity of the Father and the Son in the apostolic community indicates why Jesus' high-priestly prayer must finally be understood as a trinitarian as opposed to a merely binitarian prayer. Though the Spirit remains 'anonymous', literally unnamed, in Jesus' high-priestly prayer, his *characteristic mode of activity* cannot be missed. Indeed, there is a real sense in which the Holy Spirit is both the basis of and the answer to every one of Jesus' petitions.

As we saw in chapter 8 above, John characterizes the Spirit as the one who descends from the Father to rest and remain upon the Son so that, through the Son, he may come to rest and remain upon the disciples as well. In John 17, a very similar pattern repeatedly recurs: the Son receives a gift from the Father that he might in turn pass that gift on to others. The Son has received authority from the Father that he might pass on the gift of eternal life to his disciples (17:2; cf. 5:21, 26–27). The Son has received the Father's words that he might give those words to his disciples (17:8). The Son has received the Father's glory that he might pass that glory on to his disciples (17:22). In the light of John's earlier association of this pattern with the person of

---

[52] John of Damascus, *Fid. orth.* 1.8, 14. Perichoresis is but one version of the Father and the Son's unity. They also share a unity of divine identity/name (8:58; 10:30; 17:11 etc.) and a unity of divine action (1:3; 14:10–11 etc.). Their perichoretic unity is in view in the present context. On these three sorts of unity, see Tanner 2001: 38–41.

the Holy Spirit, it is not a stretch to suggest that the gifts of eternal life, words and glory represent but different aspects of Jesus' one messianic anointing with the Holy Spirit, an anointing he receives from the Father to bestow upon his disciples (1:33).[53] Jesus has received 'all things' from his Father that he might accomplish his mission (17:7; cf. 3:35). This full donation of the Father to the Son therefore must include the gift of the Spirit 'without limit' (3:34).

If this interpretation is indeed correct, then we may conclude that, while the Spirit is strictly speaking anonymous in the prayer of John 17, he is nonetheless the essential link in that prayer's great chain of gifting, the seal of the *pactum salutis* (cf. Eph. 1:13).[54] Viewed in this light, the gift of the Holy Spirit represents the ground and goal of Jesus' messianic mission. Jesus grounds his prayer in his pretemporal messianic investiture. He asks the Father to answer his prayer because he has received the Spirit before the world began that he might give him to his brothers. Having approached the hour of his glorification (cf. 7:39), Jesus looks to the goal of that investiture and asks the Father to apply the eternal grant of the Holy Spirit to his brothers in time, that they might come to participate in the mutual indwelling of the Father and the Son in the Holy Spirit (so 14:17, 23). In the light of this Johannine pattern, we must conclude that Augustine was right in identifying the Spirit's distinctive personal property by the title of 'the Gift'.[55] *The Spirit is the Gift of the Father to the Son, given for the sake of bringing his people into the perichoretic fellowship of the triune God.*

Augustine asks the fascinating question: Does the Spirit's identity as 'the Gift' have reference only to the messianic economy of salvation, or does his identity as the Gift belong to his eternal personhood, without reference to creation or redemption?[56] The question concerns the appropriateness of the title. Is it merely a function of the triune mission or does it say something about the triune identity itself? Jesus' high-priestly prayer suggests that this title's significance extends beyond the triune mission of salvation. For the ultimate goal of the triune mission is that the messianic community, built upon the foundation of the apostolic witness and gathered out of the world, might participate in the intra-trinitarian fellowship of love, glory and *gifting* that existed 'before the creation of the world' (17:24).[57]

---

[53] Badcock 1997: 30–31.
[54] Contra Crump 2006: 396.
[55] *Trin.* 4.29, 5.15–16.
[56] Ibid. 5.16.
[57] Barrett 1978: 514.

Father, I want those you have given me to be with me where I
am, and to see my glory, the glory you have given me because
you loved me before the creation of the world.

Righteous Father, though the world does not know you,
I know you, and they know that you have sent me. I have made
you known to them, and will continue to make you known in
order that the love you have for me may be in them and that
I myself may be in them.

(17:24–26)

The Spirit, with all his benefits, has been given by the Father to the
Son, that the Son might in turn give the Spirit to his disciples. And in
giving the Spirit to his disciples, Jesus gives them the greatest gift that
can be given: he grants them a share in the loving fellowship he has
enjoyed with the Father by the gift of the Spirit 'before the creation
of the world' (17:23–24).

Jesus' high-priestly prayer thus manifests the inner secret of the
triune plan of salvation, the secret that comprises both the foundation and the purpose of that plan. *The triune plan of salvation, the
pactum salutis, flows from, through and to the Father's eternal love for
the Son in the Spirit.* The triune God has eternally desired to bless his
people with the greatest possible gift and the greatest possible gift he
can give is nothing other than the enjoyment of his own eternal,
fecund fellowship.[58] Communion in the Son's eternal life of love,
glory and giving with the Father in the Spirit constitutes the ultimate
blessing of the gospel.[59] In the words of Herman Witsius, 'it was the
highest pitch of love that he would not be glorious without us'.[60]

Accordingly, the 'full measure of . . . joy' (17:13), which Jesus prays
his disciples will experience, must be understood as *his* joy, the joy he
has eternally known as the Father's beloved Son and eternal recipient
of the glorious gift of the Spirit (17:24).[61] This gift of glory and
joy will reach its eschatological consummation when his people,
following a time of mission and persecution (17:14; cf. 21:18–19),

---

[58] Barth *CD* IV/1: 40.

[59] Barth *CD* I/1: 480; Gruenler 1986: 129.

[60] Witsius 1990 (1822): 191. Though Jesus *shares* his glory with his brothers (17:22),
it is a share in *his* glory (17:24), the glory he enjoys in a distinctive way as God's one
and only divine Son (1:14). Jesus thus forever remains 'pre-eminent' (Col. 1:18 ESV) as
'the firstborn among many brothers' (Rom. 8:29). See Piper 2005: 158–159.

[61] Congar (1997, 1: 80) states, 'When the Spirit is given to us, he unites us to God
and each other by the same principle that seals the unity of Love and Peace in God
himself.' Cf. Torrance 1995: 250.

experience the blessed vision of the triune God (17:24; cf. 1 Cor. 13:12; 1 John 3:2; Rev. 22:4).[62]

Immanent and economic Trinity

The preceding discussion brings us into one of the most important and most hotly debated issues in trinitarian theology, namely the relationship between the 'immanent Trinity' and the 'economic Trinity', between God as he *is* (eternally) Father, Son and Holy Spirit and God as he *becomes* (in time) our Father, through the Son, by the Spirit. Debates surrounding this issue have fuelled much of the contemporary renewal of trinitarian theology.[63] Similar debates also lie behind the church's greatest schism.[64]

As we have already seen, according to the Augustinian tradition of exegesis, the triune missions reveal not only three distinct persons, but also how those three distinct persons eternally relate to one another. This view results from an interpretation of the following line of evidence. In John's Gospel, the Father is sent by no one, but instead sends the Son (e.g. 3:17; 17:3 etc.) and the Spirit (14:26). The Son is sent by the Father and sends the Spirit (15:26; 16:7).

Table 10.1   The sender–sent relationships between God the Father, God the Son and God the Holy Spirit, 1

God the Father		sends		God the Son
sender	$\rightarrow$		$\rightarrow$	sent one-turned-sender
sends	$\rightarrow$	The Holy Spirit	$\leftarrow$	sends
		sent		

Table 10.2   The sender–sent relationships between God the Father, God the Son and God the Holy Spirit, 2

God the Father	God the Son	The Holy Spirit
sender	sent	sent
sender	sender	sent
twice-sender	sent one-turned-sender	twice-sent

---

[62] Barrett 1978: 514.
[63] See Peters 1993; J. Thompson 1994; Grenz 2004; and esp. Sanders 2004.
[64] See Congar 1997, 3: 53–54.

The Spirit is sent by the Father and the Son but himself sends no one.

To this evidence Augustine then applies the following theological principle, a principle he believes is exegetically justifiable.[65] According to the Bishop of Hippo, the missions of the Son and the Spirit *in history* reveal something about the *eternal*, unchanging life of the Trinity.[66] Specifically, one can be sent in time only by someone from whom one eternally proceeds. Temporal missions reveal and are rooted in eternal processions.[67] When this principle is applied to the textual evidence concerning the triune missions, the conclusions are as follows.

The fact that the Father is not sent by anyone reveals that he does not proceed from anyone (*Trin.* 4.28). Instead, because he sends the Son and the Spirit, the Father should be recognized as the *fons divinitatis*, 'the source and origin of all deity'.[68] The fact that the Son is sent by the Father reveals that he proceeds from the Father as the Father's 'only-begotten Son' (*Trin.* 4.29).[69] The fact that the Spirit is sent, 'breathed', by the Father and the Son (Gen. 2:7; John 20:22) reveals that he proceeds from the Father and the Son (*Trin.* 4.29) as from one originating principle (*Trin.* 5.15; 15.47–48).[70] The Eastern Church does not reject this line of evidence per se, only the theological principle the Augustinian tradition applies to that evidence.[71]

Space forbids a full dogmatic discussion of this issue.[72] Nevertheless, the following points may be made. First, the case for an Augustinian

---

[65] See Augustine, *Trin.* 2.3–4; also *Civ.* 10.13.

[66] See e.g. *Trin.* 4.24, 29, 32.

[67] Ibid. 4.28–29. These 'relations of origin' are what constitute the persons *as* distinct persons. The three hold everything else in the Godhead in common, equally and identically (contra 'social' trinitarianism).

[68] Ibid. 4.32.

[69] This is the traditional interpretation of *monogenēs*, a term found in John 1:14, 18; 3:16, 18.

[70] The *filioque*. See Congar 1997, 3: 53–54.

[71] For a historical discussion of the Eastern Church's objections up to the present, see Congar 1997, 3: 57–78; for a contemporary, systematic statement of those objections, which nevertheless attempts to retain the positive significance of Augustinian teaching on this matter, see Bobrinskoy 1999: 279–303. Ultimately, Eastern theologians believe that this Augustinian principle, when applied to the trinitarian processions, compromises the Father's distinctive personal property as the *fons divinitatis* (thus e.g. Bobrinskoy 1999: 295, 302).

[72] A full dogmatic discussion would require that we engage the rest of the NT, including Paul's description of the Spirit as the Spirit *of* the Son (e.g. Gal. 4:6; cf. Rom. 8:9), as well as the history of dogma. For a very helpful introductory engagement with the present issues, see Letham 2004: 383–389; for fuller discussion and debate, see Heppe 1950: 128–132; Vischer 1981; and B. D. Marshall 2002.

reading of John does not depend upon semantics alone.[73] So, for example, while the present study follows much contemporary scholarship in translating *monogenēs* as 'only' or 'one-of-a-kind Son' instead of 'only-begotten',[74] this lexical move does not by itself defeat the Augustinian doctrine.[75] This is because, second, as with the *pactum salutis*, the case does not depend upon drawing unwarranted speculative inferences regarding the eternal Trinity from the economic data of revelation.[76] Contrary to common misunderstandings, the view that the Son eternally receives all things from the Father as his only Son (eternal generation) and that the Spirit receives all things from the Father and also the Son (dual procession) does not depend upon inference alone. Rather, this set of personal relationships (eternal generation, dual procession) is manifested *in* the economy *as* the set of relationships that *characterizes* the triune life: whether before, during or at the consummation of the economy.[77] The triune God, in other words, acts characteristically in the triune mission.[78] And he does so because revealing his true character is internal to that mission.

Thus, for example, Augustine interprets texts such as John 5:19 ('the Son can do nothing by himself; he can do only what he sees his Father doing, because whatever the Father does the Son also does') and John 5:26 ('as the Father has life in himself, so he has granted the Son to have life in himself') as referring neither to the Son's common deity with the Father (though such is implied), nor to the Son's incarnate humanity (as his 'dependence' upon the Father in these texts might imply), but instead as signifying the Son's *distinctive personal relationship* of being

---

[73] At any rate, we do not believe that the evidence against the traditional interpretation of *monogenēs* is as strong as is sometimes suggested. See Dahms 1983.

[74] See chapter 4 above.

[75] Related to this point it must be noted that the Fathers were extremely apophatic concerning what being 'eternally begotten' might actually *mean*. As Plantinga wryly observes, 'Beyond reading out of it [*monogenēs*] a mysterious, non-temporal derivation relation of Son to Father, nobody ever knew what "only-begotten" meant anyhow' (Plantinga 1991: 306). The main point affirmed in describing the Second Person of the Trinity as the 'only-begotten Son' is that the Son is God *by nature*, and not by adoption, and that the Son personally possesses what he possesses in the way of a *son*, i.e. *from* his Father. Both points are thoroughly Johannine, whether or not *monogenēs* means 'only-begotten'.

[76] Contra Reymond 1998: 326.

[77] McCabe 1987: 48–49; Rogers 2005: 117.

[78] Barth (*CD* IV/1: 198) states, 'When we have to do with Jesus Christ we do have to do with an "economy" but not with the kind of economy in which his true and proper being remains behind an improper being, a being "as if." We have to do with an economy in which God is truly himself and himself acts and intervenes in the world.'

'*from the Father*':[79] 'the life of the Son is unchanging like the Father's, and yet is *from the Father*; and . . . the work of the Father and Son is indivisible, and yet the Son's working is *from the Father* just as he himself is from the Father' (*Trin.* 2.3; italics added).[80]

It is significant for the present discussion that, according to Augustine, the Son's distinctive personal relationship of being 'from the Father' obtains *in* the economy of salvation (in their indivisible 'work') and not merely in an eternal state of affairs before, behind or beyond the economy of salvation. In other words, the Son's relationship of dependence upon the Father for all that he is and does, his relationship *to* the Father as the Son *of* the Father, characterizes his life and mission as a whole *as* the life and mission of the Son of God. 'Jesus lives out in a fully human form the mode of relationship' he eternally enjoys with the Father in the Spirit.[81] His filial mode of being belongs to his distinctive personal way of being God.[82]

In other words, the economic Trinity is not other than the immanent Trinity:[83] the economic Trinity *is* the immanent Trinity personally engaged in the gracious act of becoming *our* Father, through the Son, by the Spirit. As Hart so eloquently states, 'the economic Trinity is God in himself, graciously extending the everlasting "dance" of his love to embrace creation in its motion'.[83] When Father, Son and Holy Spirit engage in the *missio Dei*, they do not stand above or behind that mission.[84] When Father, Son and Holy Spirit engage in the *missio Dei*, they engage personally *in* that mission *as* they eternally *are*, that is, according to their characteristic interpersonal relationships.[85]

---

[79] See also Gregory of Nazianzus: 'In my opinion he is called Son because he is identical with the Father in essence; and not only for this reason, but also because he is of him' (*Or.* 30.20).

[80] Augustine's exegesis here is in keeping with the common pattern of patristic exegesis, East and West. The Fathers regularly note *three* ways the NT speaks about the *incarnate* Son of God: (1) one refers to the Son's common deity with the Father and the Spirit (e.g. 1:1: 'the Word was *God*'); (2) another refers to the Son's common humanity with us (e.g. 1:14: 'the Word became *flesh*'); and (3) a third refers to the Son's distinctive personal property of being the only Son *of* the Father, i.e. his *eternal hypostasis* (e.g. 3:16: 'his one and only Son'). See Athanasius, *C. Ar.* 3.35–36; Gregory of Nazianzus, *Or.* 29.18; 30.20; also Behr 2004: 7–8, and n. 17.

[81] Tanner 2001: 19. McCabe tantalizingly suggests that the missions are 'sacraments' of the eternal processions: 'they contain the reality they signify' (McCabe 1987: 49).

[82] Confirming the present point, it is likely that 'the one who is born of God' in 1 John 5:18 refers to *Jesus*, not to believers. For a contrary interpretation of 1 John 5:18, however, see Schnackenburg 1992: 252–254.

[83] Hart 2003: 169.

[84] As Jenson fears; see 1997: 59.

[85] Barth *CD* IV/1: 25.

This rule must apply to the Holy Spirit as well.[86] Although the traditional exegesis of John 15:26, which distinguishes the Spirit's future 'sending' by the Son from his eternal 'procession' from the Father, may be a bit too tidy an instance of theological exposition (both statements probably refer to the 'economy' of salvation),[87] it does not follow that texts such as this one are irrelevant to the question of the 'eternal procession of the Holy Spirit'.[88] Indeed, if the missions are truly the missions *of* the triune God, then we may expect that the relational pattern which unfolds in the Spirit's mission[89] belongs not merely to his saving mission but to his very identity. The Spirit, like the Father and the Son, acts in character in the economy of salvation.

After all, the point of the triune missions is that we might know 'the only true God' (17:3) and that we might enter into the trinitarian fellowship of love and glory that existed 'before the creation of the world' (17:24), before the temporal execution of the triune missions. And, if this is indeed the case, then we should regard the triune missions as necessary means to a salutary end, that of knowing God as he truly is. In trinitarian theology, the means of revelation and the content of revelation ultimately cannot be divorced, because how God gives and reveals is tied to what God gives and reveals: himself.[90]

From this brief discussion, we may draw the following summary statements about the triune identity of God.

---

[86] Crump (2006: 408) thus goes astray in assuming that because John primarily portrays the Spirit's personal identity in the context of his relationship to the disciples, therefore John has no interest in portraying the Spirit's place in 'the life of the Trinity'. The opposite is the case: by portraying the Spirit's role vis-à-vis the disciples, as one sent by the Father and the Son, we are enabled to understanding his place in the triune life.

[87] Congar 1997, 3: 49. However, as the Augustinian tradition of exegesis has commonly noted, in John 15:26 'sending' is in the future tense, whereas 'proceeding' is in the present tense. Might the former then refer to an *event* and the latter to a *characteristic relationship* that, as such, applies to the Spirit's eternal and unchanging identity?

[88] Barth *CD* I/1: 479–480. See also Carson's helpful comments in 1991: 528–529.

[89] That he is sent by the Father (14:26) *and* the Son (15:26; 16:7). More fully, see chapter 8 above.

[90] This does not require us to follow Jenson (1997: 59–60 *et passim*) and say that because the triune identity is revealed *by means of* the triune mission that the triune identity is *identical with* the triune mission. While the triune identity and the triune mission are integrally related, they are also distinct. The former is the *basis*, *means* and *goal* of the latter. The latter flows freely *from*, *through* and *to* the former. The economic Trinity thus refers to things true of God *only by virtue of his eternal decision to become 'our God'*. The immanent Trinity refers to things *always* true of God, whether before, during or at the consummation of the economy. See also Molnar 2002; and Hart 2003: 156–167.

1. *The Father is the* fons divinitatis. All that the Son and the Spirit have, they receive personally from him. The consubstantial deity of the Son and the Spirit with the Father is in no way diminished by the receptive status of the Son and the Spirit, for the Father shares with them all things (5:26; 16:13–15; 17:7),[91] except for the personal trait of being 'Father'.

The point is not that the Father, as *fons divinitatis*, generates the *divinity* of the Son and the Spirit. Divinity, by definition (Exod. 3:14!), cannot be generated. Nor do we claim that the unity of God is found only in the person of the Father. What sense, then, does it make to speak of the Father as *fons divinitatis*? Understanding this assertion requires a firm grasp of the dogmatic distinction between *essence* and *person*.[92] The Son and the Spirit, as concrete persons, are '*from* the Father'. The Father, in other words, is the 'font' of persons who are divine. However, those persons, *with* the Father, fully possess the identical, self-existent (underived, ungenerated) divine essence of the Father. In Johannine terms, Jesus has 'life in himself' (5:26) (he is the self-existent, ungenerated God) and is this God *as the Son*, who personally shares self-existence *with* the Father because he is the Son *of* the Father (5:26).[93] This leads to our next point.

[91] This includes 'self-existence' (5:26), thus safeguarding Calvin's concern to protect the Son's status as *autotheos* (Calvin, *Inst*. 1.13.19, 23, 25). It will not do to limit the scope of John 5:26 to Jesus' 'messianic investiture' (contra Reymond 1998: 326). For while Jesus' messianic investiture is no doubt in view in this verse, the whole point of the dispute in John 5 concerns Jesus' equality with God *as* God's Son. In other words, it is his *personal identity* as the Son of God, the one who has the right to receive all things from God and to do as God does, that constitutes the *basis* for his messianic investiture and activity. It should be added (also contra Reymond) that Calvin's rigorous defence of the Son's self-existence did not lead him to deny the Son's eternal generation from the Father. See Owen 2000.

[92] This distinction, we should add, is rooted in John's twofold use of 'God' in 1:1. There John uses 'God' to refer to the *person* of the Father and to refer to the *common nature* shared by the Father and the Son. See chapter 1 (pp. 43–44) in the present volume.

[93] For a brief but excellent discussion of John 5:26 in this regard, see Carson 2000: 37–38. For an analysis of Thomas' discussion of the present issue, which represents an attempt to clarify a long-standing question raised by Peter Lombard, see B. D. Marshall 2004: 55–74. For an alternative account of the present issue, which develops its thesis via interaction with Athanasius, Didymus the Blind and the Cappadocians, see Torrance 1995: 310–340. Torrance's view, it should be noted, has been influential in ecumenical dialogues between Eastern Orthodox churches and certain Reformed churches. Space forbids interacting with Torrance's thesis and its accompanying problems related to historiography. Suffice it to say that the best recent treatments of early trinitarianism paint quite a different picture from that of Torrance. See Behr 2001, 2004; and Ayres 2004.

2. *Jesus is personally distinct from the Father as his one-of-a-kind Son (1:14, 18; cf. 1 John 5:18)*. As the eternal Son, he is the filial recipient and expression of 'everything' (17:7) the Father is and has: his self-existent life, word, name and glory. As the eternal Son, he is the object of the Father's eternal delight, ever at his side (1:18; 17:24–26).

3. *The Spirit eternally proceeds from the Father as 'the gift' who rests upon and indwells God's beloved Son (1:32–34),*[94] *the one with whom the Father shares all things (3:34–35)*. But this must mean that the Spirit eternally proceeds from the Son as well (7:37–39; 15:26; 16:7; 20:22), just because the Father shares 'all things' with the Son except for the personal trait of being the Father of the Son (cf. 16:15).[95] As the Spirit of the Son (cf. Gal. 4:6), the Spirit eternally springs forth (cf. 7:38) in the fullness of the Son's joy, the joy of being the beloved Son of the Father (15:11; 17:13; cf. Luke 10:21).

Each of the preceding identifying descriptions appears in John's account of the triune missions. The claim of the present chapter is that these 'economic' relationships should be seen as characteristic of both the 'economic Trinity' and the 'immanent Trinity', and this because the whole point of the economy is to bring those given by the Father to the Son into the relationship of glory, unity and love that eternally exists between the Father and the Son in the Holy Spirit (17:24–26).

Conclusion

John's presentation of the Trinity thus lays the groundwork for later ecclesial summaries of the doctrine. Father, Son and Spirit 'are not three Gods, but one God'. Moreover, this one God eternally exists as three distinct persons: 'The Father is made of none, neither created, nor begotten. The Son is of the Father alone, not made, nor created, but begotten. The Holy Spirit is of the Father and of the Son, neither made, nor begotten, but proceeding.'[96]

---

[94] The Orthodox liturgy thus speaks of 'the Spirit who proceeds from the Father, and rests in the Son' (Bobrinskoy 1999: 99). Similarly, John of Damascus describes the Spirit as one 'who proceeds from the Father and abides in the Son' (*Fid. orth.* 1.8). Both are very Johannine formulations.

[95] Augustine's version of the *filioque*, that the Spirit proceeds from the Father and the Son *as from one principle* (*Trin.* 5.15; 15.47–48), should be acknowledged as a very Johannine formulation. Whether the *filioque* belongs in the Nicene–Constantinopolitan Creed is an entirely different matter. For a helpful discussion of the issues, see Bray 1998.

[96] Both quotations in the present paragraph are from the *Symbolum quicunque*, slightly revised from the translation of Schaff 1996 (1931).

John, we should add, sees no tension between the unity of one glorious Godhead, shared equally and identically by three persons, and a relational order, or *taxis*, among the persons, a *taxis* revealed in the salvation-historical missions of the Son and the Spirit and rooted in their eternal relationships. But neither does John attempt to explain this mystery. Rather, John simply testifies to the one God – Father, Son and Spirit – in order that we too may enter into the Father's love for the Son in the fellowship of the Spirit.

Conclusion

The gift of life: Knowing the triune God

John's Gospel was written that 'whoever believes' might receive the gift of 'life' in Jesus' name (3:16; 17:2–3; 20:31). According to the Fourth Gospel, that gift of life is characterized by a personal knowledge of God the Father, through God the Son (17:3), a knowledge enabled by God the indwelling Holy Spirit (15:26; 16:13–15). Eternal life thus consists in more than simply the removal of sin or an escape from death, though to be sure, both belong to John's teaching about salvation.[1] Eternal life has a positive, trinitarian character: 'We proclaim to you what we have seen and heard, so that you also may have fellowship with us. And our fellowship is with the *Father* and with his *Son*, Jesus Christ . . . We know that we live in him and he in us, because he has given us of his *Spirit*' (1 John 1:3; 4:13).

Eternal life consists in coming to know Jesus' Father as our Father. On the basis of the Father's eternal grant of a people to the Son (6:37; 17:6); through the Son's incarnation, crucifixion, resurrection and ascension on their behalf; and through the Father's and the Son's joint sending of the Spirit to indwell believers subsequent to Jesus' exaltation (14:23), the foundational covenant promise 'I will be your God' (e.g. Lev. 26:12) has been fulfilled in a trinitarian way. Jesus' God and Father has become our God and our Father (20:17; cf. Matt. 6:9; 2 Cor. 6:16–18).

Eternal life thus consists in sharing in the gracious overflow of the Father's eternal love for the Son in the Spirit. We share in this gracious overflow as 'children' (1:12) who have been grafted into God's beloved Son as branches into the true vine (15:1–11; 17:26). Although, as mentioned, our union with the Son commences in the Father's eternal decision, our experience of this vital union begins with our Spirit-enabled reception of Jesus and his word (1:12–13; 6:44–45; 15:3) and grows as we abide in faithful dependence upon Jesus and his word (8:31–32; 15:4–11). As in the case of Jesus, our

---

[1] See chapter 7 above.

filial relationship to the Father entails both privilege and responsibility. This responsibility includes the task of carrying on the apostolic mission (17:18; 20:21–22). Just as the Son's mission flows from, through and to the Father's love in the Spirit, so, too, the church's mission flows from, through and to its filial participation in the Father's love for the Son in the Spirit. The ultimate goal of both the privilege and responsibility of adoption is 'that the Father may be glorified in the Son' (14:13 NASB).

Eternal life also consists in the gift of the Holy Spirit who comes to rest and remain in our midst (14:17). By his presence, the Spirit continues to guide us into 'the way and the truth and the life' of Jesus (14:6; cf. 6:63; 16:13–15). Moreover, because the Spirit's coming includes the coming of the Father and the Son in so far as he mediates and manifests their presence in and among believers (14:23), the Spirit's presence establishes the trinitarian dwelling of God with his people both now and forever (14:1–3, 16). As such, the Spirit's coming is in perfect continuity with Jesus' earthly mission, and complements it in the divine economy of salvation (14:17–18). Through the indwelling of the Spirit, the ancient covenant promise (again) is fulfilled in a distinctly trinitarian way: 'I will walk among you and be your God, and you will be my people' (Lev. 26:12; cf. Rev. 21:3). God's personal presence is mediated to believers by the Spirit of the Father and the Son.

As believers come to know and adore the Father, through the Son, by the indwelling Spirit, the revelation of the biblical God of creation (1:3) and covenant (1:17) thus reaches its salvation-historical climax and destination. God's self-disclosure that in a preliminary fashion took place in the giving of the Law through Moses (1:17) was realized in a comprehensive, unparalleled and climactic fashion in the Word-become-flesh (1:14, 18; cf. 1:1; Heb. 1:1–3), who was related to God as son is to father (1:14) and who made him known out of the depth and wealth of his eternal, pre-existent relationship with him (1:1, 18; 17:5, 24). Truly, anyone who has seen Jesus has seen the Father (14:9–11), and it is only in understanding the perfect union between Jesus the Son on whom the Spirit rests and God the Father that anyone can come to believe that Jesus alone is 'the way and the truth and the life', for 'no-one comes to the Father except through' Jesus (14:6).

The focal point of God's glorious self-disclosure in Jesus, which constitutes the salvation-historical culmination of the OT and inaugurates the age of the Spirit subsequent to Jesus' exaltation (7:39), is found in what John conceives of as the glorification of the Son (12:23; 17:1), which reconceptualizes Jesus' crucifixion in Isaianic terms as the suffering Servant's being 'lifted up' (3:13; 8:28; 12:32); marks Jesus' (the sent Son's) departure from this world and his return to the Father and his pre-existent glory (13:1, 3; 14:28; 17:5, 24); epitomizes the Son's completion of his mission carried out in perfect obedience and submission to the Father (4:34; 17:4; 19:28, 30); confers true, abundant and eternal life on believers in Jesus (6:57; 10:10; 17:2);[2] and constitutes God's ultimate expression of his love for the world he brought into being in and through Jesus (3:16; cf. 13:1).

This divine self-disclosure through Jesus in word and deed, and ultimately in his willing self-sacrifice at the cross (10:15, 17–18) (truly an action that speaks louder than words) confronts the world with a critical decision that must be made and cannot be evaded.[3] Will people love darkness rather than light (3:19–21) now that the light has come into the world (1:4–5, 9–11; 8:12; 9:5), or will they believe in the light and become sons of light (12:35–36)? As Bultmann well realized in his abiding contribution to our understanding of John's theology, this 'dualism of decision' is at the heart of John's evangelistic message and pervades his Gospel as an all-encompassing, inevitable implication of the Word's coming into the world.[4] For the Word enlightens every person (1:9), but not everyone, despite the escalating series of startling manifestations of God's glory through Jesus' signs and revelatory discourses, believes that Jesus is the Christ, the Son of God (20:30–31).

Thus the divine, cruciform self-disclosure of necessity demands that 'the show must go on', or, put more appropriately, that the triune mission must continue, even past the Son's departure to his pre-existent glory. Witness must be borne to the glory seen, heard and experienced by the eyewitnesses of Jesus (1 John 1:1–4), be it through those first followers themselves (15:26–27; 21:24–25) or through later generations of believers (17:20). And in these 'greater works' (14:12), accomplished by his followers in the power of the Spirit, Jesus will continue to be active from his exalted position with the Father (14:13), so that, as Luke realized, the acts of the church, or, better, the acts of the Spirit *through* the church, will indeed, by implication, constitute 'what Jesus *continued* to do' in these last days prior to his glorious return (Acts 1:1).

---

[2] Cf. Köstenberger 1998b: 75–76.
[3] See on this Köstenberger 2005b: 19–51, 131–136.
[4] Bultmann 1971, *passim*.

When God brings an end to this world and sends his Son a second time to bring judgment to those who rejected him and to usher in the glorious consummation for those who received him and became his children (1:12), then God's purposes will be fully accomplished. For ultimately, the Father revealed his name through the Son so that by the indwelling Spirit all who believe might enter into the eternal, joyful fellowship of the triune God, a fellowship where the Father and the Son mutually glorify one another in the Spirit (12:28; 13:32; 16:14; 17:1).

With this we conclude our study of John's Gospel and the Trinity. If trinitarian doxology is indeed the end of the triune mission, then it is the only appropriate conclusion to the present study as well:

> Blest Trinity, salvation's spring
> may every soul thy praises sing;
> to those thou grantest conquest by
> the Holy Cross, rewards supply.[5]

---

[5] Venantius Fortunatus, 'Vexilla Regis', trans. Walter Kirkham Blount. Thanks to Fred Sanders for directing us to this hymn.

Bibliography

Adam, P. (2005), 'Honouring Jesus Christ', *Churchman* 119: 35–50.

Ashton, J. (1991), *Understanding the Fourth Gospel*, Oxford: Clarendon.

Athanasius (*C. Ar.*), *Orations Against the Arians*, in *The Christological Controversy*, trans. and ed. R. A. Norris, Jr., Philadelphia: Fortress, 1980, 83–101.

Augustine (*Civ.*), *The City of God*, in *A Select Library of the Nicene and Post-Nicene Fathers of the Christian Church*, ed. P. Schaff, 1886; repr. Grand Rapids: Eerdmans, 1993.

—— (*Trin.*), *The Trinity*, trans. E. Hill, Brooklyn, N. Y.: New City, 1991.

Ayres, L. (2004), *Nicaea and its Legacy: An Approach to Fourth-Century Trinitarian Theology*, Oxford: Oxford University Press.

Babcock, W. S. (1991), 'A Changing of the Christian God: The Doctrine of the Trinity in the Seventeenth Century', *Int* 45: 133–46.

Badcock, G. D. (1997), *Light of Truth and Fire of Love: A Theology of the Holy Spirit*, Grand Rapids: Eerdmans.

Baird, W. (1992), *History of New Testament Research*, vol. 1: *From Deism to Tübingen*, Minneapolis: Fortress.

Ball, D. M. (1996), *'I Am' in John's Gospel: Literary Function, Background and Theological Implications*, JSNTSup 124, Sheffield: Sheffield Academic Press.

Balthasar, H. U. von (1988, 1990, 1992, 1994), *Theo-drama: Theological Dramatic Theory*, trans. G. Harrison, 4 vols., San Francisco: Ignatius.

Bandy, A. S. (2007), 'The Prophetic Lawsuit in the Book of Revelation: An Analysis of the Lawsuit Motif in Revelation with Reference to the Use of the Old Testament', PhD diss., Wake Forest, N. C.

Barrett, C. K. (1978), *The Gospel According to St. John*, 2nd ed., Philadelphia: Westminster.

—— (1982), *Essays on John*, Philadelphia: Westminster.

Barth, K. (*CD* I–IV), *Church Dogmatics*, 4 vols., Edinburgh: T. & T. Clark, 1956–75.

Bassler, J. M. (1992), 'God in the NT', *ABD* 2: 1049–1055.

Bauckham, R. (1992), 'Jesus, Worship of', *ABD* 3: 812–819.

—— (1993), *The Theology of the Book of Revelation*, New Testament Theology, Cambridge: Cambridge University Press.

—— (1998a), *God Crucified: Monotheism and Christology in the New Testament*, Grand Rapids: Eerdmans.

—— (1998b), *The Gospels for All Christians: Rethinking the Gospel Audiences*, Grand Rapids: Eerdmans.

—— (2000), 'The Qumran Community and the Gospel of John', in *The Dead Sea Scrolls Fifty Years after Their Discovery: Proceedings of the Jerusalem Congress, July 20–25, 1997*, ed. L. H. Schiffman, E. Tov and J. C. VanderKam, Jerusalem: Israel Exploration Society and the Shrine of the Book, 105–115.

—— (2004), 'Biblical Theology and the Problems of Monotheism', in *Out of Egypt: Biblical Theology and Biblical Interpretation*, ed. C. G. Bartholomew, M. Healy, K. Moller and R. Parry, Carlisle: Paternoster; Grand Rapids: Zondervan, 187–232.

—— (2005), 'Monotheism and Christology in the Gospel of John', in *Contours of Christology in the New Testament*, Grand Rapids: Eerdmans, 148–166.

—— (2006), *Jesus and the Eyewitnesses: The Gospels as Eyewitness Testimony*, Grand Rapids: Eerdmans.

Bavinck, H. (2006 [1906–11]), *Reformed Dogmatics*, vol. 3, trans. J. Vriend, Grand Rapids: Baker.

Beale, G. K. (2004), *The Temple and the Church's Mission: A Biblical Theology of the Dwelling Place of God*, NSBT, Leicester: Apollos; Downers Grove: IVP.

Beasley-Murray, G. R. (1999), *John*, WBC 36, 2nd ed., Waco, Tex.: Word.

Behr, J. (2001), *The Way to Nicaea*, Formation of Christian Theology, vol. 1, Crestwood, N. Y.: St. Vladimir's Seminary Press.

—— (2004), *The Nicene Faith*, Formation of Christian Theology, vol. 2, Crestwood, N. Y.: St. Vladimir's Seminary Press.

Betz, O. (1963), *Der Paraklet: Fürsprecher im häretischen Spätjudentum, im Johannes-Evangelium und in neu gefundenen gnostischen Schriften*, Leiden: Brill.

Bieringer, R., D. Pollefeyt and F. Vandecasteele-Vanneuville (2001a) (eds.), *Anti-Judaism and the Fourth Gospel*, Louisville: Westminster John Knox.

—— (2001b), *Anti-Judaism and the Fourth Gospel: Papers of the Leuven Colloquium, 2000*, Assen, the Netherlands: Royal van Gorcum.

Billington, A. (1995), 'The Paraclete and Mission in the Fourth Gospel', in *Mission and Meaning: Essays Presented to Peter Cotterell*, ed. A. Billington, T. Lane and M. Turner. Carlisle: Paternoster, 90–115.

Bingham, D. J. (2005), 'Himself within Himself: The Father and His Hands in Early Christianity', *Southwestern Journal of Theology* 47: 137–151.

Block, D. I. (2003), 'Marriage and Family in Ancient Israel', in *Marriage and Family in the Biblical World*, ed. Ken M. Campbell, Downers Grove: IVP, 33–102.

Blomberg, C. L. (2001), *The Historical Reliability of John's Gospel*, Leicester: Apollos; Downers Grove: IVP.

Bobrinskoy, B. (1999), *The Mystery of the Trinity: Trinitarian Experience and Vision in the Biblical and Patristic Tradition*, Crestwood, N. Y.: St. Vladimir's Seminary Press.

Bock, D. L. (2000), *Blasphemy and Exaltation in Judaism: The Charge against Jesus in Mark 14:53–65*, Grand Rapids: Baker.

Bockmuehl, M. (2006), *Seeing the Word: Refocusing New Testament Study*, Studies in Theological Interpretation, Grand Rapids: Baker.

Boismard, M. E. (1993), *Moses or Jesus: An Essay in Johannine Christology*, trans. B. T. Viviano, Minneapolis: Fortress.

Borchert, G. L. (2002), *John*, NAC 25, Nashville: Broadman & Holman.

Boring, M. E. (1978), 'The Influence of Christian Prophecy on the Johannine Portrayal of the Paraclete and Jesus', *NTS* 25: 113–123.

Bray, G. (1998), 'The Double Procession of the Holy Spirit in Evangelical Theology Today: Do We Still Need It?', *JETS* 41: 415–426.

Brown, R. E. (1966, 1970), *The Gospel According to John*, 2 vols., AB 29, Garden City, N. Y.: Doubleday.

—— (1967), 'The Paraclete in the Fourth Gospel', *NTS* 13: 113–132.

—— (1971), 'The Spirit-Paraclete in the Gospel of John', *CBQ* 33: 268–270.

—— (1978), '"Other Sheep Not of This Fold": The Johannine Perspective on Christian Diversity in the Late First Century', *JBL* 97: 5–22.

—— (1979), *The Community of the Beloved Disciple*, New York: Paulist.

Bultmann, R. (1925), 'Die Bedeutung der neuerschlossenen mandäischen und manichäischen Quellen für das Verständnis des Johannesevangeliums', *ZNW* 24: 100–146.

—— (1951, 1955), *Theology of the New Testament*, trans. K. Grobel, 2 vols., New York: Charles Scribner's Sons.

—— (1971), *The Gospel of John*, trans. G. R. Beasley-Murray et al., Oxford: Blackwell.

Burge, G. M. (1987), *The Anointed Community: The Holy Spirit in the Johannine Tradition*, Grand Rapids: Eerdmans.

—— (2002), *The Gospel of John*, NIVAC, Grand Rapids: Zondervan.

—— (2006), 'Revelation and Discipleship in St. John's Gospel', in *Challenging Perspectives on the Gospel of John*, ed. J. Lierman, WUNT 2.219, Tübingen: Mohr–Siebeck, 235–254.

Burney, C. F. (1922), *The Aramaic Origin of the Fourth Gospel*, Oxford: Oxford University Press.

Calvin, J. (*Inst.*), *Institutes of the Christian Religion*, trans. F. L. Battles, London: SCM; Philadelphia: Westminster, 1961.

—— (*John*), *The Gospel According to St. John*, 2 vols., trans. T. H. L. Parker, Edinburgh: Oliver & Boyd, 1959, 1961.

Campbell, K. M. (2005), 'What Was Jesus' Occupation?', *JETS* 48: 501–519.

Capes, D. B. (1992), *Old Testament Yahweh Texts in Paul's Christology*, WUNT 2.47, Tübingen: Mohr–Siebeck.

Carson, D. A. (1981), *Divine Sovereignty and Human Responsibility: Biblical Perspectives in Tension*, Atlanta: John Knox.

—— (1982), 'Understanding Misunderstandings in the Fourth Gospel', *TynBul* 33: 59–89.

—— (1991), *The Gospel According to John*, PNTC, Grand Rapids: Eerdmans; Leicester: Apollos.

—— (2000), *The Difficult Doctrine of the Love of God*, Wheaton: Crossway; Leicester: IVP.

—— (2002), *Love in Hard Places*, Wheaton: Crossway.

Casey, M. (1991), *From Jewish Prophet to Gentile God: The Origins and Development of New Testament Christology*, Louisville: Westminster John Knox.

Casurella, A. (1983), *The Johannine Paraclete in the Church Fathers: A Study in the History of Exegesis*, Tübingen: Mohr–Siebeck.

Chandler, W. T. (2005), Review of A. Yong, *Beyond the Impasse*, *JETS* 48: 191–195.

Charlesworth, J. H. (2006), 'A Study in Shared Symbolism and Language', in *The Bible and the Dead Sea Scrolls: The Second*

Princeton Symposium on Judaism and Christian Origins, vol. 3: *The Scrolls and Christian Origins*, ed. J. H. Charlesworth, Waco, Tex.: Baylor University Press, 97–152.

Chennattu, R. M. (2006), *Johannine Discipleship as a Covenant Relationship*, Peabody: Hendrickson.

Childs, B. S. (1993), *Biblical Theology of the Old and New Testaments: Theological Reflection on the Christian Bible*, Minneapolis: Fortress.

Clements, R. E. (1984), 'Monotheism and the Canonical Process', *Theology* 87: 336–344.

Coloe, M. L. (2001), *God Dwells with Us: Temple Symbolism in the Fourth Gospel*, Collegeville, Minn.: Liturgical.

Colwell, E. C. (1933), 'A Definite Rule for the Use of the Article in the Greek New Testament', *JBL* 52: 12–21.

Congar, Y. (1997), *I Believe in the Holy Spirit*, trans. David Smith, 3 vols., New York: Crossroad.

Cowan, C. (2006), 'The Father and Son in the Fourth Gospel: Johannine Subordination Revisited', *JETS* 49: 115–135.

Cranfield, C. E. B. (1987), 'Some Comments on Professor J. D. G. Dunn's *Christology in the Making: A New Testament Inquiry into the Origins of the Doctrine of the Incarnation*, with Special Reference to the Evidence of the Epistle to the Romans', in *The Glory of Christ in the New Testament: Studies in Christology in Memory of George Bradford Caird*, ed. L. D. Hurst and N. T. Wright, Oxford: Clarendon, 267–280.

Croteau, D. A. (2002), 'An Analysis of the Concept of Believing in the Narrative Context of John's Gospel', ThM thesis, Southeastern Baptist Theological Seminary.

Crump, D. (2006), 'Re-examining the Johannine Trinity: Perichoresis or Deification?', *SJT* 59: 395–412.

Culpepper, R. A. (1980–1), 'The Pivot of John's Prologue', *NTS* 27: 1–31.

—— (1983), *The Anatomy of the Fourth Gospel: A Study in Literary Design*, Philadelphia: Fortress.

Dahl, N. A. (1991), 'The Neglected Factor in New Testament Theology', in *Jesus the Christ: The Historical Origins of Christological Doctrine*, ed. D. H. Juel, Minneapolis: Fortress, 153–163.

Dahms, J. V. (1983), 'The Johannine Use of *Monogenēs* Reconsidered', *NTS* 29: 222–232.

Daly-Denton, M. (2000), *David in the Fourth Gospel: The Johannine Reception of the Psalms*, AGJU 47, Leiden: Brill.

Daly-Denton, M. (2004), 'The Psalms in John's Gospel', in *The Psalms in the New Testament*, ed. S. Moyise and M. J. J. Menken, NTSI, London and New York: T. & T. Clark International, 119–137.

Das, A. A., and F. J. Matera (2002), *The Forgotten God: Perspectives in Biblical Theology*, Louisville: Westminster John Knox.

Davey, J. E. (1958), *The Jesus of St John: Historical and Christological Studies in the Fourth Gospel*, London: Lutterworth.

Davies, M. (1992), *Rhetoric and Reference in the Fourth Gospel*, JSNTSS 69, Sheffield: JSOT.

Davies, W. D. (1994), *The Gospel and the Land: Early Christianity and Jewish Territorial Doctrine*, Sheffield: JSOT.

Dixon, P. S. (1975), 'The Significance of the Anarthrous Predicate Nominative in John', ThM thesis, Dallas, Tex.

Dodd, C. H. (1953), *The Interpretation of the Fourth Gospel*, Cambridge: Cambridge University Press.

Du Rand, J. A. (2005), 'The Creation Motif in the Fourth Gospel: Perspectives on Its Narratological Function within a Judaistic Background', in *Theology and Christology in the Fourth Gospel*, ed. G. Van Belle, J. G. van der Watt and P. Maritz, Leuven: Leuven University Press, 21–46.

—— (1994), 'The Making of Christology – Evolution or Unfolding?', in *Jesus of Nazareth: Lord and Christ. Essays on the Historical Jesus and New Testament Christology*, ed. J. B. Green and M. Turner, Grand Rapids: Eerdmans, 437–452.

—— (1996), *Christology in the Making: A New Testament Inquiry into the Origins of the Doctrine of the Incarnation*, 2nd ed., Grand Rapids: Eerdmans.

—— (2007), Review of S. Gathercole, *The Pre-existent Son: Recovering the Christologies of Matthew, Mark, and Luke*, *Review of Biblical Literature*, posted at http://www.bookreviews.org.

Ebert, D. J. (1998), 'Wisdom in New Testament Christology with Special Reference to Hebrews 1:1–4', PhD diss., Deerfield, Ill.

Edwards, M. J. (2004), *John*, BBCS, Oxford: Blackwell.

Erickson, M. J. (1995), *God in Three Persons: A Contemporary Interpretation of the Trinity*, Grand Rapids: Baker.

Evans, C. A. (1987), 'Obduracy and the Lord's Servant: Some Observations on the Use of the Old Testament in the Fourth Gospel', in *Early Jewish and Christian Exegesis: Studies in Memory of William Hugh Brownlee*, ed. C. A. Evans and W. F. Stinespring, Atlanta: Scholars Press, 221–236.

—— (2000), 'New Testament Use of the Old Testament', in *New Dictionary of Biblical Theology*, ed. T. D. Alexander and B. S. Rosner, Downers Grove: IVP, 72–80.

Fee, G. D. (1994), *God's Empowering Presence: The Holy Spirit in the Letters of Paul*, Peabody: Hendrickson.

—— (2007), *Pauline Christology*, Peabody, Mass.: Hendrickson.

Ferguson, S. (1996), *The Holy Spirit*, Leicester: IVP; Downers Grove: IVP.

Fisher, M. C. (2003), 'God the Father in the Fourth Gospel: A Biblical Patrology', PhD diss., Wake Forest, N. C.

Fitzmyer, J. A. (1990–3), '*monos*', *EDNT* 2: 440–442.

Fowl, S. E. (1998), *Engaging Scripture*, Challenges in Contemporary Theology, Oxford: Blackwell.

Frey, J., and U. Schnelle (2004), *Kontexte des Johannesevangeliums. Das vierte Evangelium in religions- und traditionsgeschichtlicher Perspektive*, WUNT 175, Tübingen: Mohr–Siebeck.

Gabler, J. P. (1992 [1787]), 'An Oration on the Proper Distinction Between Biblical and Dogmatic Theology and the Specific Objectives of Each', in *The Flowering of Old Testament Theology*, ed. B. C. Ollenburger, E. A. Martens and G. F. Hasel, Winona Lake: Eisenbrauns, 493–502.

Gaffin, R. B., Jr. (1987), *Resurrection and Redemption: A Study in Paul's Soteriology*, Phillipsburg, N. J.: Presbyterian & Reformed.

Gathercole, S. (2006), *The Pre-existent Son: Recovering the Christologies of Matthew, Mark, and Luke*, Grand Rapids: Eerdmans.

Gavrilyuk, P. L. (2004), *The Suffering of the Impassible God: The Dialectics of Patristic Thought*, Oxford: Oxford University Press.

Giles, K. (2002), *The Trinity and Subordinationism*, Downers Grove: IVP.

—— (2006), *Jesus and the Father: Modern Evangelicals Reinvent the Doctrine of the Trinity*, Downers Grove: IVP.

Gnuse, R. K. (1997), *No Other Gods: Emergent Monotheism in Israel*, JSOTSup 241, Sheffield: Sheffield Academic Press.

Goldsworthy, G. (2006), *Gospel-Centered Hermeneutics: Foundations and Principles of Evangelical Biblical Interpretation*, Nottingham: Apollos; Downers Grove: IVP.

Gourgues, M. (2005), 'Le paraclet, l'esprit de vérité: Deux désignations, deux fonctions', in *Theology and Christology in the Fourth Gospel*, ed. G. Van Belle, J. G. Van Der Watt and P. Maritz, Leuven: Leuven University Press, 83–108.

Grayston, K. (1981), 'The Meaning of *Paraklētos*', *JSNT* 13: 67–82.

Gregory of Nazianzus (*Ors.* 27 – 31), *The Theological Orations*, in *Christology of the Later Fathers*, The Library of Christian Classics, ed. E. R. Hardy, 1977, Louisville: Westminster John Knox, 128–214.

Grenz, S. J. (2004), *Rediscovering the Triune God: The Trinity in Contemporary Theology*, Minneapolis: Fortress.

Grenz, S. J., with D. M. Kjesbo (1995), *Women in the Church: A Biblical Theology of Women in Ministry*, Downers Grove: IVP.

Gruenler, R. G. (1986), *The Trinity in the Gospel of John: A Thematic Commentary on the Fourth Gospel*, Grand Rapids: Baker.

Gunton, C. E. (2005), 'Towards a Trinitarian Reading of the Tradition: The Relevance of the "Eternal" Trinity', in *Trinitarian Soundings in Systematic Theology*, ed. P. L. Metzger, London: T. & T. Clark, 63–72.

Harner, P. B. (1970), *The 'I Am' of the Fourth Gospel*, Facet Books, Philadelphia: Fortress.

—— (1973), 'Qualitative Anarthrous Predicate Nouns: Mark 15:39 and John 1:1', *JBL* 92: 75–87.

Harris, M. J. (1992), *Jesus as God: The New Testament Use of* Theos *in Reference to Jesus*, Grand Rapids: Baker.

Hart, D. B. (2003), *The Beauty of the Infinite: The Aesthetics of Christian Truth*, Grand Rapids: Eerdmans.

Hartley, D. E. (1996), 'Criteria for Determining Qualitative Nouns with a Special View to Understanding the Colwell Construction', ThM thesis, Dallas, Tex.

—— (1999), 'John 1:1, Colwell, and Mass/Count Nouns in Recent Discussion', paper presented at the annual meeting of the Evangelical Theological Society, Danvers, Mass.

Hatina, T. R. (1993), 'John 20,22 in Its Eschatological Context: Promise or Fulfillment?', *Bib* 74: 196–219.

Hays, R. B. (2002), 'The God of Mercy Who Rescues Us from the Present Evil Age: Romans and Galatians', in *The Forgotten God: Perspectives in Biblical Theology*, ed. A. A. Das and F. J. Matera, Louisville: Westminster John Knox, 123–143.

Helm, P. (1997), 'Eternal Creation: The Doctrine of the Two Standpoints', in *The Doctrine of Creation*, ed. C. E. Gunton, Edinburgh: T. & T. Clark, 29–46.

Hengel, M. (1993), *Die johanneische Frage*, WUNT 67, Tübingen: Mohr–Siebeck.

—— (1999), 'Das Johannesevangelium als Quelle für die Geschichte des antiken Judentums', in *Judaica, Hellenistica et Christiana:*

Kleine Schriften II, WUNT 109, Tübingen: Mohr–Siebeck, 293–334.

Heppe, H. (1950), *Reformed Dogmatics: Set Out and Illustrated from the Sources*, trans. G. T. Thomson, Grand Rapids: Baker.

Hill, C. E. (2004), *The Johannine Corpus in the Early Church*, Oxford: Oxford University Press.

Hofius, O. (1989), '"Der in des Vaters Schoss ist", Joh 1,18', *ZNW* 80: 163–171.

Horrell, J. S. (2004), 'Toward a Biblical Model of the Social Trinity: Avoiding Equivocation of Nature and Order', *JETS* 47: 399–421.

Hoskins, P. M. (2007), *Jesus as the Fulfilment of the Temple in the Gospel of John*, Paternoster Biblical Monographs, Carlisle: Paternoster.

Hurtado, L. W. (1998a), 'First-Century Jewish Monotheism', *JSNT* 71: 3–26.

—— (1998b), *One God, One Lord: Early Christian Devotion and Ancient Jewish Monotheism*, Edinburgh: T. & T. Clark.

—— (1999), 'Pre-70 C. E. Jewish Opposition to Christ-Devotion', *JTS* 50: 35–58.

—— (2003), *Lord Jesus Christ: Devotion to Jesus in Earliest Christianity*, Grand Rapids: Eerdmans.

Jackson, H. M. (1999), 'Ancient Self-Referential Conventions and Their Implications for the Authorship and Integrity of the Gospel of John', *JTS* 50: 1–34.

Jenson, R. W. (1997), *Systematic Theology*, vol. 1, New York: Oxford University Press.

—— (2002), 'The Bible and the Trinity', *ProEccl* 11: 329–339.

—— (2003), 'How Does Jesus Make a Difference? The Person and Work of Jesus Christ', in *Essentials of Christian Theology*, ed. W. C. Placher, Louisville: Westminster John Knox, 191–205.

John of Damascus (*Fid. Orth.*), *The Orthodox Faith*, in *Saint John of Damascus: Writings*, trans. F. H. Chase, Jr., New York: Fathers of the Church, 1958.

Johnson, S. L., Jr. (1980), *The Old Testament in the New: An Argument for Biblical Inspiration*, Grand Rapids: Zondervan.

Johnston, G. (1970), *The Spirit-Paraclete in the Gospel of John*, SNTSMS 12, Cambridge: Cambridge University Press.

Juel, D. (1988), *Messianic Exegesis: Christological Interpretation of the Old Testament in Early Christianity*, Philadelphia: Fortress.

Juncker, G. (2001), 'Jesus and the Angel of the Lord: An Old Testament Paradigm in New Testament Christology', PhD diss., Deerfield, Ill.

Käsemann, E. (1968), *The Testament of Jesus*, trans. G. Krodel, Philadelphia: Fortress.

Kasper, W. (1984), *The God of Jesus Christ*, trans. M. J. O'Connell, New York: Crossroad.

Keener, C. S. (1999), 'Is Subordination within the Trinity Really Heresy? A Study of John 5:18 in Context', *TJ* NS 20.1: 39–51.

——— (2003), *The Gospel of John*, 2 vols., Peabody, Mass.: Hendrickson.

Kellum, L. S. (2004), *The Unity of the Farewell Discourse: The Literary Integrity of John 13:31–16:33*, JSNTSup 256, London: T. & T. Clark.

Kerr, A. R. (2002), *The Temple of Jesus' Body: The Temple Theme in the Gospel of John*, JSNTSS 220, Sheffield: Sheffield Academic Press.

Kierspel, L. (2007), *The Jews and the World in the Fourth Gospel: Parallelism, Function, and Context*, WUNT 2.220, Tübingen: Mohr–Siebeck.

Köstenberger, A. J. (1995a), 'The Contribution of the General Epistles and Revelation to a Biblical Theology of Religions', in *Christianity and the Religions: A Biblical Theology of World Religions*, EMSS 2, ed. E. Rommen and H. Netland, Pasadena, Calif.: William Carey Library, 113–140.

——— (1995b), 'The Seventh Johannine Sign: A Study in John's Christology', *BBR* 5: 87–103.

——— (1998a), 'Jesus as Rabbi in the Fourth Gospel', *BBR* 8: 97–128.

——— (1998b), *The Missions of Jesus and the Disciples According to the Fourth Gospel*, Grand Rapids: Eerdmans.

——— (1998c), 'Review of *Women in the Church* by S. J. Grenz', *JETS* 41: 516–519.

——— (1999a), *Encountering John: The Gospel in Historical, Literary, and Theological Perspective*, EBS, Grand Rapids: Baker.

——— (1999b), 'The Two Johannine Verbs for Sending: A Study of John's Use of Words with Reference to General Linguistic Theory', in *Linguistics and the New Testament: Critical Junctures*, ed. S. E. Porter and D. A. Carson, JSNTSS 168, Sheffield: Sheffield Academic Press, 125–143.

——— (2001a), *John*, in *Zondervan Illustrated Bible Backgrounds Commentary*, ed. C. E. Arnold, Grand Rapids: Zondervan, 2.1–216.

——— (2001b), *Studies in John and Gender: A Decade of Scholarship*, Studies in Biblical Literature 38, New York: Lang.

—— (2002), 'Jesus the Good Shepherd Who Will Also Bring Other Sheep (John 10:16): The Old Testament Background of a Familiar Metaphor', *BBR* 12: 67–96.

—— (2004a), *God, Marriage and Family: Rebuilding the Biblical Foundation*, Wheaton: Crossway.

—— (2004b), '"I Suppose" (*oimai*): The Conclusion of John's Gospel in Its Literary and Historical Context', *The New Testament in Its First Century Setting: Essays on Context and Background in Honour of B. W. Winter on His 65th Birthday*, ed. P. J. Williams, A. D. Clarke, P. M. Head and D. Instone-Brewer, Grand Rapids: Eerdmans, 72–88.

—— (2004c), *John*, BECNT, Grand Rapids: Baker.

—— (2005a), 'The Destruction of the Second Temple and the Composition of the Fourth Gospel', *TJ* 26 NS: 205–242.

—— (2005b) (ed.), *Whatever Happened to Truth?* Wheaton: Crossway.

—— (2006), 'The Destruction of the Second Temple and the Composition of the Fourth Gospel', in *Challenging Perspectives on the Gospel of John*, ed. J. Lierman, WUNT 2.219, Tübingen: Mohr–Siebeck, 69–108.

—— (2007), 'John', in *Commentary on the New Testament Use of the Old Testament*, ed. G. K. Beale and D. A. Carson, Grand Rapids: Baker; Nottingham: Apollos, 415–512.

—— (forthcoming), *The Word, the Christ, the Son of God: A Johannine Theology*, Biblical Theology of the New Testament, Grand Rapids: Zondervan.

Köstenberger, A. J., and P. T. O'Brien (2001), *Salvation to the Ends of the Earth: A Biblical Theology of Mission*, NSBT, Leicester: Apollos; Downers Grove: IVP.

Köstenberger, A. J., and S. O. Stout (forthcoming), 'The Disciple Jesus Loved: Witness, Author, Apostle: A Response to Richard Bauckham's *Jesus and the Eyewitnesses*', *BBR*.

Kruse, C. G. (2003), *The Gospel according to John*, TNTC, Leicester: IVP.

Kupp, D. D. (1996), *Matthew's Emmanuel: Divine Presence and God's People in the First Gospel*, SNTSMS 90, Cambridge: Cambridge University Press.

Lang, B. (1981), *Der einzige Gott: Die Geburt des biblischen Monotheismus*, Munich: Kösel.

—— (1983), *Monotheism and the Prophetic Minority*, Sheffield: Almond.

Larsson, T. (2001), *God in the Fourth Gospel: A Hermeneutical Study of the History of Interpretation*, Stockholm: Almquist & Wiksell International.

Leaney, A. R. C. (1972), 'The Johannine Paraclete and the Qumran Scrolls', in *John and Qumran*, ed. J. H. Charlesworth, London: G. Chapman, 38–61.

Lee, A. H. I. (2005), *From Messiah to Preexistent Son: Jesus' Self-Consciousness and Early Christian Exegesis of Messianic Psalms*, WUNT 2.192, Tübingen: Mohr–Siebeck.

Lee, D. A. (2004), 'In the Spirit of Truth: Worship and Prayer in the Gospel of John and the Early Fathers', *VC* 58: 277–297.

Leftow, B. (2002), 'Anti Social Trinitarianism', in *The Trinity*, ed. S. T. Davis, D. Kendall and G. O'Collins, Oxford: Oxford University Press, 203–251.

Lemcio, E. E. (1991), *The Past of Jesus in the Gospels*, SNTSMS 68, Cambridge: Cambridge University Press.

Letham, R. (2004), *The Holy Trinity: In Scripture, History, Theology, and Worship*, Phillipsburg, N. J.: Presbyterian & Reformed.

Levenson, J. D. (1993), *The Death and Resurrection of the Beloved Son: The Transformation of Child Sacrifice in Judaism and Christianity*, New Haven: Yale University Press.

Lincoln, A. T. (2000), *Truth on Trial: The Lawsuit Motif in the Fourth Gospel*, Peabody, Mass.: Hendrickson.

—— (2005), *The Gospel according to Saint John*, BNTC, New York: Continuum.

Loader, W. R. G. (1989), *The Christology of the Fourth Gospel: Structure and Issues*, BBET 23, New York: Peter Lang.

Louth, A. (1996), *Maximus the Confessor*, Early Church Fathers, London: Routledge.

McCabe, H. (1987), *God Matters*, London: Geoffrey Chapman, 1987; Springfield, Ill.: Templegate, 1991.

MacDonald, N. (2003), *Deuteronomy and the Meaning of 'Monotheism'*, FAT 2.1, Tübingen: Mohr–Siebeck.

—— (2005), 'Whose Monotheism? Which Rationality?', in *The Old Testament in Its World*, ed. R. P. Gordon and J. C. de Moor, Leiden: Brill, 45–67.

Machinist, P. (1991), 'The Question of Distinctiveness in Ancient Israel', in *Essential Papers on Israel and the Ancient Near East*, ed. F. E. Greenspan, New York: New York University Press, 420–442.

McGaughy, L. C. (1972), *Toward a Descriptive Analysis of EINAI as a Linking Verb in New Testament Greek*, SBLDS 6, Missoula: University of Montana.

McGuckin, J. A. (2001), *St. Gregory of Nazianzus: An Intellectual Biography*, Crestwood, N. Y.: St. Vladimir's Seminary Press.

MacLeod, D. J. (2003), 'The Eternality and Deity of the Word: John 1:1–2', *BibSac* 160: 48–64.

Marshall, B. D. (2000), *Trinity and Truth*, Cambridge Studies in Christian Doctrine, Cambridge: Cambridge University Press.

—— (2001), 'Do Christians Worship the God of Israel?', in *Knowing the Triune God: The Work of the Spirit in the Practices of the Church*, ed. J. J. Buckley and D. S. Yeago, Grand Rapids: Eerdmans, 231–264.

—— (2002), 'The Defense of the *Filioque* in Classical Lutheran Theology', *NZSTh* 44: 154–173.

—— (2004), 'In Search of an Analytic Aquinas: Grammar and the Trinity', in *Grammar and Grace: Reformulations of Aquinas and Wittgenstein*, ed. J. Stout and R. MacSwain, London: SCM, 55–74.

Marshall, I. H. (2004), *Beyond the Bible: Moving from Scripture to Theology*, Acadia Studies in Bible and Theology, Grand Rapids: Baker.

Martyn, J. L. (1977), 'Glimpses into the History of the Johannine Community', in *L'Évangile de Jean: Sources, Rédaction, Théologie*, BETL 44, ed. M. de Jonge, Leuven: University Press, 149–175.

—— (2003), *History and Theology in the Fourth Gospel*, New York: Harper & Row, 1968. 2nd ed., Nashville: Abingdon, 1979; 3rd ed., Louisville: Westminster John Knox.

Meeks, W. A. (1972), 'The Man from Heaven in Johannine Sectarianism', *JBL* 91: 44–72.

Meyer, P. W. (1996), '"The Father": The Presentation of God in the Fourth Gospel', in *Exploring the Gospel of John*, ed. R. A. Culpepper and C. C. Black. Louisville: Westminster John Knox, 255–273.

Michaels, J. R. (2004), 'Atonement in John's Gospel and Epistles', in *The Glory of the Atonement: Biblical, Historical, and Practical Perspectives*, ed. F. A. James and C. E. Hill, Downers Grove: IVP; Leicester: Apollos, 106–118.

Molnar, P. D. (2002), *Divine Freedom and the Doctrine of the Immanent Trinity: In Dialogue with Karl Barth and Contemporary Theology*, London: T. & T. Clark.

Moloney, F. J. (1980), 'From Cana to Cana (John 2:1–4:54) and the Fourth Evangelist's Concept of Correct (and Incorrect) Faith', *StudBib 1978*, II. *Papers on The Gospels*, JSNTSSup 2, ed. E. A. Livingstone, Sheffield: JSOT, 185–213.

—— (1996), *Signs and Shadows: Reading John 5–12*, Minneapolis: Fortress.

—— (1998), *The Gospel of John*, Collegeville, Minn.: Liturgical.

—— (2002), 'Telling God's Story: The Fourth Gospel', in *The Forgotten God: Perspectives in Biblical Theology. Essays in Honor of Paul J. Achtemeier*, ed. A. A. Das and F. J. Matera, Louisville: Westminster John Knox, 107–122.

Moltmann, J. (1981), 'Theological Proposals towards the Resolution of the *Filioque* Controversy', in *Spirit of God, Spirit of Christ*, ed. L. Vischer, London: SPCK, 164–173.

Moo, D. J. (2005), 'The Christology of the Early Pauline Letters', in *Contours of Christology in the New Testament*, ed. R. N. Longenecker, Grand Rapids: Eerdmans, 169–192.

Moody, D. (1953), 'God's Only Son: The Translation of John 3:16 in the Revised Standard Version', *JBL* 72: 213–219.

Morris, L. (1969), *Studies in the Fourth Gospel*, Grand Rapids: Eerdmans.

—— (1989), *Jesus is the Christ: Studies in the Theology of John*, Grand Rapids: Eerdmans.

—— (1995), *The Gospel According to John*, NICNT, rev. ed., Grand Rapids: Eerdmans.

Motyer, J. A. (1993), *The Prophecy of Isaiah: An Introduction and Commentary*, Leicester: IVP; Downers Grove: IVP.

Motyer, S. (1997), *Your Father the Devil? A New Approach to John and the 'Jews'*, Carlisle: Paternoster.

Mowvley, H. (1984), 'John 1,14–18 in the Light of Exodus 33,7–34,35', *ExpTim* 95.5: 135–137.

Muller, R. A. (2003), *Post-Reformation Reformed Dogmatics: The Rise and Development of Reformed Orthodoxy, ca. 1520–1725*, vol. 4: *The Triunity of God*, Grand Rapids: Baker.

Nicholson, G. C. (1983), *Death as Departure: The Johannine Descent–Ascent Schema*, SBLDS 63, Chico, Calif.: Scholars Press.

O'Collins, G. (1999), *The Tripersonal God: Understanding and Interpreting the Trinity*, Mahwah, N. J.: Paulist.

O'Day, G. R. (1999), '"Show us the Father, and we Will Be Satisfied" (John 14:8)', *Semeia* 85: 11–17.

O'Donovan, O. (1996), *The Desire of the Nations: Rediscovering the Roots of Political Theology*, Cambridge: Cambridge University Press.

O'Keefe, J. J., and R. R. Reno (2005), *Sanctified Vision: An Introduction to Early Christian Interpretation of the Bible*, Baltimore: The Johns Hopkins University Press.

Okure, T. (1988), *The Johannine Approach to Mission*, WUNT 2.31, Tübingen: Mohr–Siebeck.

Olsson, B. (1999), '*Deus Semper Maior*? On God in the Johannine Writings', in *New Readings in John: Literary and Theological Perspectives*, ed. J. Nissen and S. Pedersen, JSNTSup 182, Sheffield: Sheffield Academic Press, 143–171.

Olyan, S. M. (1988), *Asherah and the Cult of Yahweh in Israel*, SBLMS 34, Atlanta: Scholars Press.

Onuki, T. (1984), *Gemeinde und Welt im Johannesevangelium*, WMANT 56, Neukirchen-Vluyn: Neukirchener.

Owen, P. (2000), 'Calvin and Catholic Trinitarianism: An Examination of Robert Reymond's Understanding of the Trinity and His Appeal to John Calvin', *CTJ* 35: 262–281.

Pendrick, G. (1995), '*Monogenēs*', *NTS* 41: 587–600.

Peters, T. (1993), *God as Trinity: Relationality and Temporality in Divine Life*, Louisville: Westminster John Knox.

Piper, J. (2003), *Let the Nations be Glad! The Supremacy of God in Missions*, 2nd ed., Leicester: IVP; Grand Rapids: Baker.

—— (2005), *God Is the Gospel: Meditations on God's Love as the Gift of Himself*, Wheaton: Crossway.

Plantinga, C. (1991), 'The Fourth Gospel as Trinitarian Source Then and Now', in *Biblical Hermeneutics in Historical Perspective*, ed. M. S. Burrows and P. Rorem, Grand Rapids: Eerdmans, 303–321.

Pollard, T. E. (1957), 'The Exegesis of John 10:30 in Early Trinitarian Controversies', *NTS* 3: 334–349.

—— (1970), *Johannine Christology and the Early Church*, London: Cambridge University Press.

Porsch, F. (1974), *Pneuma und Wort: Ein exegetischer Beitrag zur Pneumatologie des Johannesevangeliums*, Frankfurt: Josef Knecht.

Poythress, V. S. (2006), 'Why Must Our Hermeneutics Be Trinitarian?', *Southern Baptist Journal of Theology* 10.1: 96–98.

Pryor, J. W. (1992), *John: Evangelist of the Covenant People. The Narrative and Themes of the Fourth Gospel*, Downers Grove: IVP.

Quast, K. (1989), *Peter and the Beloved Disciple: Figures for a Community in Crisis*, JSNTSup 32, Sheffield: JSOT.

Reinhartz, A. (1999), 'And the Word Was Begotten', *Semeia* 85: 83–104.

Rengstorf, K. H. (1964), '*Apostellō*, etc.', *TDNT* 1: 398–447.

Reymond, R. L. (1998), *A New Systematic Theology of the Christian Faith*, Nashville: Thomas Nelson.

Ricoeur, P. (1992), *Oneself as Another*, trans. K. Blamey, Chicago: University of Chicago Press.

Ridderbos, H. N. (1962), *The Coming of the Kingdom*, trans. J. de Jongste, Philadelphia: Presbyterian & Reformed.

—— (1997), *The Gospel of John*, trans. J. Vriend, Grand Rapids: Eerdmans.

Riesenfeld, H. (1972), 'A Probable Background to the Johannine Paraclete', in *Ex Orbe Religionum. Studia Geo Widengren*, SHR 21, ed. C. J. Bleeker et al., Leiden: Brill, 1.266–274.

Rogers, E. F. (2005), *After the Spirit: A Constructive Pneumatology from Resources Outside the Modern West*, Grand Rapids: Eerdmans.

Ross, A. P. (1997), '*šēm*', in *NIDOTTE* 4: 147–151.

Rowe, C. K. (2000), 'Romans 10:13: What Is the Name of the Lord?', *HBT* 22: 135–173.

—— (2002), 'Biblical Pressure and Trinitarian Hermeneutics', *ProEccl* 11: 295–312.

—— (2003), 'Luke and the Trinity: An Essay in Ecclesial Biblical Theology', *SJT* 56: 1–26.

—— (2006), *Early Narrative Christology: The Lord in the Gospel of Luke*, BZNW 139, Berlin: Walter de Gruyter.

Rusch, W. G., ed. (1980), *The Trinitarian Controversy*, Philadelphia: Fortress.

Russell, N. (2000), *Cyril of Alexandria*, Early Church Fathers, London: Routledge.

Sanders, F. (2004), *The Image of the Immanent Trinity: Rahner's Rule and the Theological Interpretation of Scripture*, Issues in Systematic Theology 12, New York: Peter Lang.

Schaff, P. (1996 [1931]), *The Creeds of Christendom: With a History and Critical Notes*, 6th ed., vol. 3, repr. Grand Rapids: Baker.

Schlatter, A. (1902), *Die Sprache und Heimat des vierten Evangelisten*, BFCT 6.4, Gütersloh: Bertelsmann.

—— (1948), *Der Evangelist Johannes*, 2nd ed., Stuttgart: Calwer.

Schnackenburg, R. (1990), *The Gospel According to St. John*, 3 vols., New York: Crossroad.

—— (1992), *The Johannine Epistles: Introduction and Commentary*, trans. R. Fuller and I. Fuller, New York: Crossroad.

Schrenk, G. (1967), *'Patēr'*, *TDNT* 5: 945–958, 974–1022.

Schürer, E. (1979), *The History of the Jewish People in the Age of Jesus Christ (175 B.C.–A.D. 135)*, vol. 2, rev. and ed. G. Vermes, F. Millar and M. Black, Edinburgh: T. & T. Clark.

Shafaat, A. (1981), 'Geber of the Qumran Scrolls and the Spirit-Paraclete of the Gospel of John', *NTS* 27: 263–269.

Smalley, S. S. (1996), '"The Paraclete": Pneumatology in the Johannine Gospel and Apocalypse', in *Exploring the Gospel of John*, ed. R. A. Culpepper and C. C. Black, Louisville: Westminster John Knox, 289–300.

Smith, D. M. (1995), *The Theology of the Gospel of John*, New Testament Theology, Cambridge: Cambridge University Press.

—— (1999), *John*, ANTC, Nashville: Abingdon.

Smith, M. S. (1990), *The Early History of God: Yahweh and the Other Deities in Ancient Israel*, San Francisco: Harper & Row.

Stibbe, M. W. G. (1991), 'The Elusive Christ: A New Reading of the Fourth Gospel', *JSNT* 44: 19–38.

—— (1993), *John*, Sheffield: Sheffield Academic Press.

—— (2006), 'Telling the Father's Story: The Gospel of John as Narrative Theology', in *Challenging Perspectives on the Gospel of John*, ed. J. Lierman, WUNT 2.219, Tübingen: Mohr–Siebeck, 170–193.

Studer, B. (1993), *Trinity and Incarnation: The Faith of the Early Church*, trans. M. Westerhoff, ed. A. Louth, Collegeville: Liturgical.

Swain, S. R. (1998), 'Truth in the Gospel of John', ThM thesis, Wake Forest, N. C.

Talbert, C. H. (1992), *Reading John*, New York: Crossroad.

Tanner, K. (2001), *Jesus, Humanity and the Trinity: A Brief Systematic Theology*, Minneapolis: Fortress.

Tennent, T. C. (2003), Review of A. Yong, *Beyond the Impasse*, *International Bulletin of Missionary Research* 27: 180–181.

—— (2004), Review of A. Yong, *Beyond the Impasse*, *Missiology* 32: 387.

Tenney, M. C. (1975), 'Topics from the Gospel of John. Part I: The Person of the Father', *BibSac* 132: 37–46.

Thompson, J. (1994), *Modern Trinitarian Perspectives*, New York: Oxford University Press.

Thompson, M. M. (1988), *The Humanity of Jesus in the Fourth Gospel*. Philadelphia: Fortress.

Thompson, M. M. (1993), '"God's Voice You Have Never Heard, God's Form You Have Never Seen": The Characterization of God in the Gospel of John', *Semeia* 63: 177–204.

—— (2000), *The Promise of the Father*, Louisville: Westminster John Knox.

—— (2001), *The God of the Gospel of John*, Grand Rapids: Eerdmans.

Tolmie, D. F. (1995), *Jesus' Farewell to the Disciples: John 13:1–17:26 in Narratological Perspective*, Leiden: Brill.

—— (1998), 'The Characterization of God in the Fourth Gospel', *JSNT* 69: 57–75.

Torrance, T. F. (1995), *The Trinitarian Faith*, London: T. & T. Clark.

Turner, M. M. B. (1977), 'The Concept of Receiving the Spirit in John's Gospel', *VE* 19: 24–42.

Vanhoozer, K. J. (2002), *First Theology: God, Scriptures and Hermeneutics*, Downers Grove: IVP; Leicester: Apollos.

—— (2005a), *The Drama of Doctrine: A Canonical-Linguistic Approach to Christian Theology*, Louisville: Westminster John Knox.

Vanhoozer, K. J., ed. (2005b), *Dictionary for Theological Interpretation of the Bible*, Grand Rapids: Baker.

Vischer, L. (1981), *Spirit of God, Spirit of Christ*, London: SPCK.

Vos, G. (1980a), 'The Doctrine of the Covenant in Reformed Theology', in *Redemptive History and Biblical Interpretation: The Shorter Writings of Geerhardus Vos*, ed. R. B. Gaffin, Jr., Phillipsburg, N. J.: Presbyterian & Reformed, 234–267. Repr. of Vos, G. (1891), *De verbondsleer in de Gereformeerde theologie*, rectoral address at the Theological School of the Christian Reformed Church in Grand Rapids, Mich.

—— (1980b) '"True" and "Truth" in the Johannine Writings', in *Redemptive History and Biblical Interpretation: The Shorter Writings of Geerhardus Vos*, ed. R. B. Gaffin, Jr., Phillipsburg, N. J.: Presbyterian & Reformed, 343–351. Repr. of Vos, G. (1927), '"True" and "Truth" in the Johannine Writings', *BRev* 12: 507–520.

Walker, P. W. L. (1996), *Jesus and the Holy City: New Testament Perspectives on Jerusalem*, Grand Rapids: Eerdmans.

Walker, W. O. (1994), 'John 1.43–51 and "The Son of Man" in the Fourth Gospel', *JSNT* 56: 31–42.

Wallace, D. B. (1996), *Greek Grammar Beyond the Basics*, Grand Rapids: Zondervan.

Ware, B. (2005), *Father, Son, and Holy Spirit: Relationships, Roles, and Relevance*, Wheaton: Crossway.

Watson, F. (2000), 'The Triune Divine Identity: Reflections on Pauline God-Language, in Disagreement with J. D. G. Dunn', *JSNT* 80: 99–124.

Webb, S. H. (1996), *The Gifting God: A Trinitarian Ethics of Excess*, New York: Oxford University Press.

Westcott, B. F. (1975 [1881]), *The Gospel according to St. John*, London: Murray.

Whitacre, R. A. (1999), *John*, IVPNTC 4, Downers Grove: IVP; Leicester: IVP.

Wiles, M. (1960), *The Spiritual Gospel: The Interpretation of the Fourth Gospel in the Early Church*, Cambridge: Cambridge University Press.

Williams, C. H. (2000), *I am He: The Interpretation of* 'ani hu' *in Jewish and Early Christian Literature*, Tübingen: Mohr–Siebeck.

Windisch, H. (1968), *The Spirit-Paraclete in the Fourth Gospel*, Philadelphia: Fortress.

Winter, P. (1953), '*Monogenēs para patros*', *ZRG* 5: 335–365.

Witherington, B. (1995), *John's Wisdom*, Peabody, Mass.: Hendrickson.

Witherington, B., and L. M. Ice (2002), *The Shadow of the Almighty: Father, Son, and Spirit in Biblical Perspective*, Grand Rapids: Eerdmans.

Witsius, H. (1990 [1822]), *The Economy of the Covenants Between God and Man*, vol. 1, repr. Kingsburg, Calif.: den Dulk Christian Foundation.

Wolters, A. (2000), 'Confessional Criticism and the Night Visions of Zechariah', in *Renewing Biblical Interpretation*, Scripture and Hermeneutics Series, vol. 1, ed. C. Bartholomew, C. Greene and K. Möller, Grand Rapids: Zondervan, 90–117.

Womack, J. A., with J. S. Horrell (2005), Review of A. Yong, *Beyond the Impasse*, *BibSac* 162.648: 489–491.

Wright, C. J. H. (2006), *The Mission of God: Unlocking the Bible's Grand Narrative*, Downers Grove: IVP; Leicester: IVP.

Wright, N. T. (1991), *The Climax of the Covenant: Christ and the Law in Pauline Theology*, Edinburgh: T. & T. Clark.

—— (1992), *The New Testament and the People of God*, Christian Origins and the Question of God 1, Minneapolis: Fortress.

—— (1996), *Jesus and the Victory of God*, Christian Origins and the Question of God 2, Minneapolis: Fortress.

Wright, N. T. (2003), *The Resurrection of the Son of God*, Christian Origins and the Question of God 3, Minneapolis: Fortress.

Yarbrough, R. W. (1995), 'Divine Election in the Gospel of John', in *The Grace of God, the Bondage of the Will*, 2 vols., ed. T. R. Schreiner and B. A. Ware, Grand Rapids: Baker, 1: 47–62.

Yeago, D. S. (1994), 'The New Testament and Nicene Dogma', *ProEccl* 3: 152–164.

Yong, A. (2003), *Beyond the Impasse: Toward a Pneumatological Theology of Religions*, Grand Rapids: Baker; Carlisle: Paternoster.

Index of authors

Index of Scripture references

Index of ancient sources